....

PRESENTED TO:

....

FROM:

....

DATE:

LIVING
— *in the* —
LIGHT

MyDaily® DEVOTIONAL

COUNTRYMAN®

A Division of Thomas Nelson Publishers

THOMAS NELSON
Since 1798

Published in Nashville, Tennessee, by Thomas Nelson. Thomas Nelson is a registered trademark of HarperCollins Christian Publishing, Inc.

Unless otherwise noted, Scripture quotations are taken from the New King James Version®. © 1982 by Thomas Nelson. Used by permission. All rights reserved.

Scripture quotations marked KJV are from the King James Version. Public domain.

Scripture quotations marked NASB are from the New American Standard Bible®, Copyright © 1960, 1962, 1963, 1968, 1971, 1972, 1973, 1975, 1977, 1995 by The Lockman Foundation. Used by permission. (www.Lockman.org).

Any Internet addresses, phone numbers, or company or product information printed in this book are offered as a resource and are not intended in any way to be or to imply an endorsement by Thomas Nelson, nor does Thomas Nelson vouch for the existence, content, or services of these sites, phone numbers, companies, or products beyond the life of this book.

ISBN 978-1-4002-1052-7

Printed in China

18 19 20 21 22 DSC 5 4 3 2 1

Introduction

Living in the Light has been compiled by fifty-one devoted men of God to reveal the light of Jesus Christ as an example of how God desires for Christians to live. Jesus reminded us, "I am the light of the world. He who follows Me shall not walk in darkness, but have the light of life" (John 8:12). As you delve into the devotions each week, allow God to reveal His light into your life.

It is our prayer for you to take that light and allow it shine for the world to see. Be a reflection of His light—obvious for all to see and benefit from, so that they too may leave the darkness and come into the Light.

Johnny M. Hunt

Dr. Johnny M. Hunt
Senior Pastor
First Baptist Church Woodstock
Woodstock, Georgia

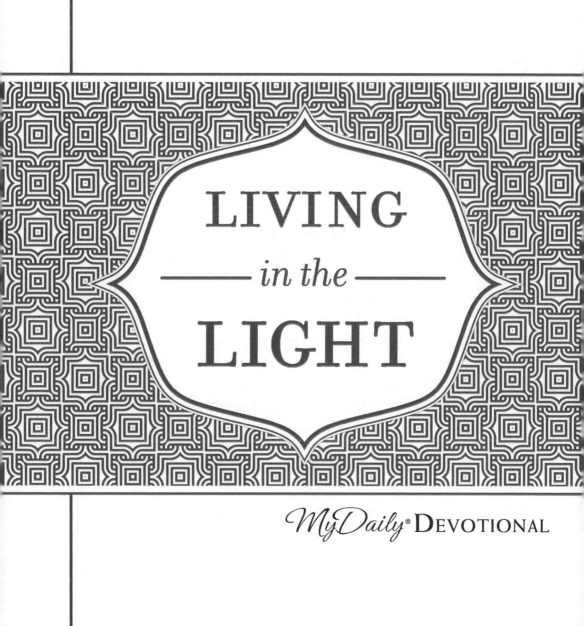

LIVING
in the
LIGHT

MyDaily DEVOTIONAL

CONTENTS

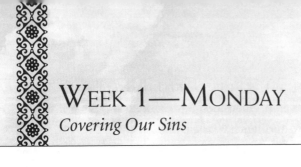

WEEK 1—MONDAY
Covering Our Sins

So when the woman saw that the tree was good for food, that it was pleasant to the eyes, and a tree desirable to make one wise, she took of its fruit and ate. She also gave to her husband with her, and he ate. Then the eyes of both of them were opened, and they knew that they were naked; and they sewed fig leaves together and made themselves coverings.

GENESIS 3:6–7

I once heard someone say, "Any sin we cover, God uncovers. And any sin we uncover, God covers." Since the beginning of time humans have attempted to cover their own sins. Solomon taught an incredible principle in Proverbs 28:13: "He who covers his sins will not prosper, but whoever confesses and forsakes them will have mercy."

Our adversary, the devil, always makes promises he has no intention of keeping. He is indeed a liar—and a subtle one at that. In the garden the enemy used fruit that looked too good to resist, and today he offers temptations we often feel we cannot live without, only to find out the results are disappointment and shame. When we are ashamed of our sins, we may attempt to use fig leaves of our own making to cover them up. But our precious heavenly Father offered the sacrifice of His Son, and His shed blood covers our sins.

May the Lord Jesus grant wisdom from heaven to help us discern good from evil. And may we not try to cover up our sins. Rather, may we find forgiveness through the shed blood of Jesus.

....

Lord Jesus, help me not be ignorant of the enemy's devices. Amen.

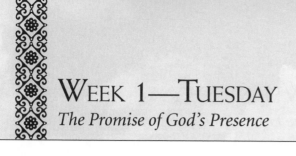

WEEK 1—TUESDAY
The Promise of God's Presence

"Behold, I am with you and will keep you wherever you go, and will bring you back to this land; for I will not leave you until I have done what I have spoken to you."

GENESIS 28:15

This passage in Genesis is an example of what many refer to as a "divine interruption." In this chapter, Jacob was forced to leave his homeland after his brother wanted to kill him, but right in the midst of his trouble, he received a comforting promise from God.

As I study the sacred text day by day, I find myself giving special attention to God's promises. When someone gets to the very bottom of God's truth, I have found no greater promise than that of God's presence: "I am with you." At the end of the day, God's greatest gift is Himself. His presence is so reassuring, comforting, overwhelming, and glorious. Often my schedule takes me to distant places, but it comforts me to know He is with me and He protects me.

Jacob enjoyed God's presence throughout his journey away from home. Similar to Jacob, you may have to leave the land of promise, but you won't lose the Lord's presence. Regardless of where you are today and whatever your need is, His presence is enough. The promise of God's presence also brings the promise of protection. He "will keep you wherever you go."

You never need to fear because God will keep you safe on your life's journey.

. . . .

Lord, You are as close as the mere mentioning of Your name. Amen.

WEEK 1—WEDNESDAY
Singing a Song to the Lord

The LORD is my strength and song, and He has become my salvation; He is my God, and I will praise Him; my father's God, and I will exalt Him.

EXODUS 15:2

D o you ever sing to the Lord? Have you ever been meditating on a passage and—unannounced—you began to sing the text to the Lord? My wife often accuses me of making up words to the songs I sing, but the truth is I sing new songs Scripture has inspired. I can hear her now, saying, "Leave the singing to the singer."

But I often respond, "You don't have to be a good singer to sing; you need only a song."

Exodus 15:1–18 is the song Moses sang after the Israelites crossed the Red Sea. The song contains four stanzas and one closing line. Each of the first three stanzas powerfully describes God's victory over the Egyptians. The fourth stanza celebrates the Lord's leadership and how His power instills fear in the enemies of the Israelites. The closing line then summarizes one great thought: our Lord reigns.

Surely the centerpiece of worship is God alone. As you sing songs of praise to the Lord, may you never forget His mighty power and love. Just as He protected the Israelites from the Egyptians, He will showcase His power in your life. Sing songs of praise to the Lord!

....

Lord, there is no other like You!

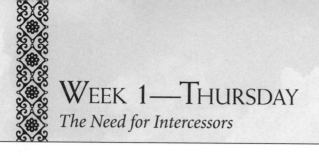

WEEK 1—THURSDAY
The Need for Intercessors

[Moses said,] "Now therefore, I pray, if I have found grace in Your sight, show me now Your way, that I may know You and that I may find grace in Your sight. And consider that this nation is Your people."

And He said, "My Presence will go with you, and I will give you rest."

EXODUS 33:13–14

Moses, in this text, interceded with the Lord on the behalf of Israel. Here we hear Moses as He talked to God, and better yet, as God spoke to Moses as a friend. Prayer is indeed a dialogue as we speak with Him and as we linger in His presence to hear the small, still voice He speaks into our lives.

In *MacLaren's Commentary: Expositions of the Holy Scripture*, he wrote, "For the end of knowing God's ways is, for the devout man, a deeper, more blessed knowledge of God Himself, who is best known in His deeds; and the highest, most blessed issue of the God-given knowledge of God, is the conscious sunshine of His favour [sic] shining ever on His servant."

When Moses interceded on the behalf of Israel, he met with God face-to-face. He was able to enjoy his presence and ask for God's blessings on His people. In like manner, we can intercede on the behalf of others and ask for God's mercies and blessings in their lives. And we can do this while knowing we are in the presence of Almighty God.

. . . .

Lord, I really do need You every hour. Amen.

Week 1—Friday
A Special Blessing

"The Lord bless you and keep you; the Lord make His face shine upon you, and be gracious to you; the Lord lift up His countenance upon you, and give you peace."

NUMBERS 6:24–26

This glorious passage of Scripture speaks of how a leader can be used by God to bless those whom he has been called to lead. In this passage, Moses received directions from heaven that led to the Lord's blessings. This blessing was to be pronounced by the high priests as they blessed the Israelites.

In this blessing, the priest would remind people of God's promised presence, His unequaled goodness, His powerful protection, and His grace. This truly was a special blessing from the Lord.

When I reflect on my life, I quickly come to the conclusion, "By the grace of God I am what I am" (1 Corinthians 15:10). He guards my life and causes my heart to beat today. I am nothing without Him. Who is more gracious than He? The blessing in Numbers 6:24–26 resounds greatly in my life.

God gives me peace as well. As Ephesians 2:14 says, "He Himself is our peace." God comforts me during the difficult seasons of life. No matter what I face, I find God's peace sustaining me at all times.

Whom should you pray this blessing over? Maybe you can write a note or send an email to a friend who needs reassurance of God's presence, goodness, protection, and grace.

....

Jesus, I am grateful for Your blessing! Amen.

DR. JOHNNY HUNT, FIRST BAPTIST CHURCH WOODSTOCK, WOODSTOCK, GA

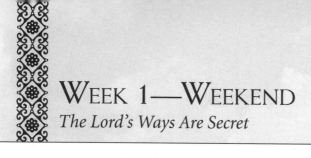

Week 1—Weekend
The Lord's Ways Are Secret

The secret things belong to the LORD our God, but those things which are revealed belong to us and to our children forever, that we may do all the words of this law.

DEUTERONOMY 29:29

In both college and seminary, my professors used to teach me that in the Old Testament the Lord Jesus is often concealed, but in the New Testament the Lord Jesus is revealed.

There is much we don't know about the Lord and His ways. We must all confess that His thoughts are not our thoughts and His ways are not our ways (Isaiah 55:8). Charles Spurgeon said, "When you can't trace His hand, trust His heart." It has also been said, "Never doubt in the dark what God told you in the light." This means that we must keep faith in God during the darkest times of life and know that He is with us even when we can't see Him.

The bottom line is that what I do know of Him has been enough to sustain me in every circumstance or crisis I have ever faced throughout my life. The old hymn says, "We will understand it better by and by." One day God's ways will be revealed to us, and we will understand Him more fully.

It is my prayer that, regardless of what I know in part or not at all, I will be obedient to what I do know.

....

Lord, continue to teach me that You are enough. Amen.

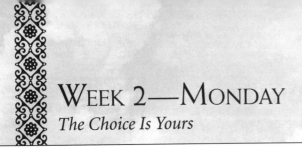

WEEK 2—MONDAY
The Choice Is Yours

I call heaven and earth as witnesses today against you, that I have set before you life and death, blessing and cursing; therefore choose life, that both you and your descendants may live; that you may love the LORD your God, that you may obey His voice, and that you may cling to Him, for He is your life and the length of your days; and that you may dwell in the land which the LORD swore to your fathers, to Abraham, Isaac, and Jacob, to give them.

DEUTERONOMY 30:19–20

As Moses stood on the plains of Moab, he delivered his last message to the people of Israel. He challenged them to make the all-important choice— the one between life and death, prosperity and adversity. Now, the correct choice was an obvious one, right? I mean, who would choose death over life, adversity over prosperity? The sad truth is many who claim to be Christians choose death and adversity on a regular basis because they choose to please themselves and do what seems right in their own eyes.

What does it mean to choose life? It means you choose to love the Lord and obey His voice. It means you say no to self and yes to Jesus in every situation, every circumstance, and every temptation. God's love and grace constantly attend those who choose life. These individuals understand the way of the Lord is always right, and they desperately strive to walk in it, regardless of what their eyes see and their flesh desires.

The most joyful people on earth are those who walk in the light with Jesus. They enjoy His love and love Him in return. They read His Word and do what He says to do. In short, they choose life because they choose Him.

....

Dear Father, I make the choice today to surrender completely to You. You alone are God, and I choose Your ways over mine. Amen.

DR. JEFF SCHREVE, FIRST BAPTIST CHURCH TEXARKANA, TEXARKANA, TX

Week 2—Tuesday
Never Alone

"The Lord will give them over to you, that you may do to them according to every commandment which I have commanded you. Be strong and of good courage, do not fear nor be afraid of them; for the Lord your God, He is the One who goes with you. He will not leave you nor forsake you."

Deuteronomy 31:5–6

The children of Israel experienced much trepidation as they prepared to cross the Jordan River and enter the promised land. They knew it was a good land God had promised them, but they also knew it was a land occupied by enemies who were fierce and strong. The people wanted to trust God, but they were afraid. So God gave them a word of comfort to calm their hearts. He promised them His enduring presence.

Perhaps you are facing a fearful situation today. Perhaps your confidence is waning, and you are starting to wonder if you are going to make it. Let me assure you that if you know Jesus as Savior and Lord, you have the promise of knowing He will never leave you or forsake you. He will fight your battles on your behalf. Your job is simply to trust Him and obey His commands. As you do this, God will see to it that those who stand in the way of your promised land will fall and flee.

Dear God, I confess I have been afraid of the obstacles I am facing today. But Lord, You are greater, and I choose to trust You. Thank You for never leaving me. I face this day with confidence because Your Word is truth. In Jesus' name, amen.

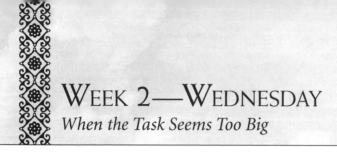

WEEK 2—WEDNESDAY
When the Task Seems Too Big

"No man shall be able to stand before you all the days of your life; as I was with Moses, so I will be with you. I will not leave you nor forsake you. Be strong and of good courage, for to this people you shall divide as an inheritance the land which I swore to their fathers to give them."

JOSHUA 1:5–6

After Moses, the servant of the Lord, died, the Lord chose Joshua to take his place. Talk about a daunting assignment. Wow! Moses was truly a spiritual giant and one of the greatest of Old Testament saints. The Bible tells us, "The LORD used to speak to Moses face to face, just as a man speaks to his friend" (Exodus 33:11 NASB). Needless to say, Joshua had huge shoes to fill!

Yet the Lord gave trembling Joshua a tremendous promise: "As I was with Moses, so I will be with you." Moses was great because God had been with him. Joshua could rest assured that the same God who helped Moses would also help him.

Are you facing a momumental assignment that has you overwhelmed and afraid? Are you in need of divine help today? Take courage! The same God who empowered Moses and empowered Joshua will also empower you. Your job is simply to trust Him.

....

Lord, it is awesome to know that as You were with Moses, You have pledged to be with me. I don't need to fear; I just need to believe Your Word, rest in Your promises, and step out in faith. Help me to glorify Christ as I walk in Your ways. Help me to be strong as I yield to Your control. In Jesus' name, amen.

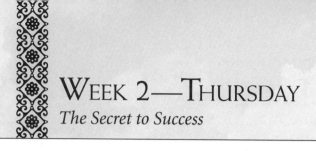

WEEK 2—THURSDAY
The Secret to Success

"This Book of the Law shall not depart from your mouth, but you shall meditate in it day and night, that you may observe to do according to all that is written in it. For then you will make your way prosperous, and then you will have good success."

JOSHUA 1:8

When Joshua took over for Moses, he was afraid. How could he follow such a huge spiritual leader as Moses? God knew Joshua was very fearful of this big assignment, so He shared with him the secret to success.

Joshua 1:8 makes it clear that prosperity and true success come from giving top priority to the Word of God. Joshua was to have the Word in his mouth, in his mind, and in his heart. The Word of God was to direct his paths and govern the people. Joshua was not just to know the Word; he was to be careful to obey the Word. Later in the New Testament, Jesus said, "If you know these things, you are blessed if you do them" (John 13:17 NASB). Blessings come to those who obey, to those who step out in faith and do what the Lord says to do.

The Bible is food for your soul. It is milk (1 Peter 2:2) and bread (Matthew 4:4) and meat (Hebrews 5:14). Begin today to increase your intake of the Word. Start memorizing a verse each week, and put God's Word into daily practice. If you do this, God will bless every aspect of your life with His grace, peace, and power. Try it and see.

....

God, I thank You for Your Word. Help me to read it and heed it so I can grow closer to You. In Jesus' name, amen.

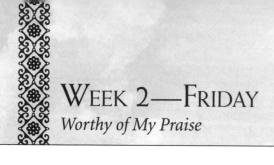

WEEK 2—FRIDAY
Worthy of My Praise

And Hannah prayed and said: "My heart rejoices in the LORD; my horn is exalted in the LORD. I smile at my enemies, because I rejoice in Your salvation. No one is holy like the LORD, for there is none besides You, nor is there any rock like our God."

1 SAMUEL 2:1–2

Poor Hannah was barren. She wanted a child more than anything, but no child would come. She brought her broken heart to the Lord, poured out all her pain to Him, and God heard her request and answered her prayer. She named her son Samuel, which means "asked of God." After Samuel was weaned, Hannah fulfilled her promise to God and took him to Eli, the high priest, to raise him as one dedicated to the Lord for life.

Can you imagine giving up your only son, the son you prayed and wept for? What a supreme sacrifice! Yet Hannah was full of praise when she presented Samuel to Eli. She rejoiced in the Lord for His goodness and grace in giving her a son. Her praise and faithfulness so honored God that He blessed her with three more sons and two daughters.

How are you doing with prayer and praise? Hannah is a great example to follow. Her prayers were from the heart, and her praise was bold and powerful. She truly blessed the Lord, and He greatly blessed her in return. He will do the same for you!

....

Father, please help me to grow in my prayer and praise. Help me share my needs from the depths of my heart. Help me always to give thanks—even in the hard times—for You alone are worthy. Amen.

DR. JEFF SCHREVE, FIRST BAPTIST CHURCH TEXARKANA, TEXARKANA, TX

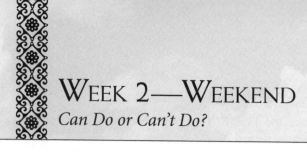

Week 2—Weekend
Can Do or Can't Do?

For You are my lamp, O Lord; the Lord shall enlighten my darkness. For by You I can run against a troop; by my God I can leap over a wall. as for God, His way is perfect; the word of the Lord is proven; He is a shield to all who trust in Him.

2 Samuel 22:29–31

One of my dear friends is Olin Owens, the facility manager at FBC Texarkana. Olin is eighty years old and still has energy to burn. One of his favorite sayings is, *"Can't is not in my vocabulary."* Olin is a can-do person.

David also was a can-do person. The source of his confidence was not himself but his God. David trusted God with all his heart. Only by the Lord could David successfully go against a troop of men or leap over a high wall. He believed Philippians 4:13 ("I can do all things through Him who strengthens me" NASB) even before it was written.

What about you? Are you a can-do or a can't-do person? Do you see difficulty in every opportunity or an opportunity in every difficulty? Maybe you are facing a seemingly impossible situation. Maybe you are thinking it just can't be done. Look to the Lord and factor Him into the equation. When you do, *impossible* becomes *I'm possible* with God.

....

Dear Lord, I want to be a can-do person. I never want to look at a situation without factoring in the Lord Jesus—my God, my Savior, and my Friend. Please give me Your light in the darkness, and show forth Your strength and power as I trust in You. Amen.

WEEK 3—MONDAY
Putting the Awe Back in Worship

Honor and majesty are before Him; strength and gladness are in His place. Give to the LORD, O families of the peoples, give to the LORD glory and strength. Give to the LORD the glory due His name; bring an offering, and come before Him. Oh, worship the LORD in the beauty of holiness!

1 CHRONICLES 16:27–29

Have you ever been to a place on your bucket list? Perhaps you've visited places such as your favorite childhood team's stadium, the Grand Canyon, the Sea of Galilee, or my favorite, the empty tomb. I was able to visit each of these places, and these are some of my most cherished memories. Each one was special in its own way. All of these places had one thing in common: they produced a sense of awe in my life. The wonder in my heart came to life as I spent time in each of these places.

King David wrote this passage about the very presence of God. Not a distant God, but a God who was near and was worthy of honor and glory. The mention of His name brought praise from David's life. Awe overcame this king so much that he proclaimed the words found in this song.

So often today, we base our worship on how our week has gone or our current life experiences. Today may we step away from everything around us for just a moment, step into the presence of a holy God, and simply stand in awe.

....

Lord Jesus, may I just stop for a moment and stand in awe of You. May I see this day in light of who You are and Your presence in my life. Amen.

RONNIE BOWERS, FLINT-GROVES BAPTIST CHURCH, GASTONIA, NC

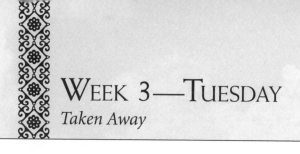

WEEK 3—TUESDAY
Taken Away

Then Job arose, tore his robe, and shaved his head; and he fell to the ground and worshiped. And he said: "Naked I came from my mother's womb, and naked shall I return there. The LORD gave, and the LORD has taken away; blessed be the name of the LORD." In all this Job did not sin nor charge God with wrong.

JOB 1:20–22

S ome verses of the Bible can keep me up at night. Today's verses are some of them because I never want to have to quote these verses from experience. But I have watched these verses come to life multiple times in our church family. Some families in our fellowship have lost children or husbands or wives. I have pastored long enough to know that tragedy and loss come today just as they did in Job's time.

Many of us have experienced the same type of losses. So how do we handle it? The portion of today's verse that is difficult for me is the phrase, "In all this Job did not sin nor charge God with wrong." How could Job do that? His faith had to be so strong and deep that it sustained him even in the face of such loss. I mentioned the circumstances earlier from my church family because I have learned from watching them. Deep faith does not avoid pain and hurt; rather, it rises above the struggle. Job trusted that somehow, even if he couldn't understand his circumstances, God would sustain him.

Friend, I do not know how deep the pain is for you today, but you are not alone. May you find strength to trust Him and still worship Him today.

Father, teach me to trust You today to a greater degree than I ever have before. Keep me from turning my heart away from You. Amen.

Week 3—Wednesday
Acquainted with Our God

Now acquaint yourself with Him, and be at peace; thereby good will come to you. Receive, please, instruction from His mouth, and lay up His words in your heart. If you return to the Almighty, you will be built up; you will remove iniquity far from your tents.

Job 22:21–23

Have you ever bought something, pulled it out of the box, looked at the instructions, and realized putting this together was going to be harder than you thought? The temptation was so great just to flip the box over, look at the big picture, and try to put it together without using the instructions. You might have said to yourself, "Forget the instructions! Surely I can do this without them!" The problem was the big picture didn't show you all the separate pieces and how they all fit together.

Life is often like that. We don't have the master plan, and we have no idea how each part of our lives fits into that plan. Job struggled with a lot of the pieces of his life and could see no real master plan. A friend reminded Job that peace doesn't come from striving to put all the pieces of life together; instead, peace comes from learning to trust the One who knows the master plan and can put each piece in place.

Sometimes we need the same reminder. We must write His Word in our hearts, receive it, trust it, and act on it. In doing so, we not only learn His teachings but we become deeply acquainted with God Himself.

....

Father, may I know You and submit my life to You today. God, You have a design for my life. Help me learn to trust You with the big picture and all of its pieces. Amen.

RONNIE BOWERS, FLINT-GROVES BAPTIST CHURCH, GASTONIA, NC

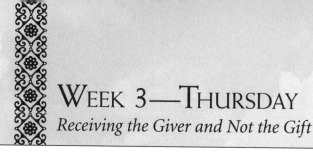

WEEK 3—THURSDAY
Receiving the Giver and Not the Gift

There are many who say, "Who will show us any good?" LORD, lift up the light of Your countenance upon us. You have put gladness in my heart, more than in the season that their grain and wine increased. I will both lie down in peace, and sleep; for You alone, O LORD, make me dwell in safety.

PSALM 4:6–8

When it came to Christmas, my wife and I opted to teach our kids to believe in Santa Claus. It was wonderful watching them rush down and find their gifts and wonder how Santa could have known just what they wanted. That was so much fun until the year they figured out the truth. The wonder was gone, and we worried our kids would think we had lied to them.

So we chose to deal with it courageously. We talked to our oldest daughter about Santa. We explained we had been the ones buying all the gifts for them every year and putting them out every Christmas morning. She held up her hand and told us politely, "I have known for years about Santa Claus."

She also told us that knowing only made Christmas better for her. She said she knew how much we really loved her if we went to all the trouble of buying things she wanted, and then arranging them in secret for her to find on Christmas morning.

Can you believe it? It was more about the giver than the gifts. In today's passage, the psalmist testified he was more content with the Lord than His gifts. Many times in our lives we settle for the gifts rather than the Giver. Today let's celebrate the Giver of good gifts and not just the gifts He blesses us with.

....

Father, may I be more satisfied today with You, the Giver of good gifts, than the gifts You bless me with. Amen.

WEEK 3—FRIDAY
Guidance Required

Give ear to my words, O LORD, consider my meditation. Give heed to the voice of my cry, my King and my God, for to You I will pray. My voice You shall hear in the morning, O LORD; in the morning I will direct it to You, and I will look up.

PSALM 5:1–3

Several years ago, a friend of mine introduced me to a new hobby: fly-fishing. After the first trip with him, I was hooked—literally! The first trip was awesome. We caught approximately fifteen fish and neither one of us ended up falling into the water. Our second trip was not as successful, though, because I forgot his instructions, which were: "Follow me and step where I step because it is deeper than it looks. Plant your feet firmly before taking the next step because it can be slick. And finally, remember the first two instructions!"

I know I don't have to tell you, but it was deeper and slicker than it looked on our second trip! After my first fall, I came up from the very cold water, and he said, "Told ya!" At that moment, I wished I had received a gentle reminder of those important instructions before heading out into the water.

Every day we need to be reminded of the instructions that situations in life can be deeper and slicker than we think. But if we just ask the Lord, He will direct our days. We must cry out to Him and ask for His instructions because we don't know what the days hold. We always need to be reminded that He holds our days and can direct our paths if we just ask Him.

Father, this is a new and exciting day. I have no idea what this day holds, but You do. Lord, guide my every step today. Amen.

RONNIE BOWERS, FLINT-GROVES BAPTIST CHURCH, GASTONIA, NC

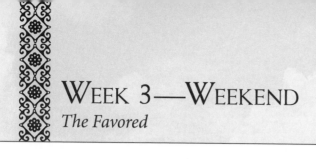

WEEK 3—WEEKEND
The Favored

But let all those rejoice who put their trust in You; let them ever shout for joy, because You defend them; let those also who love Your name be joyful in You. For You, O LORD, will bless the righteous; with favor You will surround him as with a shield.

PSALM 5:11–12

While I was teaching a group of African pastors in an open-air meeting room in Lusaka, Zambia, it began to rain. My colleagues and I kept teaching until we heard loud laughing and crying from across the field. We turned to see the pastors' wives dancing and laughing and crying in the rain, singing praises to God! It hadn't rained in months, and it wasn't the rainy season yet. Thus they were very excited.

Suddenly, we lost control of the meeting, and Pastor Zulu said, "God is pleased with this. God has surrounded us with favor. God is good and faithful." To us, it was just an afternoon shower, but to them it was a blessing raining down from God. Never will I forget the sound of God's favor and the shouts of joy as the people danced before the Lord.

The smell of an afternoon shower stills reminds me of how God provides for the righteous. May we celebrate His name and His favor today. May we also never take for granted even what appears to us to be the simplest of blessings.

....

Father, I celebrate Your name today. As I approach this day, may I recognize Your favor and may it bring joy to my life. Amen.

WEEK 4—MONDAY
My Refuge

The LORD also will be a refuge for the oppressed, a refuge in times of trouble. And those who know Your name will put their trust in You; for You, LORD, have not forsaken those who seek You.

PSALM 9:9–10

Throughout his life, David understood the real meaning of trouble because he spent many years in distress. Most certainly the sight of Goliath would have upset him. He also found himself in danger when King Saul pursued him. David's very life was often under threat, and he had to run and hide.

David was also a man who had a deep and abiding faith in God. He knew God would deliver His righteous justice. God provides refuge for all who have trouble placed on them by others, and He is the ultimate refuge for all who find themselves in trouble. God is unchanging. Those who know Him and have a personal relationship with Him can be assured He will never leave them or forsake them.

....

Dear God, I thank You for who You are. You are almighty and sovereign in all Your ways. You are the righteous Judge. You are my refuge and strength. I confess my sins to You today, and I ask You to forgive me. Thank You for enabling me to place my full confidence in You. Thank You for always being there for me. In Jesus' name I pray, amen.

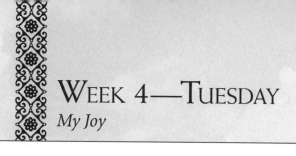

WEEK 4—TUESDAY
My Joy

But I have trusted in Your mercy; my heart shall rejoice in Your salvation. I will sing to the LORD, because He has dealt bountifully with me.

PSALM 13:5–6

At the start of this amazing psalm, David began with such a woeful lament one would think he was at the bottom of the sea! It is almost a wail of despair. His enemies were real and were on the attack. One can only imagine how he would wake up every morning surrounded by the dark circumstances of his life, and very quickly sorrow would overtake his resolve. The reality of the world in which he lived soon obliterated any perspective he had of the many blessings God had given to him.

Thus David cried out to God in this psalm. Four successive "how longs" (Psalm 13:1–2) find this great man cowering before his enemies and depressed in his heart and soul. Until, of course, he began to set his heart on God. Suddenly David recognized the splendor and majesty of the One who had set Himself apart for those who love Him. And because of God's love and mercy, David could trust in Him in every way. As a result, David's heart rejoiced. He burst into song, realizing that God's salvation is every reason to be hopeful in spite of his circumstances. All of a sudden, the bountiful blessings of God replaced David's despair.

Dear God, I confess my heart has not been set on You as it should. Thank You for loving me. Thank You for the bountiful blessings of my life. In Jesus' name, amen.

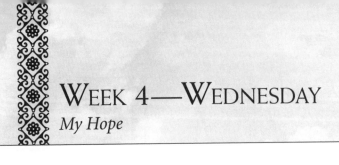

Week 4—Wednesday
My Hope

Therefore my heart is glad, and my glory rejoices; my flesh also will rest in hope.
For You will not leave my soul in Sheol, nor will You allow Your Holy One to see
corruption. You will show me the path of life; in Your presence is fullness of joy; at Your
right hand are pleasures forevermore.

Psalm 16:9–11

These three verses find David expressing great joy. His heart burst with gladness from the very core of his being. His "glory" was the reminder that he was created in the very image of God, and his hope was made complete in the full affirmation of the eternal splendor of God. David also highlighted the very reason why his "flesh" could "rest in hope." He saw God as his Deliverer and Provider, and he knew God would save him from an eternity in Sheol. This was also a reference to how God would not allow Jesus Christ ("Your Holy One") to be confined to death and would in fact raise Him triumphantly from the grave. Because of this promise of a future resurrection, David had a living hope, and he found himself in a state of ecstatic joy.

After this, David pointed out how God reveals himself to His people. Because His right hand contains all the pleasures of His promises, God could show David the "path of life." In like manner, God directs all of His children on this same path, and His very presence fills His children with inexpressible joy.

....

Dear God, thank You for the joy of knowing You as Savior and Lord. Thank You for rescuing me from the grave, and thank You for filling my life with Your presence. I have real hope in You. In Jesus' name I pray, amen.

DR. DON WILTON, FIRST BAPTIST CHURCH, SPARTANBURG, SC

WEEK 4—THURSDAY
My Petition

Hear a just cause, O LORD, attend to my cry; give ear to my prayer which is not from deceitful lips. Let my vindication come from Your presence; let Your eyes look on the things that are upright.

You have tested my heart; You have visited me in the night; You have tried me and have found nothing; I have purposed that my mouth shall not transgress.

PSALM 17:1–3

God is not only our loving heavenly Father, He is also our righteous and holy Judge. We can approach His throne of grace with anything that concerns us. Nothing falls outside of His divine jurisdiction, and everything matters to Him. For example, in Philippians 4:6, Paul exhorts believers to bring everything before God in prayer. Nothing is off limits.

This is exactly where we find David in Psalm 17. He was in a law court—God's law court. David stood before the ultimate Chief Justice of the world. This is His world, and without Him was not anything made that was made. David approached the divine court and appealed to God to respond to him and recognize David's relationship with Him. The manner in which he petitioned God was one of great humility. David pleaded his case by testifying about his personal faithfulness to God. God had tested him and visited him in times past, even when few were watching. David knew God had found him to be upright and faithful and, therefore, would look on him with favor. David had confidence that God would reward his faithfulness.

. . . .

Dear God, how deeply I confess my sin before You. Search my heart and know my thoughts. Please grant me Your favor. In Jesus' name I pray, amen.

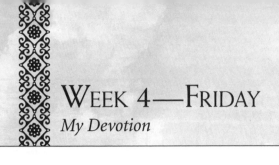

WEEK 4—FRIDAY
My Devotion

I will love You, O LORD, my strength. The LORD is my rock and my fortress and my deliverer; My God, my strength, in whom I will trust; My shield and the horn of my salvation, my stronghold. I will call upon the LORD, who is worthy to be praised; so shall I be saved from my enemies.

PSALM 18:1–3

Everything the psalmist said about his Lord flowed out of his devotion to God. And this devotion is the ultimate mark of his love for God. David expresses tender intimacy with God. His vibrant and real love laid the foundation for his total submission to God. And because he was devoted to God, David was able to speak with such confidence about being "saved from [his] enemies." He knew God would protect him at all times.

A heart in tune with God is a heart in touch with God's actions. So David's outburst of love for the Lord formulated this essential testimony of his entire life. His devotion to God enabled him to affirm God is the mighty Warrior. It is the Lord who was able to provide for His servant, David. He was all David needed, regardless of the challenging and tough times he faced.

Dear God, I want to tell You just how much I love You today. I am totally devoted to You. Thank You for Your divine power and protection in my life regardless of the circumstances I face. In Jesus' name I pray, amen.

DR. DON WILTON, FIRST BAPTIST CHURCH, SPARTANBURG, SC

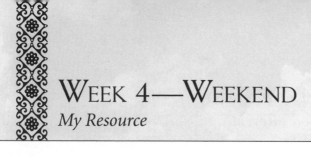

WEEK 4—WEEKEND
My Resource

As for God, His way is perfect; the word of the LORD is proven; He is a shield to all who trust in Him. For who is God, except the LORD? And who is a rock, except our God? It is God who arms me with strength, and makes my way perfect.

PSALM 18:30–32

One can only imagine the loneliness of David as he found himself constantly hounded and challenged. Saul was relentless in his pursuit of David. The king used every means possible to demean David and make certain David knew his very life was at stake. As a result, David found himself constantly on the run. The enemy lurked in the shadows, poised to attack at any moment. This unrelenting threat of attack produced a heavy burden on his heart. Time and again he plunged into depression and despair.

Except for the resource he knew he had in God, David could not have survived, and this is what Psalm 18:30–32 recognizes. Rather than bragging about his own abilities, David pointed out the power of the Lord. Rather than making a display of his fighting prowess, David humbly relied on the Lord. And because of this David was able to depend on what he knew to be true: God was his ultimate resource. He was the One to whom David could turn. He was totally trustworthy because all His ways are perfect. His words are true. His protection is sure. David knew beyond a shadow of a doubt that God was the Rock upon which he could stand. God gave him all the strength necessary to survive. In the end, David knew God would save him from the hand of King Saul.

Dear God, You are my Rock and my Fortress. Thank You for always being there for me. In Jesus' name I pray, amen.

WEEK 5—MONDAY
How to Receive God's Revelation

The law of the LORD is perfect, converting the soul; the testimony of the LORD is sure, making wise the simple; the statutes of the LORD are right, rejoicing the heart; the commandment of the LORD is pure, enlightening the eyes; the fear of the LORD is clean, enduring forever; the judgments of the LORD are true and righteous altogether.

PSALM 19:7–9

In today's Bible reading we find a sixfold description of God's special revelation.

The Law: This is God's revealed will. It restores the soul.

The Testimony: This is God's truth. It makes the simple person wise.

The Statutes: These are God's injunctions. They make our hearts rejoice.

The Commandments: These are authoritative words from God. They bring enlightenment to the eyes of the reader.

The Fear: This connotes a reverential trust in the heart of the believer.

The Judgments: These are the decisions that relate to our human situations that lead us to righteous choices.

The psalmist tells us that following the revelation of God leads to great reward and keeps us from error. This obedience is like gold in our pockets. It is like sweet honey to the taste. Disobedience leads to poverty and bitterness.

For God's revelation to be beneficial, one must read the Word, believe the Word, obey the Word, and apply the Word.

Lord, enlighten me by Your Word so that I make wise decisions and fair judgments. Amen.

DR. TED H. TRAYLOR, OLIVE BAPTIST CHURCH, PENSACOLA, FL

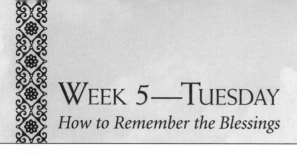

WEEK 5—TUESDAY
How to Remember the Blessings

For You meet him with the blessings of goodness; You set a crown of pure gold upon his head. He asked life from You, and You gave it to him—length of days forever and ever. His glory is great in Your salvation; honor and majesty You have placed upon him. For You have made him most blessed forever; You have made him exceedingly glad with Your presence.

PSALM 21:3–6

This is a royal psalm of thanksgiving where David acknowledged God as the ultimate King who had established David's kingdom. David spoke in verse three about the blessings of God. Christians should strive every day to remember the many benefits God has bestowed up them.

All good things come down from the Father. He is the Author of all. Blessings come in various shapes: finances, jobs, health, friends, family, church, and much more. Thank God for His blessings.

Of course some blessings don't appear to be blessings when they first arrive. Sometimes the rough spots turn out to be blessings in disguise. David had those. He confronted Goliath, and out of that came encouragement for every generation of future believers. King Saul turned on David, and from that came the psalms David never would have penned if he hadn't faced difficult times. His own son Absalom even rebelled against him. Throughout that family tragedy, David still recognized God's hand was upon him.

God never wastes a painful period in your life. God has a plan to work things out for your good.

Lord, today I give You praise for the many blessings in my life. You are a good, good Father. In Jesus' name, amen.

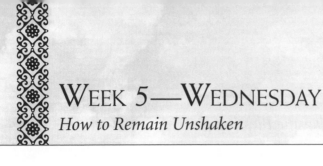

WEEK 5—WEDNESDAY
How to Remain Unshaken

His glory is great in Your salvation; honor and majesty You have placed upon him. For You have made him most blessed forever; You have made him exceedingly glad with Your presence. For the king trusts in the LORD, and through the mercy of the Most High he shall not be moved.

PSALM 21:5–7

David continued in this royal psalm to speak of his trust in almighty God. In verse seven the shepherd king spoke of his confidence in the Lord. He then gave us a most important word (found in the NASB translation of this passage): *lovingkindness*. This word gave the king stability. He would not be shaken.

Lovingkindness is a translation of the Hebrew word *hesed*. We find it more than 200 times in the Old Testament. It means a steadfast love, and it stresses the idea of being in a loving relationship. We find it often in the verses speaking of God's faithful love toward an unfaithful people.

The book that illustrates this word most pointedly is Hosea. Gomer had gone away in unfaithfulness, and Hosea was called to display *hesed* toward his wife. God commanded Hosea to love her even though she was an adulteress (Hosea 3:1). This is a picture of how even though His people turned to other gods, God's faithful love for them never wavered.

David pointed out that having this kind of relationship with the Most High God leads to a stance where we are unshaken. We should remain mindful this day of God's lovingkindness toward us.

....

Thank You, dear Father in heaven, for Your lovingkindness and unfailing pursuit of me. In Jesus' name, amen.

DR. TED H. TRAYLOR, OLIVE BAPTIST CHURCH, PENSACOLA, FL

Week 5—Thursday
How the Good Shepherd Cares for Us

*The Lord is my shepherd; I shall not want. He makes me to lie down in green
pastures; He leads me beside the still waters. He restores my soul; He leads me in the
paths of righteousness for His name's sake.*

Psalm 23:1–3

As a college student I made my first trip to Israel where I met my first
shepherd. My group was walking and came upon a group of lambs, and
we decided we wanted to touch one of them. As we approached the animals,
we heard a scream. A young boy came out from the rocks where he was watching. Along with his voice, he raised a stick. Needless to say, we backed off and
did not touch the sheep. This young shepherd was willing to lay down his
life—or ours—for the sheep. Psalm 23 came alive to me that day.

As followers of Jesus, we have a Shepherd. He is a Guide, Protector, and
constant Companion. In John 10:11 Jesus tells us He is the Good Shepherd
and He lays down His life for the sheep. In 1 Peter 5:4 we read that Jesus is the
Chief Shepherd and will come again one day for His sheep. We must never
forget that He watches over us.

As you go about your everyday life, He is with you. The Good Shepherd is
present. Trust Him with your life. He knows more than you know, and He
loves you more than you love yourself.

*Father, I'm glad You know my path today before I walk it. I choose to trust You.
Lord, I confess there are days I need restoration. Make me strong in Your Spirit.
Teach me to slow down and rest by the still waters You provide on the path today.
Today I want nothing other than to know You! Amen.*

Week 5—Friday
How to Walk Forward to Heaven

Yea, though I walk through the valley of the shadow of death, I will fear no evil; for You are with me; Your rod and Your staff, they comfort me. You prepare a table before me in the presence of my enemies; You anoint my head with oil; my cup runs over. Surely goodness and mercy shall follow me all the days of my life; and I will dwell in the house of the Lord forever.

Psalm 23:4–6

As a minister of the gospel, I have walked some tough, dark days with the terminally ill. Although salvation may be secure and the follower of Christ knows the promises of Scripture, anxiousness is a normal response to the unknown.

One particular saint who was in the final stage of cancer taught me a valuable lesson along this line. I had stopped by his home to find him in excruciating pain. He was silent most of the visit. But as I knelt at his bedside to pray, he gathered his breath to whisper in my ear.

"Pastor, I have known Psalm 23 most of my life, but I have never understood what 'shadow of death' meant until now. The day is dark, but I have peace. I realize there is no shadow without light. And it is that light, my Lord, who is with me. And however many days remain, goodness and mercy are behind me, moving me forward to dwell in heaven forever."

Do you know someone grappling with peace in his or her final days on earth? Be encouraged that no matter how many steps are left on his or her journey, God is with this individual. All the way.

Dear Lord, fear can grip my heart and steal my joy at times. Thank You for this psalm to remind me what You are doing to move me toward heaven. Amen.

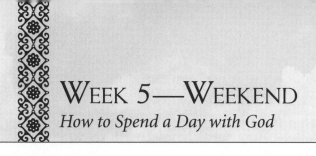

WEEK 5—WEEKEND
How to Spend a Day with God

Show me Your ways, O LORD; teach me Your paths. Lead me in Your truth and teach me, for You are the God of my salvation; on You I wait all the day.

PSALM 25:4–5

Every day is a gift. We have a choice of what to do with it. Tomorrow it will be gone forever. We should desire to make each day worthwhile.

In Psalm 25:4–5 we find actions to take daily if we want to please the Lord.

Show me Your ways. Jesus taught us to pray not our will, but for His to be done. Discernment is vital as we long to understand the mysterious dealings of the Spirit. God will make His ways known to us. Listen for His voice saying, "This is the way; walk in it."

Teach me Your paths. Like parents who guide their child who is just learning to walk, God is our Father and will instruct us on which paths to take. A fork in the road is not a simple choice for Christians. We must heed the Father's direction, and then walk in it.

Lead me in the truth. This is where we must have ears to hear. Stop and listen because the Father is speaking. He often uses three pointers in helping us discern the way. Bible passages are one source of help. The Holy Spirit offers direction in following God's will. The wisdom of saintly counselors also offers godly advice to follow.

Make the most of the gift of today with God.

....

Lord, as I live today show me the steps to take. I have big decisions to make. Help me learn in the small steps so I will be prepared for the larger ones. In Jesus' name, amen.

WEEK 6—MONDAY
A Little Secret with a Big Reward

Who is the man that fears the LORD? Him shall He teach in the way He chooses. He himself shall dwell in prosperity, and his descendants shall inherit the earth. The secret of the LORD is with those who fear Him, and He will show them His covenant. My eyes are ever toward the LORD, for He shall pluck my feet out of the net.

PSALM 25:12–15

D o you like to be let in on a secret? If you're anything like most people, the answer to that question is yes. That's why the shelves of bookstores are filled with volumes of titles that begin something like this: *The Secret of How to . . .* You see, most people are naturally intrigued by some secret that will equip or enhance their lives.

In Psalm 25:12–15 David shared a little secret with a big reward. He said the person who fears God will be instructed by God's Word. The Lord confides in those who revere Him, and the result is abounding blessings. Learn this little secret—the fear of the Lord isn't just the beginning of wisdom (Proverbs 9:10), it is also the beginning of the only successful, safe, and truly satisfying walk in this life. When we learn to fear God we learn to trust Him, and when we trust Him, He reveals to us His will for our lives.

....

Lord, help me to revere and trust You. Let me not lean on my own understanding, but encourage me look to You for the answers to this life. Protect me from the snares of the enemy, and enable me to walk in such a way that honors You. Amen.

DR. BRAD WHITT, ABILENE BAPTIST CHURCH, MARTINEZ, GA

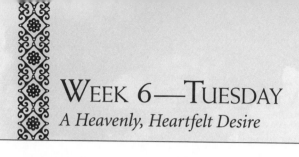

WEEK 6—TUESDAY
A Heavenly, Heartfelt Desire

One thing I have desired of the LORD, that will I seek: that I may dwell in the house of the LORD all the days of my life, to behold the beauty of the LORD, and to inquire in His temple. For in the time of trouble He shall hide me in His pavilion; in the secret place of His tabernacle He shall hide me; He shall set me high upon a rock.

PSALM 27:4–5

What a heavenly, heartfelt desire is found in these verses! David shared the lifelong goals he sought: to dwell and behold and inquire in the temple of the Lord. What is surprising about this proclamation by David is that he wrote this psalm when he was on the run. We read here an undeniable expression of his confidence in the promises of God. He knew in the midst of the fight that God would ultimately give him the victory and he would enjoy the Lord's presence.

That's a lesson we must learn. Even though things may not be going the way we want, and even though we may face fierce foes, our God is greater, and in His presence is joy forevermore. He will hide us from our troubles and set us high upon a rock. We must trust Him to do what only He can do and live in ways that express our complete confidence in Him.

....

Lord, in the midst of a world that seeks to draw me away from You and cause me to doubt Your promises, let me seek You with my whole heart and live a life that is pleasing in Your sight. In Jesus' name, amen.

WEEK 6—WEDNESDAY
Hearing God's Voice

Hear, O LORD, when I cry with my voice! Have mercy also upon me, and answer me.
When You said, "Seek My face," my heart said to You, "Your face, LORD, I will seek."
Do not hide Your face from me; do not turn Your servant away in anger; You have been
my help; do not leave me nor forsake me, O God of my salvation.

PSALM 27:7–9

H ave you ever cried out to God only to hear nothing but your own voice? If so, you can understand some of the emotions David experienced as he penned this psalm. Yet even when David heard no audible response, he knew deep down that God was near him.

So many times we cry out to God, desiring to see His face and enjoy His presence. We feel so far away from Him. What we fail to realize is that God desires us even more than we desire Him. He wants to fellowship with us because He loves us with an everlasting love. Yet our sin creates the distance and barriers between Him and us. That's why we must seek Him with our whole hearts. We must remove the obstacles in our lives that keep us from enjoying and experiencing His presence. The greatest thing to realize is that even when we don't hear His voice, even when we feel far away from God, God is never far away from us. He will never leave us or forsake us.

Lord, help me to remove the obstacles that keep me from a close fellowship with You. May I stay close and know You are the God of my salvation. In Jesus' name, amen.

DR. BRAD WHITT, ABILENE BAPTIST CHURCH, MARTINEZ, GA

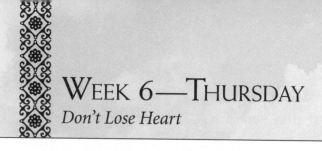

WEEK 6—THURSDAY
Don't Lose Heart

I would have lost heart, unless I had believed that I would see the goodness of the LORD in the land of the living. Wait on the LORD; be of good courage, and He shall strengthen your heart; wait, I say, on the LORD!

PSALM 27:13–14

The key to real success in this life and the life to come is in the heart. If an athlete loses heart, he or she will most likely lose the game. If a soldier loses heart, he or she will most surely lose the battle. David also needed not to lose heart, and in the midst of a crisis, he cried out to God and the Lord strengthened his heart.

In this psalm, David, a man after God's own heart, told of the absolute necessity of waiting on the Lord. That's a tough task to complete, but it is the key to encouragement and strength in our lives. Through waiting on the Lord we gain strength and rise up on wings of eagles! Therefore, no matter what we face, no matter the burden we bear, we must not lose heart. We must wait on the Lord and be encouraged, knowing He will strengthen us.

....

Lord, I concur with David that unless I believe I will see Your goodness in the land of the living, I will lose heart. But my confidence is in You and Your strength. That's why today I wait patiently on You and trust You to strengthen my heart. In Jesus' name, amen.

Week 6—Friday
God, Our Strength and Shield

Blessed be the LORD, because He has heard the voice of my supplications! The LORD is my strength and my shield; my heart trusted in Him, and I am helped; therefore my heart greatly rejoices, and with my song I will praise Him.

PSALM 28:6–7

Faith touches God's heart and moves His hand, and His hand controls all of creation. No wonder David broke out into a song of exaltation! He trusted God and experienced deliverance. When he was worn out, God became His strength. When wicked men attacked him, God was his shield. What a powerful picture of God's provision and protection in the life of someone who placed his trust in Him.

Are you sobbing today? Are you worn out and run down? Are you pierced through by the arrows of the enemy? Turn to the Lord and trust Him. He will be your strength and shield. He will make a way where there seems to be no way. He will put a song in your heart and praise on your lips that enable you to cry out, "Blessed be the Lord!"

....

Lord, I praise You for hearing my prayers. I thank You for taking care of every need and overcoming every enemy in my life. I exalt You for Your abounding goodness, and I declare to the world that You are my strength and my shield. My heart rejoices in You today, and with my lips and life I will praise Your name. Amen.

DR. BRAD WHITT, ABILENE BAPTIST CHURCH, MARTINEZ, GA

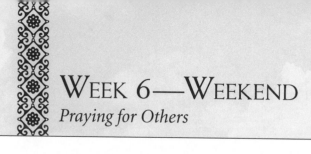

WEEK 6—WEEKEND
Praying for Others

The LORD is their strength, and He is the saving refuge of His anointed. Save Your people, and bless Your inheritance; shepherd them also, and bear them up forever.

PSALM 28:8–9

We live in a selfish world, and we are prone to be selfish people. Too many times we are concerned only about ourselves—what we need, enjoy, and want. How refreshing and striking it is, then, to read where David took the focus off himself and began to pray for others. This was specifically a prayer for Israel, and David prayed for his people's salvation. He prayed that the Lord would shepherd them—guide and provide for them—and exalt them.

Do you pray this way for others? Do you pray for the salvation of your family, friends, coworkers, or classmates? Do you pray God will guide your spouse and children? Do you pray He will lift up your boss or teacher? Great blessing is found in praying for others and seeing God work in their lives in response to your prayers. Ask the Lord to touch your heart and help you to become a powerful prayer warrior who intercedes on behalf of others.

Lord, place on my heart those who are in need. Help me to be aware of those around me, and then prompt me to pray for them. Please hear my prayers for my family, friends, and acquaintances. Lord, You are a saving refuge. Help me to run to You for salvation, strength, and sustenance. Bless Your people and save souls today, I pray. Amen.

WEEK 7—MONDAY
Our Only Gift

Give unto the LORD, O you mighty ones, give unto the LORD glory and strength. Give unto the LORD the glory due to His name; worship the LORD in the beauty of holiness. The voice of the LORD is over the waters; the God of glory thunders; the LORD is over many waters. The voice of the LORD is powerful; the voice of the LORD is full of majesty.

PSALM 29:1–4

Psalm 29 talks about what you can give the Lord. Have you ever considered the only thing you can give God? You could give him your life, but He gave it to you first. You could give Him your tithe, but He gave it to you first. The only thing you truly can give God is your worship. Your worship is what He desires from you. The Bible says, "But the hour cometh, and now is, when the true worshippers shall worship the Father in spirit and in truth: for the Father seeketh such to worship him" (John 4:23 KJV). What are some of the reasons people go to church on Sunday? To fellowship with others? To hear a sermon? In actuality, the number one reason you should go to church is to worship God!

Worship is not about your clothing, your denomination, or your circumstances in life. Do not allow what is wrong with you to stop you from worshipping what is right with God. Worship is about exalting God for who He is and praising Him for what He has done.

I spent most of my ministry making workers out of people. If I could go back and start over again, I would make worshippers out of them instead. That is what God desires most!

....

Lord, make me a worshipper! In Jesus' name, amen.

DR. BENNY TATE, ROCK SPRINGS CHURCH, MILNER, GA

Week 7—Tuesday
God Is Good

Oh, how great is Your goodness, which You have laid up for those who fear You, which You have prepared for those who trust in You in the presence of the sons of men! You shall hide them in the secret place of Your presence from the plots of man; You shall keep them secretly in a pavilion from the strife of tongues.

Psalm 31:19–20

A deacon once spoke up in a church service and with great excitement stated, "God am good!"

The pastor corrected him by stating, "God is good."

And the deacon replied, "He sure am. He sure am."

It wasn't correct grammar, but the deacon was correct. God is good, and He is good to us all of the time. This is what Psalm 31:19–20 teaches.

A verse I cling to during difficult times in life is Romans 8:28, "And we know that all things work together for good to them that love God" (KJV). I am glad the verse doesn't say *some, many,* or *most,* but *all*! The good, the bad, and the ugly! God works them all for our good and His glory.

And consider that Paul was the man to make this statement. Yes, the man who was beaten five times with thirty-nine stripes and three times with rods. He was stoned, shipwrecked, betrayed, and falsely accused. But he still said God worked everything for his good. God is too loving to be unkind! Remember, God's sovereignty will help you keep your sanity.

....

Lord, thank You for Your goodness! In Jesus' name, amen.

Week 7—Wednesday
God Will Guide You

You are my hiding place; You shall preserve me from trouble; You shall surround me with songs of deliverance. I will instruct you and teach you in the way you should go; I will guide you with My eye.

Psalm 32:7–8

There have been times in almost thirty-five years of marriage that I started to reveal something in a group setting and got a certain look from my wife, Barbara. Yes, I could see in her eyes and sense she was saying, *Don't go there!* She was guiding me with her eyes.

How encouraging to know that God also guides us with His eyes, which is what Psalm 32:8 asserts. God wants to guide and direct our lives because He has a plan and purpose for our existence.

One of the ways God guides our lives is through the Holy Spirit. The Holy Spirit came upon people in the Old Testament to accomplish certain tasks; after Pentecost He came to live within all believers. Our Savior even said it was more beneficial for the invisible Holy Spirit to be on the earth than the visible Jesus (John 16:7). Today we have a privilege that Moses, David, and Daniel did not have—we can experience the Holy Spirit living within our hearts to guide and direct us. If we yield to the Holy Spirit, He will show us which doors to walk through and which ones we should close.

....

Lord, guide me in the paths of righteousness for Your name's sake. Amen.

WEEK 7—THURSDAY
God Knows Best

Our soul waits for the LORD; He is our help and our shield. For our heart shall rejoice in Him, because we have trusted in His holy name. Let Your mercy, O LORD, be upon us, just as we hope in You.

PSALM 33:20–22

I often am an impatient person. I even want the microwave to hurry up! But the Bible teaches me to wait on God. Many times I prayed for outcomes and events and became discouraged because an answer did not come quickly. Yet I truly believe God was teaching me the importance of waiting. Learning to wait is what David alludes to in Psalm 33:20–22.

I believe God wants to teach us three lessons through waiting. First, God wants to teach persistence. Persistence is what got the snail on the ark! A mushroom will come up in my yard in six hours, but an oak tree takes thirty years. I have often said, "I am an oak tree because an oak tree is only a nut that refused to quit." Persistence is important.

Second, God wants Christians to learn the importance of preparation. We would not give a five-year-old child the keys to the car because he or she is not mature enough. Many times we simply are not ready for what we are aspiring to. We must prepare ourselves for the future.

Third, God wants us to learn His plans are better than ours. Mary and Martha wanted Jesus to come and heal their sick brother, Lazarus, but Jesus waited four days before arriving! Why? Mary and Martha wanted their brother healed, but Jesus wanted to perform a resurrection. God's plans for our lives are always better than our plans. The secret is to wait on Him.

God, help me to wait on You. Amen.

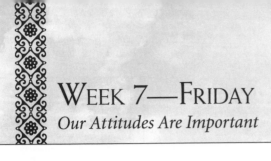

Week 7—Friday
Our Attitudes Are Important

I will bless the LORD at all times; His praise shall continually be in my mouth. My soul shall make its boast in the LORD; the humble shall hear of it and be glad. Oh, magnify the LORD with me, and let us exalt His name together.

PSALM 34:1–3

This portion of Scripture was written during a very difficult time in David's life. He was on the run for his life from King Saul. To protect himself, he sought refuge among the Philistines. As we can see in Psalm 34, his circumstances were not good, but he maintained a positive attitude.

We can learn three lessons in the midst of tough periods. First, our attitudes begin with the will. David said, "I will bless the LORD at all times." David determined within himself to praise the Lord even in his difficult circumstances.

Second, our attitude will determine our emotions: "My soul shall make its boast in the LORD." David had a good attitude about the Lord's provision, and his emotions showed it. This is what David exhibited while praising God.

Third, attitude spreads to others. David asserted, "The humble shall hear of it and be glad." Our attitudes are contagious! Others will see how we praise the Lord in spite of our difficult circumstances, and then they too will praise the Lord. We must never underestimate the importance of our attitudes.

Lord, help me to think properly. Amen.

DR. BENNY TATE, ROCK SPRINGS CHURCH, MILNER, GA

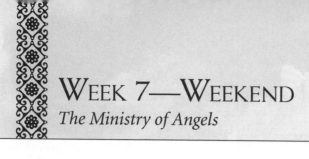

Week 7—Weekend
The Ministry of Angels

I sought the Lord, and He heard me, and delivered me from all my fears. They looked to Him and were radiant, and their faces were not ashamed. This poor man cried out, and the Lord heard him, and saved him out of all his troubles. The angel of the Lord encamps all around those who fear Him, and delivers them.

PSALM 34:4–7

In Psalm 34:4–7, David sang of how God uses angels to protect His children. I remember better than a decade ago I was walking through one of the most difficult times of my life and ministry. My sleep was greatly affected. I remember being wide awake early one Sunday morning, so I got up on this cold winter morning and went to a local walking track because I expected no one would be there. After I had walked several laps, a woman appeared out of nowhere. She stopped and looked at me and said, "Cheer up. Give it to God, and it will all work out." Then she disappeared. I have always believed it was an angelic encounter—and by the way, it did all work out!

The Bible tells us, "Be not forgetful to entertain strangers: for thereby some have entertained angels unawares" (Hebrews 13:2 KJV). Yes, angels still can manifest in human bodies as they did in biblical days! And apparently, often we do not recognize them in our lives. God also uses angels to escort us into the presence of God when we pass from this life (just as the angels did for Lazarus in Luke 16:22).

Angels have a great ministry!

··

God, help me to be aware of angels. In Jesus' name, amen.

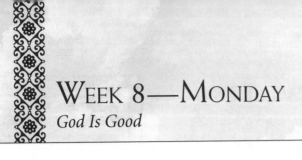

Week 8—Monday
God Is Good

Oh, taste and see that the LORD is good; blessed is the man who trusts in Him! Oh, fear the LORD, you His saints! There is no want to those who fear Him. The young lions lack and suffer hunger; but those who seek the LORD shall not lack any good thing.

PSALM 34:8–10

One of the first prayers many of us learn as children begins, "God is great. God is good." The goodness of God is a major theme throughout the Bible. God's goodness is not just something to talk about; it is something to experience. In this psalm David said, "Taste and see." He invited his readers to experience the goodness of God as he had already experienced it. We experience the goodness of God by trusting Him, fearing ("revering") Him, and seeking Him. The unbelieving, the irreverent, and the complacent can never fully experience the goodness of God.

This text reveals three ways God manifests His goodness toward us. First, He makes us happy: "Blessed is the man who trusts in Him!" Because God is good we need not be sad. Second, by establishing a covenant relationship with us, God reveals His goodness. The use of "saints" does not refer to humans in their natural state. Rather, it refers to people's spiritual state after salvation. We are saved because God is good. Third, through providing for our needs God demonstrates His goodness. Because God is good we "shall not lack any good thing." We should be very thankful!

Father, thank You for Your goodness toward me today. I have not earned Your kindness, and I certainly do not deserve it, but You have chosen to bestow it on me. I love You, Lord. In Jesus' name, amen.

DR. ROBERT C. PITMAN, BOB PITMAN MINISTRIES, MUSCLE SHOALS, AL

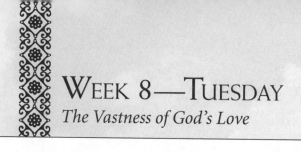

Week 8—Tuesday
The Vastness of God's Love

Your mercy, O Lord, is in the heavens; Your faithfulness reaches to the clouds. Your righteousness is like the great mountains; Your judgments are a great deep; O Lord, You preserve man and beast.

PSALM 36:5–6

In Ephesians 3:18, the apostle Paul prayed the believers might comprehend the full measure of the love of God. That is quite a prayer! In his hymn, "The Love of God," Frederick Lehman wrote,

> *Could we with ink the ocean fill, / And were the skies of parchment made,*
> *Were every stalk on earth a quill, / And every man a scribe by trade;*
> *To write the love of God above / Would drain the ocean dry;*
> *Nor could the scroll contain the whole, / Though stretched from sky to sky.*

In our text for today, "mercy" refers to God's lovingkindness, which is one of the greatest attributes of God found in Scripture. Because God is love He is also faithful, righteous, and just. Infidelity, unrighteousness, and injustice can never be in the presence of God.

Out of His great love He cares for all living creatures, both humans and animals. That means He cares for you! He cares about your life and all that your life involves. He cares for your physical, spiritual, emotional, and financial well-being. O how He loves you!

··

Father, thank You for loving me. Today I ask You to help me live in such a way others may see Your love through me. In Jesus' name, amen.

WEEK 8—WEDNESDAY
The House of the Lord

How precious is Your lovingkindness, O God! Therefore the children of men put their trust under the shadow of Your wings. They are abundantly satisfied with the fullness of Your house, and You give them drink from the river of Your pleasures. For with You is the fountain of life; in Your light we see light.

PSALM 36:7–9

In this text David described the lovingkindess of God, which can be found in His house. Because of God's lovingkindess, His dwelling is a "precious" house, which means it is very special.

God's house is precious because it is a *loving* house. One of the great tragedies of this fallen culture is that so many houses have no love inside them. Many husbands and wives share no love for each other. Countless numbers of children grow up in homes where they are unloved. Not so in God's house. His house overflows with His lovingkindness.

God's house is precious because it is a *safe* house. In far too many houses today people live in fear. Sometimes they fear home invaders. Sometimes those within the house cause the fear. Domestic violence is a blight on modern society. Child abuse is an offense to God and an embarrassment to the nation. But God's house is safe because in it we are under the shadow of His wings.

God's house is precious because it is a *happy* house. No hunger, thirst, or want are ever known in His house. His house is always full of abundance, and we "drink from the river of [His] pleasures." God's family all live in His precious house.

....

Father, thank You for the blessings of living in Your house. In Jesus' name, amen.

DR. ROBERT C. PITMAN, BOB PITMAN MINISTRIES, MUSCLE SHOALS, AL

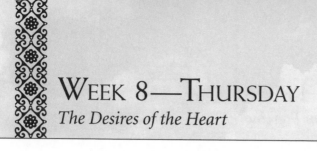

WEEK 8—THURSDAY
The Desires of the Heart

Trust in the LORD, and do good; dwell in the land, and feed on His faithfulness. Delight yourself also in the LORD, and He shall give you the desires of your heart.

PSALM 37:3–4

In Galatians 5:17 the apostle Paul reminded us that Christians possess two natures. One of those natures he described as the Spirit and the other he described as the flesh. He also informed us these two natures constantly struggle against each other to be in charge. The heart of the flesh contains evil desires (Galatians 5:19–21), but the heart of the Spirit desires godly things (Galatians 5:22–23).

How can we be sure the desires of our hearts are good desires and not evil ones? The Holy Spirit inspired David to give us some clues about this long before the New Testament was written. Note five principles from the text:

1. Develop a strong faith ("Trust in the LORD").
2. Live a godly life ("Do good").
3. Be mindful of biblical boundaries ("Dwell in the land").
4. Fill your heart with truth ("Feed on His faithfulness").
5. Put God first ("Delight yourself also in the LORD").

God will give you the desires of your heart when your desires come from a heart in love with Jesus and controlled by the Holy Spirit!

....

Father, today I ask You to guard my heart so my desires will be in accordance with Your perfect will for my life. In Jesus' name, amen.

WEEK 8—FRIDAY
How to Keep from Fretting

Commit your way to the LORD, trust also in Him, and He shall bring it to pass. He shall bring forth your righteousness as the light, and your justice as the noonday. Rest in the LORD, and wait patiently for Him; do not fret because of him who prospers in his way.

PSALM 37:5–7

*T*o *fret* means to be extremely anxious about something. In today's psalm, the word refers to being jealous of others' blessings. God's people need to be careful as they ponder the possessions of others. Sometimes those possessions may have been gotten by unethical or unscrupulous methods. That can spark the fire of anger in a believer's heart—even so, this attitude is unhealthy to have for an extended period of time. At other times the manner of getting possessions is not the issue; it is the possessions themselves. A child of God can become obsessed with the possessions of others. On the other hand, Christians should be able to rejoice in the blessings of others instead of coveting their blessings.

If we are not right in our hearts concerning the possessions of others, we are not right with God. David called us to commit ourselves completely to the Lord, to trust Him in every situation, and to wait until He makes all things right. He will provide for all of our needs.

....

Father, today I ask You to help me keep my eyes on You. Do not let me be jealous or angry because of what others may have. Teach me to be satisfied in You. In Jesus' name, amen.

DR. ROBERT C. PITMAN, BOB PITMAN MINISTRIES, MUSCLE SHOALS, AL

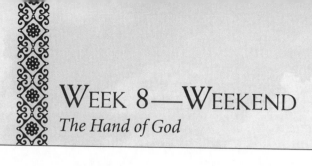

WEEK 8—WEEKEND
The Hand of God

The steps of a good man are ordered by the LORD, and He delights in his way. Though he fall, he shall not be utterly cast down; for the LORD upholds him with His hand.

PSALM 37:23–24

In 2 Timothy 4:7, the apostle Paul said, "I have finished the race." But he began his race long before he finished his race. It really began on the day of his salvation. When God saved you, He set before you a race to run. The course He set before you at times may seem smooth, but at other times it may seem exceedingly rough. Sometimes you will walk through green pastures, but not always. Also, you do not always run your race at a fast pace. The child of God sometimes crawls through rugged ravines and limps through deep valleys. On the course set before you will be great victories, but you will also face some defeats along the way. You will enounter times of great joy as well as times of deep sorrow.

In Psalm 37, David talked about a person whose life is committed to God. That person's course is "ordered by the LORD." You are not a victim of fickle fate as you go through life; you are a traveler on a divine path. As you follow His guidance, you please Him, and then He blesses you.

You may stumble as you run, but it will only be temporary because God holds your hand throughout the entire journey. He will never leave you lying in the dust; He will always pick you up again.

....

Father, thank You for holding my hand today. In Jesus' name, amen.

Week 9—Monday
Rejoice in the Rescue

I waited patiently for the LORD; and He inclined to me, and heard my cry. He also brought me up out of a horrible pit, out of the miry clay, and set my feet upon a rock, and established my steps. He has put a new song in my mouth—praise to our God; many will see it and fear, and will trust in the LORD.

PSALM 40:1–3

Life contains too few moments when nothing tempts us to worry and all things are in perfect order. Unfortunately, many deep pits and miry bogs appear along life's way. The worst of all is the pit of sin and the bog of emptiness. But our Lord rescues from both of these and ensures for us a dynamic and settled future.

In today's text, the psalmist expressed his trust in the Lord for rescuing him in all of life's circumstances. The imagery the psalmist used is indicative of life events that feel like deep pits and miry clay. Like the psalmist, we find ourselves in impossible situations at times.

I grew up in north Georgia. There is a substance called Georgia clay. It will leave a person stuck, incapable of moving. So too will certain situations of life. But the Lord removes us from the clay to rock-solid footing for His glory.

The imagery of verse one pictures God giving acute care to His child. I never cease to be amazed that the God of the universe listens to me and He constantly cares for me. The result of this grace is a new song, a song of praise that draws others to Christ.

....

Lord, help me to trust You in all situations. In Jesus' name, amen.

MICHAEL ORR, FIRST BAPTIST CHURCH CHIPLEY, CHIPLEY, FL

WEEK 9—TUESDAY
Trust and Be Happy

Blessed is that man who makes the LORD his trust, and does not respect the proud, nor such as turn aside to lies. Many, O LORD my God, are Your wonderful works which You have done; and Your thoughts toward us cannot be recounted to You in order; if I would declare and speak of them, they are more than can be numbered.

PSALM 40:4–5

As people saved from our sins, we should be the happiest people alive. Yet we often are not. Why is this? Because we do not trust God fully. Those who trust Him are "blessed," says the psalmist. Basically the word *blessed* means to be happy, to have a settled joy. How is it possible to experience life and have this joy?

First, we reflect on our redemption. In verse 5 the psalmist declared the many works the Lord had done. And there is no greater work than the work of redemption through Jesus Christ on our behalf. If we can trust Him with our eternal existence, we can trust Him with our temporary circumstances.

Second, we must call to mind the fact God has a purpose for us. He made us and He saved us for His glory. We have a glorious future. If we live obediently for His glory, we will fulfill His purpose for us, and our lives will be effective and not wasted.

Third, we must express our trust by obeying His Word. It is an act of faith to obey the Word of God and not to trust human wisdom and fall for cultural philosophies. Rather, we find joy in obeying our Lord (Luke 11:28).

Lord, help me to trust and obey. In Jesus' name, amen.

Week 9—Wednesday
He Can Handle It

Why are you cast down, O my soul? And why are you disquieted within me? Hope in God, for I shall yet praise Him for the help of His countenance.

Psalm 42:5

While in college I worked part-time as an assistant to my New Testament professor. One day I was scheduled to proctor an exam for a class while my wife took our baby girl to the doctor for tests. Our daughter had been sick and losing weight. We thought she might have cystic fibrosis. I was scared to death. I felt as if someone had kicked me in the stomach. I could not go with my wife to the appointment, and I remember sitting at a desk in front of the class as the students took the exam.

I was in anguish as I prayed silently, *Lord, help me. Heal my daughter.* My Bible was lying on the desk. I picked it up and happened to turn to the same verses from today's text and read. Tears welled up in my eyes and peace flooded my heart. The Lord reminded me, "I've got this." No matter the outcome, God had everything handled. And true to His word, and every gracious, our God took care of our daughter and she didn't have cystic fibrosis or any other disease. She had been suffering only from allergies.

The verse for today is a reminder to pray about all things with fervor and persistence. Prayer is our expression of trust. God chooses to work through the prayers of His people (James 5:16). Furthermore, we must praise Him. When He takes care of a situation or gives us strength to endure it, we should express our thanks. May we never forget He can handle all of our problems.

....

Lord, help me trust You with everything. In Jesus' name, amen.

MICHAEL ORR, FIRST BAPTIST CHURCH CHIPLEY, CHIPLEY, FL

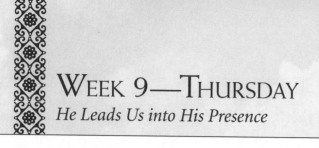

WEEK 9—THURSDAY
He Leads Us into His Presence

Oh, send out Your light and Your truth! Let them lead me; let them bring me to Your holy hill and to Your tabernacle. Then I will go to the altar of God, to God my exceeding joy; and on the harp I will praise You, O God, my God.

PSALM 43:3–4

Following the truth of God's Word results in a life of worship. It leads to a life that glorifies God. The psalmist desired to follow God's guidance, which resulted in coming into His presence to fellowship with Him and worship Him. These verses also imply something even more profound. Reception to the gospel light, the ultimate truth of the gospel, brings people into the direct presence of God. While on earth, we fellowship with Him through the Holy Spirit. But one day we will arrive in the very dwelling place of God!

The day I wrote this devotion marked the one-year anniversary of my mother's going home to heaven. Shortly before my mother passed I read an autobiography she had written in her college freshman English class. She told of the most important event in her life, which was when she accepted Christ. Throughout her life my mother walked with Jesus, served Him, and witnessed to others. And on a bitterly cold February day, with her family gathered around her bedside, she breathed her last. She left the room and this realm to arrive in the city of God.

I encourage anyone reading this: If you have not received Jesus—do so now. Repent of your sins and trust Christ to save you. Surrender to Him as Lord; He will guide you while on you're on earth and take you to His very presence one day.

....

Lord, help me follow You until You take me home. In Your name I pray, amen.

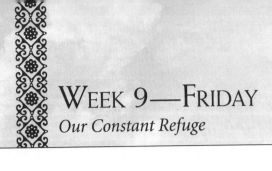

Week 9—Friday
Our Constant Refuge

God is our refuge and strength, a very present help in trouble. Therefore we will not fear, even though the earth be removed, and though the mountains be carried into the midst of the sea; though its waters roar and be troubled, though the mountains shake with its swelling.

Psalm 46:1–3

I will never forget September 11, 2001. It began as any other Tuesday morning until I received a phone call to turn on the television and see what had happened. I sat stunned by what I saw. An unfathomable attack had occurred against the nation, and life would never be the same. Church members called the church office that day just to talk. People stopped by my office, and we wept together as we discussed the events of the day. I knew we needed to be together as a church family that night, so I called a prayer meeting. While preaching, I spoke from Psalm 46. We needed to be reminded that nothing takes our Lord by surprise. He is our help in time of trouble. He actively strengthens us during tribulations—and He did that night.

The text for today is a great promise that no matter the disaster, whether natural or man-made, God is over all. We must not fear! God will work all things according to the counsel of His will (Ephesians 1:11). He will provide the strength to weather the storm. Furthermore, He will use the disaster for our benefit as well as for His glory (Romans 8:28).

....

Lord, You are my Refuge and my Strength. Keep me safe. In Jesus' name, amen.

MICHAEL ORR, FIRST BAPTIST CHURCH CHIPLEY, CHIPLEY, FL

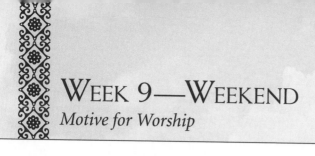

WEEK 9—WEEKEND
Motive for Worship

We have thought, O God, on Your lovingkindness, in the midst of Your temple. According to Your name, O God, so is Your praise to the ends of the earth; Your right hand is full of righteousness. Let Mount Zion rejoice, let the daughters of Judah be glad, because of Your judgments.

PSALM 48:9–11

Churches battle over music styles. We call these battles *worship wars*. I know of one church that decided to sing some modern praise songs as well as hymns. When the modern songs were sung, one group stood to sing, while the more traditional group sat and didn't sing. The opposite occurred when the traditional songs were sung. That is no way to worship!

Today's text provides us with a foundation for worship, one that results from reflecting on the attributes of God. The practice evokes a response of worship no matter the style of music.

First, to worship one must reflect on God's love. A simple reflection on the love of God demonstrated by the sacrifice of the Lord Jesus leaves us awestruck. Second, He is sovereign over all. All of creation praises Him to the ends of the earth. When we worship God, we join in this praise. Third, all He does is perfect. He makes no mistakes. This should motivate us to worship our holy, righteous God. Fourth, He exercises perfect justice. His judgments are always sound and fair. We worship a God who shows justice to all.

To think on these attributes opens our hearts to the greatness of God as we worship Him.

. . . .

Lord, help me reflect on Your greatness as I worship. Amen.

Week 10—Monday
A Clean Heart

Create in me a clean heart, O God, and renew a steadfast spirit within me. Do not cast me away from Your presence, and do not take Your Holy Spirit from me. Restore to me to the joy of Your salvation, and uphold me by your generous Spirit.

PSALM 51:10–12

David had sinned greatly, and in this psalm he revealed some of the damaging effects sin has on believers. Sin creates a barrier between us and God, and it causes us to lose the joy that comes from being forgiven and walking with God. In general sin makes us heavyhearted and burdened. Though our sin affects other people, our sin is first against God Himself.

David recognized his heart as the source of his sin. Thus David asked God to deal with the cause of his sin by creating within him a new heart. David realized only God can change a person's heart.

The New Testament teaches that the Holy Spirit lives in all believers, and He is the seal who ensures our salvation will be complete someday (Ephesians 1:13–14). David did not lose his salvation—just his joy. David did not request that God restore His salvation; he wanted his joy back.

Christ died to pay for every sin we have committed or will commit. His shed blood means our sins are forgiven forever. Even so, we should make every effort to avoid it because sin causes us to lose our joy.

Father, I realize the desire to sin originates within my heart and is the cause of trouble in my life. I ask the same as David did: please create a new heart in me. Amen.

WEEK 10—TUESDAY
Like a Green Olive Tree

But I am like a green olive tree in the house of God; I trust in the mercy of God forever and ever. I will praise You forever, because You have done it; and in the presence of Your saints I will wait on Your name, for it is good.

PSALM 52:8–9

The first seven verses of this psalm address the wicked—those opposed to God and who reject Him as Lord of their lives. But then verse 8 begins to contrast the fate of the wicked with those who trust in God.

Verse 5 says the wicked will be uprooted, whereas David would be like a green olive tree in verse 8. David believed this because the wicked around him trusted in their actions and riches, which are only temporary, while he trusted in the mercy of God, which endures forever.

In verse 9 David wrote, "You have done it"—without saying what God did. The point is God has already acted against those who reject Him as well as on behalf of those who love Him. God's plans have already been set in motion, and His people wait for these plans to be manifested.

To please God one must live by faith. This means to believe what He says. God knows all things, so nothing will come along to surprise Him. When He says in His Word that He will not treat the wicked the same as those who trust Him, we can believe Him and wait on Him to act. In the interim, we're to praise His name because He has done great things already in the past and He will do great things in the future.

··

Lord, I know You will make things right in the end. Help me wait on You. Give me eyes to see eternity and a voice to praise You. Help me trust You more. In Jesus' name, amen.

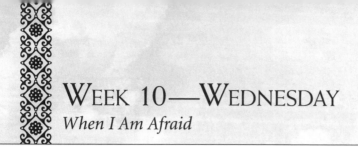

WEEK 10—WEDNESDAY
When I Am Afraid

Whenever I am afraid, I will trust in You. In God (I will praise His word), in God I have put my trust; I will not fear. What can flesh do to me?

PSALM 56:3–4

A lot of things make us afraid. Even David admitted he was afraid at times, and Psalm 56 gives guidance on what to do when we are afraid.

David had learned to turn his thoughts to God. God is all-powerful, all-knowing, and always present. And nothing happens He doesn't know about or doesn't allow to happen. This may not bring us much comfort in and of itself, but this is the essence of trust. And it's a test of our faith. Each time we trust Him our faith grows stronger.

David reminded himself that when he was afraid he would trust God. To trust God means to trust His Word. To trust God means not to trust ourselves. David was a courageous man, but he had limitations. God has none. Whatever people do to us has no effect on what God has already done for us or will do for us in the future.

Regardless of what we are afraid of—health problems, financial issues, relationship dilemmas—we must entrust them to God. He is good and merciful, and He has promised to supply our needs.

....

Lord, help me overcome the fears I have in life. Help me praise You even when I am afraid. Please increase my faith in You. Amen.

Week 10—Thursday
God Is Our Refuge

But I will sing of Your power, yes, I will sing aloud of Your mercy in the morning; for You have been my defense and refuge in the day of my trouble. To You, O my Strength. I will sing praises; for God is my defense, my God of mercy.

PSALM 59:16–17

Psalm 59:16 starts with "But" and refers to earlier verses in the psalm where David related how his enemies were always pursuing him. Yet David would sing in spite of the fact that men were searching for him in order to end his life.

David told us why he sang even though his enemies sought to kill him. God had defended him in the past, and He had been David's refuge. God was faithful, so the fact that He had defended David before indicated He would do so again.

God shows no favoritism and is unchanging. So God will do the same for any of us who seek refuge in Him. But we must have a relationship with Him. David referred to God as his "defense" and "Strength." The basis of this relationship was God's mercy, which David rightly praised.

We may not have an assassin chasing us, but we do have an enemy prowling around like a lion (1 Peter 5:8), and God is certainly stronger than this enemy and can keep us safe. Like David, we can be confident that God will protect us from both our earthly foes as well as our spiritual adversary.

Lord, thank You for Your mercy and for Your willingness to be my Refuge just as You were for David. I am not always as confident as I should be. Please provide me Your strength in my times of weakness. Help me to praise Your name. Amen.

Week 10—Friday
The Rock That Is Higher Than I

Hear my cry, O God; attend to my prayer. From the end of the earth I will cry to You, when my heart is overwhelmed; lead me to the rock that is higher than I. For You have been a shelter for me, a strong tower from the enemy. I will abide in Your tabernacle forever; I will trust in the shelter of Your wings.

PSALM 61:1–4

We're busy. There is always something more that needs to be done. Many times we feel as though we'll never be able to complete anything. We feel overwhelmed. But we're in good company because David felt the same way.

Our lives can be chaotic, but when we take a few minutes with God, our lives improve. Something within us longs to be with God, and when we're not with Him, we feel something is missing.

All we have to do is call on God. He hears us no matter where we are, even to the ends of the earth. When we call on Him, He leads us to a higher place—a place above the hectic activities.

The rock David referred to was a secure place of safety, a place bigger and stronger than he. The tabernacle was the house of God, where God's presence dwelt. David wanted to be near God in His house. When David communed with God, he felt so comfortable and at peace he never wanted to leave.

The peace we feel being so close to the One who loves us and who protects us is a peace that surpasses all understanding. We should emulate David and seek to fellowship with God on a daily basis. Only then will we find peace in the midst of our chaotic lives.

Lord, lead me to the rock that is higher than I. Amen.

WEEK 10—WEEKEND
We Can Trust Him

My soul, wait silently for God alone, for my expectation is from Him. He only is my rock and my salvation; He is my defense; I shall not be moved. In God is my salvation and my glory; the rock of my strength, and my refuge, is in God. Trust in Him at all times, you people; pour your heart out before Him; God is a refuge for us.

PSALM 62:5–8

In this psalm, David waited for God alone. God was his rock and salvation, his defense, his glory, and his refuge. Since he trusted no other, he waited on God.

If we do not trust God alone, our faith in Him is incomplete. When we pick and choose what to trust Him with and to what extent, we act as if we are wiser than He. But to look for answers and help from any other is to seek counsel from a lesser being.

If we've ever stepped off a dock into a boat and felt the boat move, it likely made us uncomfortable. That's how many of us live as Christians. We trust Jesus enough to make some changes in our lives, but we have not yet fully surrendered to Him. In the process we're miserable and we are not fully effective witnesses for God.

We should decide whether God is trustworthy or not. If He is, we must trust Him completely. We'll need help with this from time to time, and God is capable of helping us. But in the end, our faith in Him will be rewarded.

. . . .

Lord, I need to trust You more. Please show me the areas in my life where trust is lacking, and help me strengthen them. Thank You for Your patience with me. Amen.

WEEK 11—MONDAY
The Parched Soul

O God, You are my God; early will I seek You; my soul thirsts for You; my flesh longs for You in a dry and thirsty land where there is no water. So I have looked for You in the sanctuary, to see Your power and Your glory.

PSALM 63:1–2

Sometimes we feel out of sync because life has hit us with the blows of pressures and struggles. It seems so overwhelming to us that in spite of our best efforts we find our thoughts drifting off to waterless places.

In this psalm David taught us that in the midst of spiritual dryness we should seek the Lord. Why should we do this? We seek Him because He's our God, and He has blessed us with another day of living, giving us an opportunity to influence someone's life for His glory and honor. What a blessing we have!

When experiencing a dry spell, David thought back to the sanctuary, the tabernacle in which God's presence dwelt on earth. Because of Jesus' death on the cross, we have access to a refreshing, indwelling tabernacle during our parched season. Because of the Holy Spirit, we can enter into God's presence whenever we need our thirsty spirit revived by His power.

No matter what we're facing right now, we can know that the refreshing of our inner tabernacles is available through the power of prayer!

Heavenly Father, thank You for allowing me to hear Your voice and for quenching my thirst when I am suffering a spiritually dry season. Amen.

BISHOP A. B. VINES SR., NEW SEASONS CHURCH, SPRING VALLEY, CA

WEEK 11—TUESDAY
Refreshing in Hard Times

Because Your lovingkindness is better than life, my lips shall praise You. Thus I will bless You while I live; I will lift up my hands in Your name. My soul shall be satisfied as with marrow and fatness, and my mouth shall praise You with joyful lips.

PSALM 63:3–5

This passage continues the previous devotion where David described a spiritually dry time in his life. Yet his tone changed in verse 3. How true these words are in times of trouble. This passage reminds us we have another chance to see the goodness of the Lord in our lives. David reminded us we should bless the Lord even in weariness of life. How wonderful to hear David say he would lift up his hands in spite of his head hanging so low.

What a remarkable declaration to praise God with joyful lips that are cracked from the dryness of the desert. This is an illustration of a real sacrifice of praise during difficult times. David's decision was to bless the name of the Lord regardless of his current situation. In like manner, praise helps us to understand that if we turn back the pages of our lives, we can reflect on the fact God has been good and His love endures forever.

Dear Lord, help me to remember: "Even though the fig trees have no blossoms, and there are no grapes on the vines; even though the olive crop fails, and the fields lie empty and barren; even though the flocks die in the fields, and the cattle barns are empty, yet I will rejoice in the LORD! I will be joyful in the God of my salvation" (Habakkuk 3:17–18, NLT). In Jesus' name, amen.

WEEK 11—WEDNESDAY
Rejoicing During the Night Watch

When I remember You on my bed, I meditate on You in the night watches. Because You have been my help, therefore in the shadow of Your wings, I will rejoice. My soul follows close behind You; Your right hand upholds me.

PSALM 63:6–8

All of us have bad nights where we stay awake and worry about difficult situations. But when was the last time we stayed up throughout the night remembering the goodness of the Lord? Reflecting on the Lord's blessings is a good way to pass the long nights when we can't sleep.

In our preceding passage, David talked about God's tender love for us in trying times, but he now found himself praising God again for being faithful during the night watch. Often during the night watch all of life seems to decelerate, so we can meditate about the events of the day. We can comprehend that it actually was a day the Lord had made and we should rejoice and be glad (Psalm 118:24). This never-ending assurance of our Lord keeps us focused in uncertain times.

....

Dear Lord, help me in the quietness of the night to reflect on and celebrate the blessings of my life. Let Your calming Spirit enable me to keep still and stay focused on Your goodness and the joy of Your salvation. I know my peace truly does not come from this earth but from You. I commit my thoughts and my actions to You. In Jesus' name, amen.

BISHOP A. B. VINES SR., NEW SEASONS CHURCH, SPRING VALLEY, CA

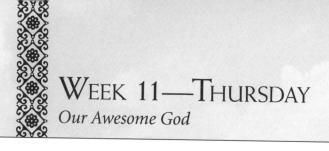

Week 11—Thursday
Our Awesome God

Make a joyful shout to God, all the earth! Sing out the honor of His name; make His praise glorious. Say to God, "How awesome are Your works! Through the greatness of Your power Your enemies shall submit themselves to You. All the earth shall worship You and sing praises to You; they shall sing praises to Your name."

Psalm 66:1–4

What an awesome God we serve—period! The psalmist stated this in three different ways in this passage. The first evidence of our awesome God is the grandeur of His worthiness. Our God is worthy of all praise and adoration. The prophet Nehemiah said, "You alone are the LORD; You have made heaven, the heaven of heavens, with all their host, the earth and everything on it, the seas and all that is in them, and You preserve them all. The host of heaven worships You" (9:6).

The second way we see how God is awesome is in the genius of His handiwork. What can compare to what the Lord has done when it comes to creation? It's just breathtaking! Just think: there are more than 400,000 species of flowering plants in the world along with 31,000 species of fish and 340 breeds of man's best friend. All different, all amazing, and all made by the same God!

Finally, we see the awesomeness of God when we understand the magnitude of God. How can we not praise Him? "From the rising of the sun to its going down the LORD's name is to be praised" (Psalm 113:3). This sort of admiration comes from a thankful heart and a mind focused on His goodness to us and the world.

....

Thank You, Lord, for Your splendor and excellent works. My vocabulary is too limited to describe You, so I can only use words of praise. Hallelujah! Amen!

Week 11—Friday
Serving Is Worship

Blessed be the Lord, who daily loads us with benefits, the God of our salvation! Our God is the God of salvation; and to GOD the Lord belong escapes from death.

PSALM 68:19–20

When we are in the day-to-day hustle and bustle of life, we may sometimes forget how to bless the Lord. Well, I found myself in this very state a while ago. Yes! The preacher man was in a rut—so what did I do? I picked myself up and made some pastoral care and hospital visits to disciples who were sick and shut in. Wow! What a breath of fresh air to be able to minister and serve at a personal and intimate level. What does this have to do with blessing the Lord? Well, it forced me to go back to my purpose. God chose me to serve and minister to the people of God. And when life pulls me in so many directions, it is a blessing just to get back to the basics and touch those whom I serve.

You may not be in the ministry, but you should be ministering to those around you. You have the benefit of being the Lord's hands and mouth to His brokenhearted people. The Lord has chosen you to help bless this hurting world with the gospel of peace. So, remember, if you can't find a sense of praise, then serve, and then watch His Spirit overtake you with joy—unspeakable joy full of hope and glory.

··

Dear Lord, thank You for the opportunity to comfort and encourage Your people the same way You have blessed me with the gospel of peace. Amen.

BISHOP A. B. VINES SR., NEW SEASONS CHURCH, SPRING VALLEY, CA

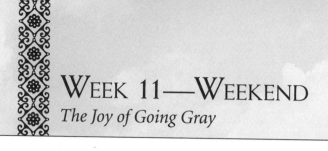

WEEK 11—WEEKEND
The Joy of Going Gray

O God, You have taught me from my youth; and to this day I declare Your wondrous works. Now also when I am old and grayheaded, O God, do not forsake me, until I declare Your strength to this generation, Your power to everyone who is to come.

PSALM 71:17–18

While searching Google on the topic of gray hair, I was amazed to find almost 8 million hits on how to go gray gracefully. But I was astonished to see almost 250 million hits on how to stop from getting gray hair. In this world of denial (where forty is the new twenty and fifty is the new thirty), what ever happened to the blessing of wisdom that comes with old age?

In this psalm David rejoiced that he served a God who protected him in his youth, and this same unchanging God continued to sustain him during his later years. This passage lists a specific request by David. David asked that the Lord would not abandon him until he was able to declare the Lord's strength and power to this generation and the generations to come. David wanted everyone to hear about the Lord's strength and power.

Let us celebrate our Lord who protects us throughout the various stages of our lives. In our attempts to stay young, let us not forget to tell the stories of our awesome God to this generation and the ones to come.

. . . .

Lord Jesus, thank You for allowing me to see another day so I can communicate the story of Your compassion throughout every stage of life. Help me to appreciate the ability to pass on wisdom. Amen.

Week 12—Monday
The Comfort of God's Presence

Nevertheless I am continually with You; You hold me by my right hand. You will guide me with Your counsel, and afterward receive me to glory. Whom have I in heaven but You? And there is none upon earth that I desire besides You.

PSALM 73:23–25

I have wondered at times if God was listening to me. There have been moments when I struggled through life and thought my prayers were not being answered. Yet God proved in the end that He always hears and answers my prayers. As Psalm 73 asserts, He has always been right alongside me.

Never has there been a time when God did not exist. He is eternal and He will always be God. As believers, we find comfort in knowing that because He is eternal, we serve a God who is more than capable of addressing our every need. The Bible tells us, "Elijah was a man with a nature like ours, and he prayed earnestly that it would not rain, and it did not rain on the earth for three years and six months" (James 5:17 NASB). Elijah knew he could trust God to answer his prayers. He also knew God would demonstrate His power and authority over creation to prove His presence.

Scripture says, "The effective prayer of a righteous man can accomplish much" (James 5:16 NASB). God assures us He is with us and understands our needs. He upholds us by the might of His power in every situation. His guiding counsel helps us to avoid sin, and His Spirit directs us in the paths of righteousness.

Lord, I can rest knowing You are always with me. Thank You for Your love. Amen.

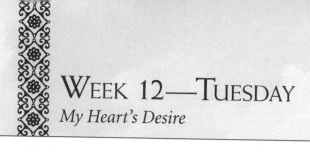

WEEK 12—TUESDAY
My Heart's Desire

Whom have I in heaven but You? And there is none upon earth that I desire besides You. My flesh and my heart fail; but God is the strength of my heart and my portion forever.

PSALM 73:25–26

God created us to be in a relationship with Him. That relationship is based on the love that God demonstrated to us in His Son, Jesus Christ. The totality of the Christian life centers on the heart. God transforms our lives when we give our hearts to Jesus. God's delivering us from iniquity is also a matter of the heart, which is where sin hides unseen and unexposed to others. Our hearts settle on trusting our Lord when we surrender to Him completely. When we realize no one else can do for us what God can do, our hearts yearn for Him more. The psalmist wrote, "As the deer pants for the water brooks, so my soul pants for You, O God" (Psalm 42:1).

Arriving at the place where the heart seeks after God continually is a part of the process of maturing in Christ. Within that process, we often experience failure, frustration, and disappointment. David mentions some of these frustrations in Psalm 73:25–26. We encounter these obstacles because of the flesh and our desires to walk in the flesh. Yet we must strive to overcome the desires of our flesh. In doing so, we will please God.

....

Lord, I bend my heart toward You, and I surrender myself to Your will. I trust You will be everything to me and Your grace will be enough. Heavenly Father, lead me in helping others give their hearts to You. In Jesus' name, amen.

WEEK 12—WEDNESDAY
Magnify the Lord

Teach me Your way, O LORD; I will walk in Your truth; unite my heart to fear Your name. I will praise You, O Lord my God, with all my heart, and I will glorify Your name forevermore. For great is Your mercy toward me, and You have delivered my soul from the depths of Sheol.

PSALM 86:11–13

In a world that changes so drastically over a short period of time, we sometimes struggle to differentiate between the truth and falsehood. Many question whether absolute truth even exists. We live in a world that is becoming increasingly anti-Christian, but more importantly, moving further away from God. One must understand that in these times, God has never changed. The Bible tells us "Jesus Christ is the same yesterday and today and forever" (Hebrews 13:8 NASB). Therefore, we can find comfort in knowing we can walk in God's truth. This psalm of praise invites the heart to rejoice in the presence of the Lord. It moves the heart to celebrate the grace and mercy of God because He has rescued our souls from the grave.

With every opportunity, we should magnify the name of the Lord! He has provided an unmerited salvation to humankind, and He took upon Himself the punishment we deserve. How great is His mercy! The desire of every disciple of Christ should be to want to know more of Him day by day.

Lord, I praise Your name for Your goodness, Your kindness, and Your mercy. Help me to lead others to salvation through Your name. Amen.

BRYON J. BARMER, BRIGHT HOPE COMMUNITY CHURCH, SPRING VALLEY, CA

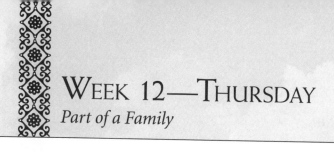

WEEK 12—THURSDAY
Part of a Family

Blessed are the people who know the joyful sound! They walk, O Lord, in the light of Your countenance. In Your name they rejoice all day long, and in Your righteousness they are exalted.

PSALM 89:15–16

As a young child growing up in a large urban community, I had an easy time finding a group of which to be a part. Whether you find yourself in family groups, groups at school, or hanging out with friends at work, it is not hard to find a place to belong. God also has created such a place for those who believe in Him. Psalm 89:15–16 references the community of faith believers enjoy.

The people of God belong to Him, and that makes Christians part of a family. Not only are we a family, but God created us to live forever as a family in the presence of Him. This is a spiritual family into which we must be born. Jesus told Nicodemus, "Unless one is born again, he cannot see the kingdom of God" (John 3:3). Being a part of God's family has several benefits. The main benefit is we do not have to pay the price for our sins because Jesus has paid it all for us. Other blessings include eternal life in heaven, where we will never know sin again nor ever grow old.

Part of the joy of being a child of God involves knowing we have a relationship with the Father that will never end. With that comes a myriad of blessings on this side of eternity.

....

Lord, I rejoice in knowing You have made a way for me to be a part of Your family forever. Thank You for gifting me with what I do not deserve. Amen.

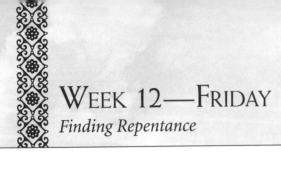

WEEK 12—FRIDAY
Finding Repentance

Return, O LORD! How long? And have compassion on Your servants. Oh, satisfy us early with Your mercy, that we may rejoice and be glad all our days!

PSALM 90:13–14

Emptiness, loneliness, and desperation are just some of the emotions one experiences because of sin. In Psalm 90 Moses expressed how the Israelites once knew God as their "dwelling place" (v. 1) but had sinned against Him. Moses recognized that God's wrath had consumed them, and he now sought God with a penitent heart on behalf of the people.

The Bible teaches God will forgive us of all sin when we confess. This was why Christ died on the cross at Calvary. Christ's death, burial, and resurrection are the foundation of our eternal salvation. Belief in Jesus as Savior and confession of our sins are the central components that lead to salvation.

The Bible says, "If we confess our sins, He is faithful and righteous to forgive us our sins and to cleanse us from all unrighteousness" (1 John 1:9 NASB). When we sin, we should do just what Moses did on behalf of the Israelites in Psalm 90:13–14. We should cry out to the Lord for forgiveness.

The consequences for remaining in a state of unforgiven sin are too costly. For the unbeliever, the price is eternal separation from God in hell. For the believer, unconfessed sins cause a disruption of fellowship with God. Prayers won't be answered until confession of sin is made to God. Confession and repentance are necessary to restore the sinner's relationship with God.

> *Lord, forgive me of the sins I have committed and the iniquities of my heart. Grant mercy and compassion to Your servant, so I may follow wherever You lead. In Jesus' name, amen.*

BRYON J. BARMER, BRIGHT HOPE COMMUNITY CHURCH, SPRING VALLEY, CA

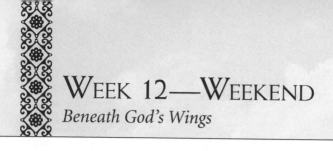

WEEK 12—WEEKEND
Beneath God's Wings

He who dwells in the secret place of the Most High shall abide under the shadow of the Almighty. I will say of the LORD, "He is my refuge and my fortress; my God, in Him I will trust."

PSALM 91:1–2

US military service personnel are committed to protecting our nation against all enemies, both foreign and domestic. I served in law enforcement for nearly thirty years, and I believed it was my duty to protect all citizens of the community in which I served. But no branch of the military and no law enforcement agency in the world can provide the security and protection that God can.

God provides for and protects those who belong to Him. The language of this passage suggests that God provides a covering for the believer. It paints the picture of a bird—such as an eagle—hovering over and shading its young. So it is with God. When we choose to find refuge in God, He hovers over us with His protection. He causes us to rise above our circumstances. When we choose to dwell with God, He overshadows us so we can say, "He is my refuge and my fortress; my God, in Him I will trust."

....

Lord, You are my Strong Tower, my Buckler, and my Shield. I trust in You for Your protection and provision. Keep me from all hate, harm, and danger as I seek to do Your will. Amen.

WEEK 13—MONDAY
Our Divine Protector

For He shall give His angels charge over you, to keep you in all your ways. In their hands they shall bear you up, lest you dash your foot against a stone.

PSALM 91:11–12

For many people, the world has become a very scary place. Whenever I am talking with a group of people about current events, someone will usually bring up the subject of fear. We can find people all around us who are drowning in fear. Most of the fears we struggle with are situations beyond our control. We have no control over the government, the stock market, the environment, or the actions of others. Even though we cannot control the things that make us fearful, we can control how we respond when we are tempted to live in fear. Psalm 91:11–12 teaches that we don't have to be afraid because God's angels protect us.

Further, how we respond to the attacks of Satan is critical as we mature in our relationship with the Lord. Responding in faith helps us to overcome our fears when we place all of our trust in Jesus. Satan used the very words from our text today when he tempted Jesus in the wilderness (Matthew 4:5–7). He twisted the verses in an attempt to make Jesus stumble. He does the same to you and me. Whenever Satan misuses Scripture, we must follow the example of Jesus and properly apply biblical teaching. This is why we need to meditate on the Word and fill our hearts with its truth! Whenever we are tempted to retreat in fear, we should respond in faith and trust our Lord to protect us.

Dear Lord, I choose today to trust You in all things. Help me to live faithfully as I seek to glorify Your holy name. Amen.

BRENT THOMPSON, HEFLIN BAPTIST CHURCH, HEFLIN, AL

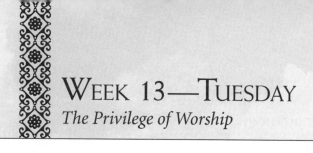

WEEK 13—TUESDAY
The Privilege of Worship

It is good to give thanks to the LORD, and to sing praises to Your name, O Most High; to declare Your lovingkindness in the morning, and Your faithfulness every night. . . . For You, LORD, have made me glad through Your work; I will triumph in the works of Your hands.

PSALM 92:1–2, 4

As children of God, we should be grateful for the privilege of worship. When we worship God, we declare His worth. The psalmist teaches us that worship includes giving thanks, singing, and publicly declaring the faithfulness of God. We give thanks not only for what He has done for us, but simply for who He is. He is our holy, sovereign, omnipotent, omniscient, and omnipresent Lord. We sing because He has put a "new song in [our] mouth[s]—praise to our God; many will see it and fear, and will trust in the LORD" (Psalm 40:3). We publicly declare His worth by the words we speak and how we conduct our daily lives.

The psalmist also teaches us the results of God's faithfulness, which are seen in His mighty works. One of His greatest works is bringing joy and peace to the hearts of those who have been called by His name. The works of His mighty hands will make glad the hearts of His children as they rejoice in Him.

. . . .

Dear Lord, remind me of the importance of daily worship. Let not my heart drift from my first love. You alone are worthy of all praise. Thank You for the joy and victory You bring into my life. I love You, and I bless Your name! Amen.

WEEK 13—WEDNESDAY
The Source of Our Strength

Unless the LORD had been my help, my soul would soon have settled in silence. If I say, "My foot slips," Your mercy, O LORD, will hold me up. In the multitude of my anxieties within me, Your comforts delight my soul.

PSALM 94:17–19

We all know what it's like to need help. No one can build a healthy life without developing relationships with others who can provide help during times of need. As we focus on building healthy relationships with other believers, we must remember to base the health of our earthly relationships on the health of our heavenly relationship with our Lord. He is our divine Helper and the source of all our strength. He alone is the one who sustains us in our shortcomings by His infinite mercy. As children of God, we are grateful recipients and His Word reminds us: He is "rich in mercy" (Ephesians 2:4). No one is as merciful as the Lord.

The psalmist declared the Lord is the one who held him up and provided for his safety. Every child of God must not forget that when he or she is in the Lord's holy grip, he or she is safe and secure for eternity. No one else can provide the security the Lord provides.

In addition to being merciful to us, God also comforts us about our fears. This world is filled with problems that cause anxiety to build in our lives. The apostle Peter pointed us to the place of relief from our worries: "Casting all your care upon Him, for He cares for you" (1 Peter 5:7). No one can match the comfort and peace that comes from the Lord.

....

Dear Lord, remind me daily You alone are my help. I cast all my cares upon You because You care for me. In Jesus' name, amen.

BRENT THOMPSON, HEFLIN BAPTIST CHURCH, HEFLIN, AL

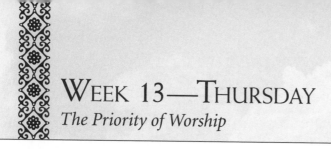

WEEK 13—THURSDAY
The Priority of Worship

Oh come, let us sing to the LORD! Let us shout joyfully to the Rock of our salvation. Let us come before His presence with thanksgiving; let us shout joyfully to Him with psalms. For the LORD is the great God, and the great King above all gods.

PSALM 95:1–3

P salm 95 is one of my favorite psalms. It speaks directly to the heart of worshipping our heavenly Father. We must never forget that worship involves our emotions, engages our minds, and touches our hearts. Many people try to suppress their emotions in worship for fear of appearing to be fanatical. Others base all of their worship on their feelings. Both of these extremes can cause us to miss the ultimate purpose of our worship experience. Whether we worship privately or corporately, we should not suppress our abilities to see, feel, hear, or think. God created us to do all these things, and each should be involved each time we worship God.

The psalmist in today's text sang and shouted joyfully with thanksgiving in the presence of God. Yes, he was emotional, but clearly his heart and mind were also engaged as he worshipped. He ended this psalm by declaring the greatness of our God and King. In worship, we can come before our God knowing that no one is greater than He! The search is over. We have found the greatest of the great!

Dear Lord, as I enter Your holy presence today, I want to engage my heart, mind, and emotions to experience Your greatness! I love You, Lord, and I dedicate this day to You. Amen.

WEEK 13—FRIDAY
He's Already There

In His hand are the deep places of the earth; the heights of the hills are His also. The sea is His, for He made it; and His hands formed the dry land.

PSALM 95:4–5

Our Lord is our divine Creator! Everything was made by Him and for His glory. As the psalmist continued to declare the glory of the Lord in Psalm 95, he focused on the aspect of God's physical creation in today's text. He referenced four areas of creation in particular: the "deep places," the hills, the sea, and the dry land. Regardless of where we are, we abide on a portion of His creation. And not only do we abide on His creation, we can also abide in His presence.

We all know what it's like to travel through the "deep places" of life. We often refer to them as *valleys* or *times of spiritual drought*. In my personal experience, I have learned the valleys and times of drought were beneficial to my spiritual maturity. Those experiences caused me to extend my roots deeper into God's Word, which strengthened my relationship with Him. We are not allowed the luxury of determining the depth of the valley or the duration of our stay, but we can persevere with the promise of His presence. Thus, throughout our life experiences, we learn not to allow our worship to lose its intensity in the deep places. We learn to worship God joyfully regardless of whether we're on the highest hill or in the lowest valley. Wherever we are, He's already there.

Dear Lord, thank You for the days I have spent in the valleys of life. During those times You taught me so much about Your holy character. Thank You for loving me. Amen.

BRENT THOMPSON, HEFLIN BAPTIST CHURCH, HEFLIN, AL

WEEK 13—WEEKEND
The Privilege of Being His

Oh come, let us worship and bow down; let us kneel before the LORD our Maker. For He is our God, and we are the people of His pasture, and the sheep of His hand.

PSALM 95:6–7

Our Lord is not only our divine Creator, He is our Master who designed us. He has specifically crafted us by His hand down to the smallest detail. Another psalm says, "I will praise You, for I am fearfully and wonderfully made" (Psalm 139:14). Have we ever stopped and thought about the complexity of the human body? It's nothing short of a miracle! Every person has a specific genetic code that makes him or her very unique. What's even more amazing is that God Himself designed each person by His own hands.

Friends, Psalm 95:6–7 gives us a great reason to bow down and kneel before our Lord. We find many reasons to sing, shout joyfully, and magnify the name of our Jehovah God! He designed us for His glory and created us to dwell with Him. He called us to represent His holy character to a world that is completely lost without Him. We are pilgrims on this earth, heading toward our heavenly home, where we will live eternally in the presence of our great God.

As you worship with other believers, take time to praise God for designing you and calling you to be one of His own. Thank Him for walking by your side and for never deserting you. Remember, He is the Good Shepherd, and being one of His sheep is a privilege.

Dear Lord, as I worship You today, I'm grateful for the privilege of being Yours. In Jesus' name, amen.

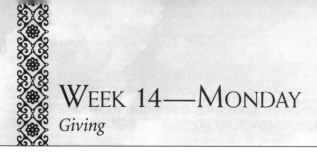

WEEK 14—MONDAY
Giving

Give to the LORD, O families of the peoples, give to the LORD glory and strength. Give to the LORD the glory due His name; bring an offering, and come into His courts. Oh, worship the LORD in the beauty of holiness! Tremble before Him, all the earth.

PSALM 96:7–9

An Operation Christmas Child shoebox spokesperson shared a personal story about giving a simple gift. She spoke of her opportunity to go to Russia and help deliver shoeboxes to school children. One little boy was very excited to have a roll of Smarties candy in his box. He was so exicted that he offered his enticing new roll of candy to the lady who had delivered him the shoebox. At first she refused to accept it. The Holy Spirit then convicted her, saying, "This child has never had anything new to give. Don't you dare steal this child's joy of giving." As a result, she accepted the gift.

God is a giving God. He is so giving that God gives the gift of giving. He does this by allowing His people to give. What can we give to God? Psalm 96:7–9 answers this question. First, as the people of God, we can give God our witness. We can make much of His name. Second, we can give God our wealth. Third, we can give God all of our worship. God is worthy of every person's worship; therefore, every person of every tribe, language, or people group can praise Him.

Father, Your holiness is beautiful and Your name is high above all names. Forgive me for where I have not shared in the gift of giving. Thank You for allowing me to give. Give me an opportunity to give. In Jesus' name, amen.

DR. SAM GREER, RED BANK BAPTIST CHURCH, CHATTANOOGA, TN

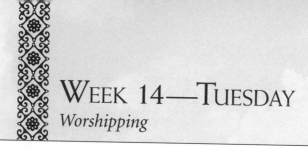

WEEK 14—TUESDAY
Worshipping

Know that the LORD, He is God; it is He who has made us, and not we ourselves; we are His people and the sheep of His pasture. Enter into His gates with thanksgiving, and into His courts with praise. Be thankful to Him, and bless His name. For the LORD is good; His mercy is everlasting, and His truth endures to all generations.

PSALM 100:3–5

Some forms of worship are unacceptable to God. First, idolatry was forbidden in the Old Testament. Another form of unacceptable worship is failing to give God the praise He deserves. This transpired in the days of Malachi when the Jews offered less than their best to God. Finally, while at Mars Hill Paul noticed an altar to "the unknown god." He condemned this ignorant form of worship. Unlike these unacceptable forms of worship, Psalm 100 paints a picture of worship that is acceptable to God, and it answers the who, how, and why of worship.

First, whom should we worship? We should worship the One who made us. God made us in His image. Creation should never be worshipped. The Creator should always be worshipped.

Second, how should we worship? We should worship by making much of the One who made us. We were made by God to make much of God.

Third, why should we worship? God is self-sustaining. He doesn't need our worship, but God wants us to worship Him. We show our love for Him by worshipping Him.

....

Gracious Father, You are good, loving, and faithful. You alone are worthy of my worship. Forgive me for offering to You unacceptable worship. Help me to worship You today in spirit and truth. In Jesus' name, amen.

Week 14—Wednesday
Hoping

Of old You laid the foundation of the earth, and the heavens are the work of Your hands. They will perish, but You will endure; Yes, they will all grow old like a garment; like a cloak You will change them, and they will be changed. But You are the same, and Your years will have no end.

PSALM 102:25–27

Too many people are hoping without any hope. Hoping without any hope is eternally dangerous. Some people put their hope in a lottery ticket, a job promotion, a relationship, drugs, alcohol, success, education, hobbies, abilities, or the American dream. What happens when all falls apart? As followers of Jesus, we know our hope is the confident assurance of who Jesus is and what He promises to those who love Him. Even in times of suffering, such as the death of a loved one, hardship, injustice, persecution, and separation, followers of Jesus react differently from those who have no hope.

According to Psalm 102, God's people have a past, present, and future reason to hope. In the past, God was at work. In the present, God is still at work. In the future, God will continue to work. God's creation changes and will one day come to an end, but God, the Creator, never changes and will never end.

Followers of Jesus have every reason to hope. People who refuse to follow Jesus have no reason to hope. Will you confess and turn from your sins and place your faith in Jesus alone? If so, you will begin hoping with hope!

Father, I praise You for the works of Your hands, which give great hope. Thank You for giving me the confident assurance of Your Word. Help me to live my life as one who is hoping with hope. In Jesus' name, amen.

DR. SAM GREER, RED BANK BAPTIST CHURCH, CHATTANOOGA, TN

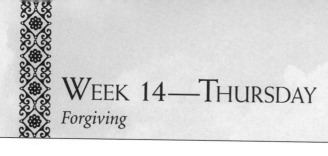

WEEK 14—THURSDAY
Forgiving

For as the heavens are high above the earth, so great is His mercy toward those who fear Him; as far as the east is from the west, so far has He removed our transgressions from us. As a father pities his children, so the LORD pities those who fear Him.

PSALM 103:11–13

Robert Ebeling is a retired NASA engineer who worked on the 1986 *Challenger* launch that killed all seven occupants. Ebeling and four other engineers anticipated the very failure that led to this tragedy. Their pleas to delay the launch were rejected by NASA. The night before the launch Ebeling even told his wife the *Challenger* would blow up. After three decades of suffering deep depression and heavy guilt, Ebeling still admits he could have done more to prevent the explosion. Clearly, Ebeling has been unable to forgive himself for the tragedy that took place.

Forgiveness may not be popular, but it is biblical. Forgiveness is easier to receive than it is to give. Forgiveness is even messy, but forgiveness is not an option for those who have been forgiven. Jesus also reminds us the forgiven should forgive, the forgiven must forgive, and the forgiven can forgive (Matthew 6:14–15).

In Christ, you are forgiven! Are you willing to forgive yourself and others?

Father, I praise You for Your forgiveness. Help me to forgive anyone I have yet to forgive. Grant me the compassion of Jesus to forgive. Thank You for the height and depth of Your forgiveness. In Jesus' name, amen.

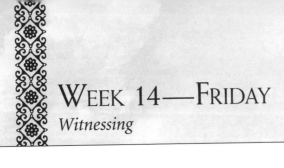

WEEK 14—FRIDAY
Witnessing

Sing to Him, sing psalms to Him; talk of all His wondrous works! Glory in His holy name; let the hearts of those rejoice who seek the LORD! Seek the LORD and His strength; seek His face evermore! Remember His marvelous works which He has done, His wonders, and the judgments of His mouth.

PSALM 105:2–5

One hot and humid Mississippi day, I was jogging on a neighborhood street. The last leg of the run was uphill. About halfway up the hill, I noticed an SUV coming down the hill. While panting for air and pouring sweat, I realized the vehicle was drawing closer to me. The window rolled down and an arm extended out with a cold, refreshing soft drink in hand. I grabbed the soft drink and said, "Thank you!"

At that moment, I heard the lady in the front seat of the SUV scream, "Wait! Stop!"

I stopped. The lady who handed me the drink said, "Could you open this bottle for me?"

As they pulled away, the lady in the front seat laughingly said, "He thought the drink was for him."

The ladies in that SUV held what would have quenched my thirst, but they kept it to themselves. As followers of Jesus, we hold what a lost and thirsting world needs. All people need the gospel of Jesus. Psalm 105 lays out how to take personal evangelism personally. Remember, all gospel conversations begin with a conversation. With whom will you have a gospel conversation today?

....

Father, please give me the boldness and opportunity to have a gospel conversation today. In Jesus' name, amen.

DR. SAM GREER, RED BANK BAPTIST CHURCH, CHATTANOOGA, TN

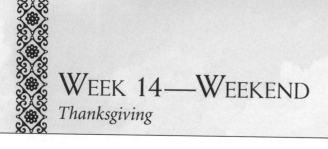

WEEK 14—WEEKEND
Thanksgiving

Oh, that men would give thanks to the LORD for His goodness, and for His wonderful works to the children of men! For He satisfies the longing soul, and fills the hungry soul with goodness.

PSALM 107:8–9

I have heard it said a "complaining Christian is an oxymoron." Yet as a pastor, I have heard some head-scratching complaints from church members throughout the years. One that stands out was a complaint in regard to the volume of the music in corporate worship. An older gentlemen, as he shouted in my ear, said to me, "Pastor, the music is too loud! I can't hear it!"

How do we as followers of Christ guard against complaining? According to the Bible, gratitude destroys a complaining spirit.

Psalm 107 helps us to think about God so we can thank Him. Psalm 107 reminds us of whom and for what we can be thankful. We should always give thanks to God because He is good, and He alone is good. We should always give thanks to God because He is great. God's greatness is seen in all of His creation. We should also always give thanks to God because He is God. God alone satisfies the longing souls of men, women, boys, and girls.

Father, I thank You for being good. Thank You for being great. Thank You for being God. Help me to destroy a complaining spirit with gratitude. Help me to think of You more so I will thank You more. In Jesus' name, amen.

WEEK 15—MONDAY
Healing

He sent His word and healed them, and delivered them from their destructions. Oh, that men would give thanks to the LORD for His goodness, and for His wonderful works to the children of men! Let them sacrifice the sacrifices of thanksgiving, and declare His works with rejoicing.

PSALM 107:20–22

On a day like any other day, I received word that JR, a church member, had been in an accident and was in the hospital. He was on life support. The outlook was grim.

While JR was in the hospital, a faithful lady stood beside his bed and prayed. As she prayed, the monitors recording the downward spiral of his health reversed and began to show immediate improvement. God was at work!

Throughout the weeks ahead, JR slowly improved as God healed him, miraculously granting him life. Weeks later, God delivered JR from intensive care, and he was transferred to a rehabilitation facility near his home. It was an exciting day!

The psalmist pointed out in today's passage that when God does something amazing, thanksgiving is the natural result. I recently entered our worship center for a Sunday morning service and there sat JR and his family. As I recognized him publicly that morning and he stood, the church knew it was witnessing a miracle. Thanksgiving and rejoicing were sweet that day.

I do not know your situation, but God does. The same God who met JR's needs can meet yours as well. Spend time with Him right now. He cares. He's near!

....

Dear Lord, help me to recognize Your miracles at work in the lives of Your people. Amen.

DR. BYRON MCWILLIAMS, FIRST BAPTIST CHURCH, ODESSA, TX

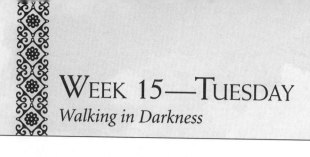

Week 15—Tuesday
Walking in Darkness

Unto the upright there arises light in the darkness; he is gracious, and full of compassion, and righteous. A good man deals graciously and lends; he will guide his affairs with discretion. . . . He will not be afraid of evil tidings; his heart is steadfast, trusting in the LORD.

PSALM 112:4–5, 7

Every person experiences darkness in life. At times it seems the tide has gone out and refuses to come back in. In these dark times, Christians can easily forget basic truths about their Father in heaven. Maybe we need a reminder. In today's text, the psalmist declared three truths about God.

God is gracious to His children! This means God pours out His favor on us even when we are unable to recognize that the blessings come from Him. He never stops extending grace to us. He always longs to bless.

God shows compassion to His children! When we hurt, God feels our pain and responds with tender mercies. He heard the Israelites' cries of pain from Egypt. Jesus felt compassion as He stood before the grave of Lazarus and watched how death impacted those whom He loved. On our darkest days, our Lord still has sweet compassion as we suffer.

God is righteous! He can never be credited with evil, but is always crowned with good. We can always trust the sand of circumstances that sift through His perfect hands.

Yes, we sometimes walk in darkness, but we do not walk alone. God guides His children through the trials of life.

....

Dear Lord, help me never to forget basic truths about Your grace, compassion, and righteousness. Amen.

WEEK 15—WEDNESDAY
Divine Benefits

What shall I render to the LORD for all His benefits toward me? I will take up the cup of salvation, and call upon the name of the LORD. I will pay my vows to the LORD now in the presence of all His people.

PSALM 116:12–14

Have you paused lately to thank God for the wonderful divine benefits you've received from His hand? Here are a couple thoughts from Psalm 116 to get you started.

First, you've drunk from the cup of salvation and experienced the greatest exchange possible when you were transferred from death to life. You were spiritually dead in your sins, but were made alive through Christ Jesus! Now you no longer are bound by sin and death; you are an overcomer! You need not live enslaved when you've been set free by the Savior of the world. Thank Him for your freedom!

Second, because of all you've received from God, you now have the great joy of living daily for Him as you fulfill your vows to Him. When I married my wife many years ago, we stood in front of our pastor and exchanged vows. We promised to love, honor, and cherish each other all the days of our lives. We made these vows to each other before the Lord. In an even greater way, when you called upon the name of Jesus and received salvation, you committed to living for Him and daily fulfilling your vows of obedience to your King. Are you doing that? Are you living daily to love, honor, and cherish the Lord Jesus?

....

Dear Lord, help me to be thankful for the salvation You've given me, and help me to remain faithful to my vows to You. Amen.

DR. BYRON MCWILLIAMS, FIRST BAPTIST CHURCH, ODESSA, TX

WEEK 15—THURSDAY
Brother Walter Was Right

The stone which the builders rejected has become the chief cornerstone. This was the LORD's doing; it is marvelous in our eyes. This is the day the LORD has made; we will rejoice and be glad in it.

PSALM 118:22–24

I n a previous pastorate, I met an elderly saint named Brother Walter. He and his wife resided at the local, small-town nursing home. He was bound to a wheelchair, unable to walk, but that had little impact on his mobility. When I walked into the facility, I'd find Brother Walter pulling himself along with one foot, smiling and heading in my direction.

What I will never forget is the joy this sweet saint had as he lived daily for Jesus. When others were depressed or angry, he found joy and happiness. When others grew bitter, Brother Walter grew content. What was the key for his delightful outlook on life?

Every time I visited the nursing home and Brother Walter rolled up, he would personalize one of the verses we read that day. He would say, "This is the day the Lord has made. *I* will rejoice and be glad in it." And did he ever!

Brother Walter had figured out the key to joyous living regardless of conditions. He understood life was a gift of God's grace, and he was determined to see through the clouds to find the sunshine regardless of the storms he encountered. He could do this for one simple reason: he had met the stone the builders had rejected, the Lord Jesus Christ, and he had come to know Him intimately.

This is the day the Lord has made. Rejoice in His goodness!

....

Dear Lord, help me to rejoice in every day You've given me on this earth. Amen.

Week 15—Friday
It's Friday and God Is Good

God is the LORD, and He has given us light; bind the sacrifice with cords to the horns of the altar. You are my God, and I will praise You; You are my God, I will exalt You. Oh, give thanks to the LORD, for He is good! For His mercy endures forever.

PSALM 118:27–29

When the clock "alarms" us on Friday, it is often the easiest day to hop out of bed because the weekend is at hand. Fridays are for rejoicing! Fridays are for thanksgiving!

Today, the psalmist encouraged us to participate in a time of thanksgiving. The referenced sacrifice was a thanksgiving offering bound and placed on the altar to acknowledge the ongoing goodness of God. With the sacrifice in place, the writer burst into a declaration of praise from an overflowing heart. He then closed by stating two distinct facts about the character of God: He is good and His mercy endures forever. What does this mean for us?

Everything God does is good. His interaction with His children is a perfect picture of goodness on display. Out of this goodness, our God chooses to bless rather than curse. God's goodness always reigns supreme—even on Mondays when the going gets tough.

God is always merciful! He delights to show mercy to His children. Mercy is the discretionary act of a judge who is within his right to invoke the death penalty but chooses to pardon instead. That's what our Lord did for us. When we deserved death, God sent forth His Son as a sacrifice on the altar of a Roman cross. As the old hymn says, "Morning by morning new mercies I see."

It's Friday! Let's give thanks to the Lord!

....

Dear Lord, thank You for Your goodness and mercy. I give praise to Your name! Amen.

DR. BYRON MCWILLIAMS, FIRST BAPTIST CHURCH, ODESSA, TX

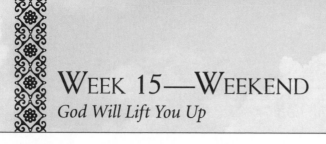

Week 15—Weekend
God Will Lift You Up

My soul clings to the dust; revive me according to Your word. I have declared my ways, and You answered me; teach me Your statutes. Make me understand the way of Your precepts; so shall I meditate on Your wonderful works.

PSALM 119:25–27

As a pastor, I often encounter anxiety, depression, and stress in the lives of those I counsel. These conditions are not new; for many millennia they have impaired God's children. In the words we read today, we see the psalmist so depressed he felt at the point of death.

What is the answer for those who suffer like this? What can you do when your "soul clings to the dust"? Here's a plan that will help.

First, spend time in Scripture! He says, "Revive me according to your word." Christians should find spiritual dividends every time they open God's Word. Turn to your Bible. Read for spiritual encouragement and not only for knowledge. God will be present.

Second, spend time in prayer! The psalmist had had his requests answered before because he said, "You answered me." Time spent in prayer is never wasted! When a problem cannot be fixed by human solutions, prayer is your answer. God beckons you to call to Him. He delights to respond!

Third, spend time at the feet of Jesus! No better place can be found than sitting at the Master's feet. There you will learn as He teaches you His precepts. Turn to the Gospels and let the Savior speak to your heart!

Finally, spend time rejoicing! Little combats depression and darkness more than time spent rejoicing in the Savior who loves you. Why not start right now?

....

Dear Lord, when my "soul clings to the dust," let me find my joy in You. Amen.

WEEK 16—MONDAY
Committed to the End

Teach me, O LORD, the way of Your statutes, and I shall keep it to the end. Give me understanding, and I shall keep Your law; indeed, I shall observe it with my whole heart. Make me walk in the path of Your commandments, for I delight in it.

PSALM 119:33–35

N othing seems to last very long in this world. Primitive cultures rarely threw things away because every item produced was seen as something with intrinsic value to be used again and again to its fullest extent. Modern culture throws away much: food, consumer goods, and sadly, even items of great value such as marriage and family. Being committed to something forever is a steadfastness seldom found among us. Yet the psalmist declared his intent to keep God's commandments "to the end."

The best way to keep God's commandments is to ask for His help and guidance in doing so. The writer called on God to "teach me," to "give me understanding," and to "make me walk." An imperfect human made each of these requests to a perfect God for His help to do something that is difficult for an imperfect human to do. But the psalmist didn't only ask for heavenly assistance—he made his own commitment. A life committed to the keeping of God's Word is accomplished by a heart saturated with the passionate faith rooted in the delights of Scripture. Such a passion creates a self-determination to take whatever steps are necessary to be committed to the end.

Father, help me always to remember Your faithfulness to me. Let me know Your Word, do Your Word, and be committed to Your Word to the end. In Jesus' name, amen.

DR. FRED M. EVERS, NORTHSIDE BAPTIST CHURCH, TIFTON, GA

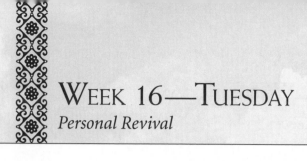

WEEK 16—TUESDAY
Personal Revival

Your word is a lamp to my feet and a light to my path. I have sworn and confirmed that I will keep Your righteous judgments. I am afflicted very much; revive me, O LORD, according to Your word.

PSALM 119:105–107

F ew of us doubt the need for spiritual revitalization in our lives. In like manner, the psalmist asked God to bring him revival, a personal renewal of his relationship with God. We use such terms as *recommitment* or *rededication* to describe our commitment to personal revival. The conviction of our sin brings an "affliction" of the soul. Such a wounded soul is a good inspiration for personal renewal. If a malady of sin afflicts us in such a way, perhaps it is time to pray for revival.

True revival does not happen simply because we ask God for it. We must comprehend that a change in our direction is required if we want to avoid an afflicted soul. This text contains both admittance and commitment. First, we must admit that God's Word is the light that illuminates the direction we should go. The lamp of the text was likely the small, oil-burning lamp of the ancient world. It showed only a small distance in front of the walker on a dark path. By carefully holding up the lamp the walker move forward in safety— similarly should one use Scripture as illumination. Second, the text calls for a commitment. We must commit ourselves to obey the righteous judgments of God we have neglected.

....

Father, forgive me for my failures. Let me confirm the standards of Your Word in my life and look to the light of Your Word to lead me in the direction I should go. In Jesus' name, amen.

Week 16—Wednesday
The Lord Is Our Keeper

The LORD is your keeper; the LORD is your shade at your right hand. The sun shall not strike you by day, nor the moon by night. The LORD shall preserve you from all evil; He shall preserve your soul. The LORD shall preserve your going out and your coming in from this time forth, and even forevermore.

PSALM 121:5–8

P salm 121 may have been a pilgrimage song the Jews used as they traveled to Jerusalem. On their way, they faced the dangers of the heat of the sun, the coldness of the night, or even the attacks of thieves. They sang this song to remind themselves of God's protection.

We are also on a pilgrimage. But in all the journeys of life the Lord is our keeper. We should not feel that God will spare us from all difficulties and trials. But we can know our souls stand under the providential shadow of His protection. No event in life occurs when He is not with us and no calamity falls upon us that He cannot use for His glory and for our spiritual maturation.

Such is the testimony of the saints. There would not have been a Joseph if it were not for his time in prison. There would not have been a Moses if it were not for his birth in slavery. God holds us in the palms of His hands no matter the trials we go through, and then He uses those trials to mold us into living testimonies of His faithfulness as our Keeper.

....

Father, remind me daily that no valley is too deep nor danger so difficult to keep me out of the shadow of Your eternal strength. In Jesus' name, amen.

DR. FRED M. EVERS, NORTHSIDE BAPTIST CHURCH, TIFTON, GA

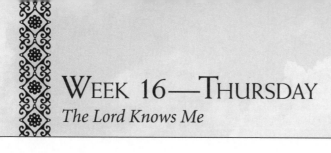

WEEK 16—THURSDAY
The Lord Knows Me

O LORD, You have searched me and known me. You know my sitting down and my rising up; You understand my thought afar off. You comprehend my path and my lying down, and are acquainted with all my ways. For there is not a word on my tongue, but behold, O LORD, You know it altogether.

PSALM 139:1–4

There is nothing about me the Lord does not know. Psalm 139 uses the word "know" multiple times. The usage connotes a deep and intimate knowledge of another person. God knows all the activities of our lives: our sitting, standing, going, and even sleeping. He even knows what we will say before we say it. His observation of us is not for the purpose of gaining knowledge—He wants to know us because of His compassionate care and oversight.

When a mother brings home a newborn, she holds the child as she feeds him. Her loving observation soaks up every aspect of the child's being. Her overwhelming love soaks in every detail. She knows the dimples of his chin, the curls of hair on his head, the birthmark on the bottom of his right foot, and the deep blue of his eyes. Nothing about him goes unnoticed. A mother's love for her baby is a great love, but such love pales in comparison to the love God has for us. His watchful gaze of love soaks up every part of us.

....

Father, thank You for watching me with Your eyes of love. Remind me that no aspect of my life unknown to You. Amen.

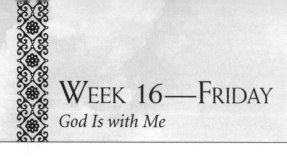

WEEK 16—FRIDAY
God Is with Me

Where can I go from Your Spirit? Or where can I flee from Your presence? If I ascend into heaven, You are there; if I make my bed in hell, behold, You are there. If I take the wings of the morning, and dwell in the uttermost parts of the sea, even there Your hand shall lead me, and Your right hand shall hold me.

PSALM 139:7–10

God's omnipresence is His unique ability to be present in all places at the same time. The presence of God in this passage is His specific and continual presence in every aspect of our lives. The God who was present at all the miracles of the Bible and the God who was present with all the prophets and apostles is present with us. There is no place we can go where He is not present. Even if we could fly at the speed of the light from the morning sun and go to the lowest depths of the sea—He is already present.

His presence is far more than just being in our location. He is present as our Friend, Comforter, Defender, and Father. He is always our God no matter where we are. This is the promise Jesus gave His disciples in Matthew 28:20: "I am with you always, even to the end of the age." No path exists where He will not be present to lead us. There is no calamity in our lives where He will not hold us with His right hand. God is with us always.

Father, thank You for Your presence in my life. May I always remember You are with me. Amen.

DR. FRED M. EVERS, NORTHSIDE BAPTIST CHURCH, TIFTON, GA

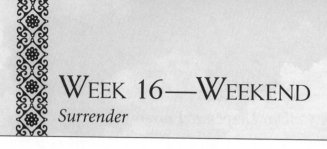

WEEK 16—WEEKEND
Surrender

Search me, O God, and know my heart; try me, and know my anxieties; and see if there is any wicked way in me, and lead me in the way everlasting.

PSALM 139:23–24

David ended Psalm 139 with a statement of absolute surrender to God. Almost every verb in this passage is an imperative. David called on God in the strongest terms to look even deeper within his being and to find any flaw that would keep him from complete intimacy with God.

The word "know," used twice in these two verses and multiple other times in the psalm, underscores knowledge of the deepest intimate relationship. God knows us, His eyes search out the innermost parts of who we are, and there is nothing about us He does not know. God is with us always; there is no place we can go where He is not present. In light of God's passionate pursuit, how can we not respond in total surrender to Him?

The animals offered in the Old Testament sacrificial system had to be without blemish. The priest would examine the animals to look for any mark of imperfection that would disqualify them as gifts to a perfect God. But David requested far more than just an outer examination. He called on God to check out every nook and cranny, look under every rug, and plunder every closet. He wanted God to find any sin or imperfection that would keep him from complete intimacy with His heavenly Father.

....

Father, search all of me and let me surrender to You with all my heart. Amen.

WEEK 17—MONDAY
Desperate Times Call for Desperate Prayers

Answer me speedily, O LORD; my spirit fails! Do not hide Your face from me, lest I be like those who go down into the pit. Cause me to hear Your lovingkindness in the morning, for in You do I trust; cause me to know the way in which I should walk, for I lift up my soul to You.

PSALM 143:7–8

Have we ever been truly desperate? Some moments in life are so paralyzing they leave us reeling with the notion that no solution is possible. David likely wrote this psalm while Saul was trying to kill him. Though David was confident in his relationship with God, Saul's relentless pursuit and oppression left him wondering if his trials were the result of spiritual compromise on his behalf.

David called out for God not to hide His face from him. The beautiful simplicity of his plea reminds us that seeing the face of God is more important than freedom from our enemies. Like a child in need of parental affirmation, we need the eyes of God upon us and the will of God guiding us. This prayer admonishes us to look for our Savior rather than solutions when life unravels.

Awareness of God's love and assurance of His continued guidance are more important than easy remedies that do not require sustained dependence upon Him. David's commitment to lift His soul to the Lord is his recognition that satisfaction in God is just as important as strength received from God.

....

Father, help me to rest in You as I navigate life's complexities and challenges. Remind me of Your faithfulness when I doubt Your presence or Your plans. Forgive me for valuing my personal comfort more than my relationship with You. Amen.

DR. ADAM B. DOOLEY, SUNNYVALE FIRST BAPTIST CHURCH, DALLAS, TX

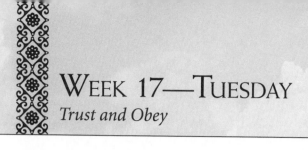

WEEK 17—TUESDAY
Trust and Obey

Cause me to hear Your lovingkindness in the morning, for in You do I trust; cause me to know the way in which I should walk, for I lift up my soul to You. Deliver me, O LORD, from my enemies; in You I take shelter. Teach me to do Your will, for You are my God; Your Spirit is good. Lead me in the land of uprightness.

PSALM 143:8–10

When was the last time the Lord intervened on your behalf? Maybe as David wrote in this psalm, it was the removal of a trial or the defeat of an enemy. Though the Lord welcomes our petitions for relief and often answers them, the greatest evidence of our trusting God is how we endure trials. Not knowing the ultimate solution to his dilemma, David yearned to be aware of God's love, to grasp God's direction, to understand God's will, and to experience God's righteousness.

Certainly we should believe that God is able to meet our needs instantaneously, but substantive faith requires more of us than momentary belief. The presence of difficulty forces us to accept God's love without conditions and to follow God's directions without explanations. Real trust does not waver when answers are in short supply. Demonstrating that we love God more than the solace He offers necessitates finding ourselves in situations where relief does not come. Such difficult moments are less a test of what God is able to do and more a proving ground for how much we are willing to trust Him.

So when hard times come we should feel free to seek an exit strategy from the Lord, but we also need to be ready to rest in His love and walk in His ways even if the intervention we hope for does not come.

......

Lord, help me learn to trust You in everything I face. In Jesus' name, amen.

WEEK 17—WEDNESDAY
More Than a Song

Great is the LORD, and greatly to be praised; and His greatness is unsearchable. One generation shall praise Your works to another, and shall declare Your mighty acts. I will meditate on the glorious splendor of Your majesty, and on Your wondrous works. Men shall speak of the might of Your awesome acts, and I will declare Your greatness.

PSALM 145:3–6

I s praise a real part of our lives? Certainly we all have moments when circumstances compel us to voice our adoration and appreciation for God's intervention. Unfortunately, those instances are far too infrequent for many Christ followers. Though our petitions remain continually before the Lord, our praise tends to mimic the deafening silence of a forgetful heart.

By extolling God's various attributes, David remained captivated by the unfathomable glory and greatness of his heavenly Father. His pattern of worship is instructive for us today because he worshipped God for who He is, what He had done, and what He would do. Along with past generations, future followers would declare the magnificence of our God and King as they observe His wonderful works and provisions.

This psalm teaches us that praising God is more than an obligatory addition to our prayers. No, we worship because our adulation is true and our God is a worthy recipient of unending reverence. In addition, our continued esteem is to our personal benefit because it fulfills the purpose for which God created us. Each of us exists to glorify our Creator. Does our lack of praise indicate that we have made Christianity more about us than our Savior?

....

Father, I worship You for being a good God who is worthy of my adoration. Amen.

DR. ADAM B. DOOLEY, SUNNYVALE FIRST BAPTIST CHURCH, DALLAS, TX

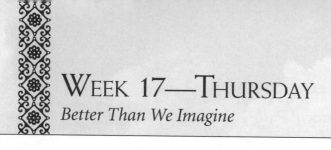

WEEK 17—THURSDAY
Better Than We Imagine

The LORD upholds all who fall, and raises up all who are bowed down. The eyes of all look expectantly to You, and You give them their food in due season. You open Your hand and satisfy the desire of every living thing.

PSALM 145:14–16

How benevolent is our God? Initially we tend to answer this question by recalling the specific works of the Lord in our lives. Indeed, doing so leads us to praise our heavenly Father (Psalm 145:4, 6–7).

Have we ever stopped to consider, however, the gracious activity of God in the lives of those who do not know Him? David acknowledged God's sustaining compassion toward all who fall and His generous provision for all who are hungry and needy. In fact, true satisfaction in life flows out of the open hand of our loving and attentive Creator. God not only feeds the birds of the air and clothes the lilies of the field (Matthew 6:26–29), He also furnishes sunlight and rain for the just and unjust alike (Matthew 5:45). In other words, believers do not earn the gracious gifts that come down from heaven because God also dispenses them to those who refuse to worship Him.

Certainly saints are more aware of God's benevolence, but they should recognize God is also patient and kind with His enemies. Why should we care? And why should this drive us to worship more enthusiastically? We mustn't forget that at one point all of us were enemies of God. We cannot scoff at the notion of God's universal generosity because we were once on the receiving end of it.

....

Lord, thank You for loving those who reject You. Help me to do the same as I remember how I used to live before accepting Jesus as my Savior. Amen.

WEEK 17—FRIDAY
Walking the Straight Path

Trust in the LORD with all your heart, and lean not on your own understanding; in all your ways acknowledge Him, and He shall direct your paths.

PROVERBS 3:5–6

Would we like to live with the certainty that God is directing our paths? Doing so requires two basic commitments from those who belong to the Lord. First, we must learn to trust God rather than our own understanding. Solomon was not bemoaning common sense here, but instead our tendency to value human reason over divine revelation. Total trust in God comes from a commitment to honor the Word of God. As disciples of Jesus, we must value what God says more than what we think. Direction from the Lord will always be consistent with the teachings of Holy Scripture.

Second, when we acknowledge God in all things we can have confidence that He will guide us. Many people miss the will of God simply because they do not care to look for it. When we realize that God put us on earth to glorify Him rather than ourselves, we are free to watch Him unfold His particular plans for our lives. God promises to make His path obvious to those who are anxious to honor Him each step of the way. All Christians have the same purpose even if their paths vary in scope and design.

Father, I long for You to direct my path. Help me to trust You without reservation while acknowledging You in every part of my life. Use the Bible, Your Spirit, and the body of Christ to make Your will readily apparent to me. Thank You for guiding me. Amen.

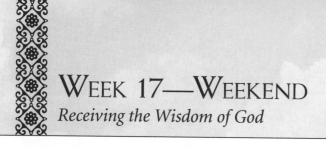

Week 17—Weekend
Receiving the Wisdom of God

I have taught you in the way of wisdom; I have led you in right paths. When you walk, your steps will not be hindered, and when you run, you will not stumble. Take firm hold of instruction, do not let go; keep her, for she is your life.

Proverbs 4:11–13

Understanding Proverbs requires identifying the wisdom Solomon referred to throughout the book. Though various nuances accompany the king's teaching, grasping that Jesus is the fulfillment of wisdom is key. Since Christ is the wisdom of God (1 Corinthians 1:24, 30), growing in our relationship with our Savior is equivalent to growing in wisdom. Thus, the way of wisdom is the way of Jesus.

When He transforms our hearts, we not only find the right paths but also live without hindrance or stumbling. This admonition does not promise freedom from adversities or trials but instead assures us that resting in Christ will protect us from the many heartaches that sin brings into our lives. Clinging to Him allows us to receive instruction and live accordingly.

Though our disobedience will always require repentance that results in changed behavior, such transformation is possible only when we cultivate a daily, genuine relationship with the Son of God. When we seek the Lord in His Word, yield to Him through our prayers, and journey together in the body of Christ, the roots of wisdom will run deep into our hearts as the evidence of biblical faith blossoms.

....

Father, thank You for sending a Savior to die for me. Help me to embrace Jesus in every area of my life. Give me the wisdom that comes only through knowing Your Son. Prevent me from deviating from the right path. In Jesus' name, amen.

Week 18—Monday
God's Wisdom Leads to Life

My son, give attention to my words; incline your ear to my sayings. Do not let them depart from your eyes; keep them in the midst of your heart; for they are life to those who find them, and health to all their flesh. Keep your heart with all diligence, for out of it spring the issues of life.

PROVERBS 4:20–23

Proverbs 4 speaks of the value of God's wisdom. The wisdom of God comes from His words to us. We should seek to know the wisdom of God about all things. God's Word gives us His perspective.

When we listen to what God says to us about life, something dynamic occurs in our lives. We receive fresh, reviving life. Something unique begins to flow through us, and it brings the healing we need in life.

God's wisdom leads to life! When we begin to experience these moments with God, we do not want to lose them. They become like the springtime that follows a tough wintry season.

We receive God's wisdom because we determine to listen to what God says to us about life from His dynamic Word. From this moment on, our entire perspectives change and our decision-making is impacted.

We see the very source of life and healing for us personally because our futures come from one thing: doing what God commands us to do in His Word. This is what revives our lives!

....

Dear God, give me ears to hear what You say to me from Your Word. Create reviving life within me and may Your life be expressed through me—not just to heal me, but also to become healing for others. In Jesus' name, amen.

DR. RONNIE FLOYD, CROSS CHURCH, SPRINGDALE, AR

WEEK 18—TUESDAY
God Will Protect You

The fear of man brings a snare, but whoever trusts in the Lord shall be safe. Many seek the ruler's favor, but justice for man comes from the Lord. An unjust man is an abomination to the righteous, and he who is upright in the way is an abomination to the wicked.

PROVERBS 29:25–27

We live in a very dangerous world. Evil abounds. Terrorism occurs not just outside the borders of America, but even inside its borders. Each of us knows that all kinds of places could be the next location where evil fulfills its wicked intent to interrupt, intimidate, or even destroy human life.

Fear is real in the world.

But God does not give us a spirit of fear! He does not want us to succumb to living in sheer terror. Nor does God want us ever to fear what people can do to us. In this passage Solomon taught us whom we should fear. God wants us to fear (or revere) Him. He wants us to live in ways that respect and honor God by entrusting our care to Him every day.

God is not just able to protect us; He will protect us. Do we believe this? If so, we must trust God to do it. Now. Today. Wherever we are located.

While the government of this nation is mandated to protect our national security, God will protect us with His divine security when we trust Him.

....

Lord, I pray now for your protection over the public places in my community. Also, please protect me. Amen.

WEEK 18—WEDNESDAY
There Is No Time like God's Time

What profit has the worker from that in which he labors? I have seen the God-given task with which the sons of men are to be occupied. He has made everything beautiful in its time. Also He has put eternity in their hearts, except that no one can find out the work that God does from beginning to end.

ECCLESIASTES 3:9–11

From the moment we get up each morning to the moment we go to bed each night, we live by the clock. Time does not just instruct us as it should; rather, it rules us. This leads us to think of ourselves more highly than we should. It also leads us to equate busy lives with meaningful lives. Yet the two do not often connect.

God says something in Ecclesiastes that should stop us in our tracks: He has made everything beautiful in its time.

There is no time like God's time. He is the Creator of the times and seasons of life. Therefore, everything, yes, everything He has made is appropriate or beautiful in its time. Problems and interruptions—they never seem to come at the right time. Yet there is no time like God's time.

If we have walked with Him for any time, we often wonder when He is going to answer our prayers or show up in our situations as we have asked Him to do. Then we learn God is never too late, never too early, but always on time. There is no time like God's time.

....

Lord, I trust You that You are making all things beautiful in Your time. Amen.

DR. RONNIE FLOYD, CROSS CHURCH, SPRINGDALE, AR

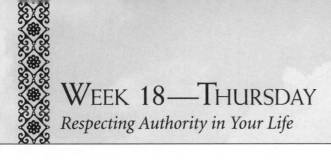

WEEK 18—THURSDAY
Respecting Authority in Your Life

I say, "Keep the king's commandments for the sake of your oath to God. Do not be hasty to go from his presence. Do not take your stand for an evil thing, for he does whatever pleases him."

Where the word of a king is, there is power; and who may say to him, "What are you doing?" He who keeps his command will experience nothing harmful; and a wise man's heart discerns both time and judgment.

ECCLESIASTES 8:2–5

The way you respond to authority tells a great deal about your spiritual maturity.

The authority figures in your life are not perfect. Your employers, your bosses, your parents, your teachers, your presidents, your pastors, your government officials, or your family: none of them are perfect. But each is your authority.

If people have responsibility of any kind over you, then you have the responsibility to accept their authority. People often forget God has placed authority over them. Man or woman has no authority except the authority entrusted to them by God.

The verses here are clear: When you walk in agreement with those over you, God keeps you safe from harm. On the other hand, when you have a position of authority, God expects you to act properly too. When the time comes to make an appeal to your authority about something, you are to show good timing and judgment.

....

Dear God, give me the humility to live under those in authority in my life. Amen.

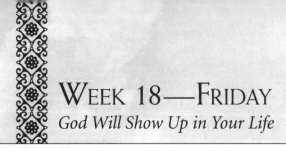

Week 18—Friday
God Will Show Up in Your Life

"Behold, God is my salvation, I will trust and not be afraid; 'For Yah, the Lord is my strength and song; He also has become my salvation. Therefore, with joy you will draw water from the wells of salvation.'"

Isaiah 12:2–3

Storms will come in your life. There will be moments when you know that if God does not show up in a specific situation, you are in deep trouble. Living through these storms is not fun. The prophet Isaiah wrote about such difficult times in the text for today. But when God shows up, you know He will intervene in this situation and save you powerfully. There is nothing like God revealing Himself in the situations of your life.

When He showed up in the form of a burning bush, God changed Moses' life forever. Moses' direction and confidence relating to his future took on a new trajectory. Just as with Moses, when God shows up in your life, it impacts you forever.

Many times it alters only your perspective and confidence, but other times it changes the direction of your life. This energizes you with new spiritual strength! Your vision and energy become impacted, and you want to brag on Jesus and what He is doing in your life. Jesus makes you want to sing . . . again. Jesus gives you joy . . . again. Jesus becomes as rivers of living water in your life . . . again.

All this occurs in your life when God shows up in the midst of those times when your needs are the greatest. When God shows up, He always gives You strength.

....

Lord, You know my needs. Come! I need You! In Jesus' name, amen.

DR. RONNIE FLOYD, CROSS CHURCH, SPRINGDALE, AR

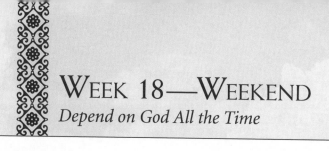

WEEK 18—WEEKEND
Depend on God All the Time

You will keep him in perfect peace, whose mind is stayed on You, because he trusts in You. Trust in the LORD forever, for in YAH, the LORD, is everlasting strength.

ISAIAH 26:3–4

Depending on ourselves can lead to misery and disaster. When we become burdened about something and carry it personally rather than giving it to God, often we become miserable and overwhelmed by what is upon us. This is never healthy and results in unrest.

Yet when we depend on God all the time, He gives us perfect peace. This happens only when our minds stay upon Him all the time. When this occurs, not only does our load lighten, our strength increases. When we depend on God all the time, our perspectives change and our attitudes rise to a different altitude. Looking up to God in our lives always lifts us up.

Carrying our burdens through life weighs us down. It discourages us. It can even depress us. This is never God's will and way for us. Whatever the problem, God is able. Whatever the decision, God is able. Whatever awaits us, God is able.

This weekend, spend time reflecting upon the times in your life when you focused on God and depended on Him daily. Determine this weekend that when Monday comes, you will start your day with God.

God is always waiting to meet with you. In the early mornings or even in the late nights, God is there for you. Resolve now to depend on God all the time.

....

Lord, I will depend on You all the time. Amen.

WEEK 19—MONDAY
Whom Do You Trust?

Therefore the LORD will wait, that He may be gracious to you; and therefore He will be exalted, that He may have mercy on you. For the LORD is a God of justice; blessed are all those who wait for Him.

ISAIAH 30:18

The first seventeen verses of this chapter are a rebuke to Judah for not seeking God's will concerning the nation of Assyria. King Hezekiah's advisors urged him to turn to the Egyptians and not to God for help. After all the Lord had done for His people, they turned away from Him and sought the help of feeble Egypt. Unlike their leaders of old—Moses, Joshua, David—the rulers of Jerusalem did not seek the will of God. They listened to the words of men. The prophet Isaiah told the people what would happen to Judah because they had rejected God and turned to follow the lies of men (Isaiah 30:12–14).

As we come to our verse, the prophet turned from the subject of rebellion to the subject of restoration. Since Judah would not wait on the Lord to deliver, God would wait to be gracious to the nation. Discipline would be meted out, but then restoration would come. We need to remember that God is a God of love but also of justice. When we sin, we face God's judgment, but we can also rejoice in knowing He offers forgiveness and restoration.

....

Lord, teach me to trust Your Word and know You want what's best for me. May I rest in Your grace and follow Your Word and will for my life. In Jesus' name, amen.

DR. ROB ZINN, IMMANUEL BAPTIST CHURCH, HIGHLAND, CA

WEEK 19—TUESDAY
The Lord Is My Treasure

The LORD is exalted, for He dwells on high; He has filled Zion with justice and righteousness. Wisdom and knowledge will be the stability of your times, and the strength of salvation; the fear of the LORD is his treasure.

ISAIAH 33:5–6

This passage in Isaiah was directed against Sennacherib because of his treachery against Judah, which is found in 2 Kings 18. Israel had been carried off into captivity by the nation of Assyria, and now the Assyrian army was invading Judah. Showing a lack of faith, King Hezekiah tried to buy off the Assyrians (2 Kings 18:13–15), but Sennacherib broke his word and invaded Judah anyway. Jerusalem was now surrounded and in deep trouble. Isaiah had promised that God would be gracious to His people if they would only trust Him (Isaiah 30:18–19), so a few devout followers prayed to God (Isaiah 33:2). As today's text promised, the Lord would be exalted in the defeat of Assyria.

We must learn to trust the Lord in a crisis, in uncertain times, or when we don't understand. As Solomon wrote, "Trust in the LORD with all your heart, and lean not on your own understanding; in all your ways acknowledge Him, and He shall direct your paths" (Proverbs 3:5–6). The king did a foolish thing when he took the temple treasures and tried to bribe Sennacherib, but the Lord forgave Hezekiah and reminded him, "The fear of the LORD is [your] treasure" (Isaiah 33:6).

Unbelief looks to human resources for help, but faith looks to God. If we keep our focus on God, we won't be disappointed.

....

Lord, remind me that You are my supply and in Christ all my needs are met. In Jesus' name, amen.

WEEK 19—WEDNESDAY
A Precious Promise

He gives power to the weak, and to those who have no might He increases strength.
Even the youths shall faint and be weary, and the young men shall utterly fall, but
those who wait on the LORD shall renew their strength; they shall mount up with wings
like eagles, they shall run and not be weary, they shall walk and not faint.

ISAIAH 40:29–31

Let's be very honest—we all have days when everything seems to be against us. Things just are not going well, we're tired, or we feel overworked! Instead of praising the Lord, we just complain. Sometimes we feel as though God is against us rather than for us. We know that's not true, but that's how we feel.

Deep down we know we don't live by feelings but faith. Yet the enemy works hard to discourage us. Today's passage is a promise to hold on to—a verse to hide in our hearts and to remind us of the promise of God. The Lord always knows how we feel and what we're facing in life. He is able to meet our needs and give us the strength and energy to go on. Remember, "I can do all things through Christ who strengthens me" (Philippians 4:13).

The concept of waiting on the Lord does not mean to sit around and do nothing. Rather, it means to hope and to look to the Lord for all that we need. It involves remembering His love and character, meditating on His Word and promises, and seeking to glorify Him. We exchange our power for His power, and He enables us to soar and meet the challenges before us.

Lord, give me the grace to wait on You! Amen!

DR. ROB ZINN, IMMANUEL BAPTIST CHURCH, HIGHLAND, CA

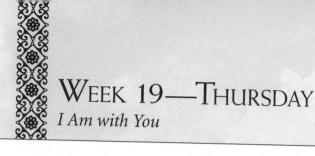

WEEK 19—THURSDAY
I Am with You

"Fear not, for I am with you; be not dismayed, for I am your God. I will strengthen you, yes, I will help you, I will uphold you with My righteous right hand."

ISAIAH 41:10

One of the tools of Satan is fear. People who do not know the Lord live in fear of darkness, fear of the unknown, fear of death, and so on. In Isaiah's day, Israel lived in fear of the Gentile nations. Today we live in fear of war, ISIS, and a very unstable political environment. But we have God's promise: "Fear not, for I am with you."

Some might say, "But He was speaking to the nation of Israel." My friends, if we are in Christ He is speaking to us. As Jesus said also to His disciples, "And lo, I am with you always, even to the end of the age" (Matthew 28:20).

The truth is we may be unfaithful to Him, but He is always faithful to us. We may turn our backs on Him, but when we turn back around, He will still be there. He is there to lead us, guide us, give us strength in our weakness, help us, and uphold us with His right hand. We serve the living God, and nothing is too difficult for Him! We are not called to live in fear, but to live by faith!

....

Lord, thank You for loving me, filling me, and using me. Give me a boldness to share Your love with others. Keep me focused on You. In Jesus' name, amen.

WEEK 19—FRIDAY
Look to the Future

"Do not remember the former things, nor consider the things of old. Behold, I will do a new thing, now it shall spring forth; shall you not know it? I will even make a road in the wilderness and rivers in the desert."

ISAIAH 43:18–19

To the nation of Israel, this was a message of hope that God would redeem His people and deliver them. They were not to look at what the Lord had done in the past for He would do something new.

Now as we meditate on this passage, God also speaks to us. We can choose to live in the past, or we can look toward the future. Some can't let go of past sins even though God has forgiven them and the sins are gone (Jeremiah 31:34). And some resist change because they are not comfortable with the new. It is good to remember what the Lord has done and what He has taught us. He has plans for where we are right now and where we are going.

Today is the first day of the rest of your life. God loves you and has a plan for you. Walk in the light you have and continue to grow in His grace. Never stop learning. Whatever new thing God does in your life is always for your good and His glory. Keep moving forward and follow the direction God gives you.

Lord, thank You for all You have done for me and how blessed I am. Give me the grace to follow as You lead. In Jesus' name, amen.

DR. ROB ZINN, IMMANUEL BAPTIST CHURCH, HIGHLAND, CA

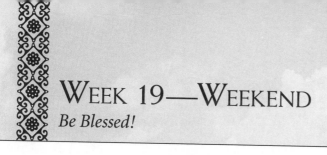

WEEK 19—WEEKEND
Be Blessed!

Thus says the LORD, your Redeemer, the Holy One of Israel: "I am the LORD your God, who teaches you to profit, who teaches you in the way you should go. Oh, that you had heeded My commandments! Then your peace would have been like a river, and your righteousness like the waves of the sea."

ISAIAH 48:17–18

God is a God who blesses! He desires to profit us, grow us, and use us to bear fruit. He is also a loving Father, and as such He will discipline us when we do not obey. Hebrews 12:7 reminds us: "If you endure chastening, God deals with you as with sons; for what son is there whom a father does not chasten?" Also, Samuel told Saul, "To obey is better than sacrifice" (1 Samuel 15:22). And Jesus said, "If you love Me, keep My commandments" (John 14:15). Clearly, the Bible teaches the importance of obedience.

Why do so many believers not understand that God will not bless disobedience? Look again at Isaiah 48:18: "Oh, that you had heeded My commandments!" How many blessings have we missed because we did not pay attention and do what God told us to do? Jesus asked, "Why do you call Me 'Lord, Lord' and not do the things which I say?" (Luke 6:46). If we want to be blessed, then with a joyful heart we must trust and obey. This will ensure God's blessings on us.

....

Lord, give me a heart to do Your will, to follow Your instruction manual, and to love Your Word. I choose to be Your obedient servant. In Jesus' name, amen.

Week 20—Monday
Never Forgotten

"Can a woman forget her nursing child, and not have compassion on the son of her womb? Surely they may forget, yet I will not forget you. See, I have inscribed you on the palms of My hands; Your walls are continually before Me."

ISAIAH 49:15–16

When our middle child, Bryant, was only about ten years old, we inadvertently left him by himself. Yes, poor parenting I know, but we left him at his aunt's house while the rest of the family went to see a movie during the Christmas break. Of course, once we realized he was not with us, we rushed back and got him. Oh, the look of betrayal on his face!

To err is indeed human. But God never errs; He never makes a mistake, and He never forgets His own. Jesus redeemed us by His shed blood, and we are forever engraved on His palms of love and our faces are forever before Him. What a powerful God He is!

If the devil tempts you to question God's goodness or he tells you God has forgotten you, do not listen to his lies. Remember this wonderful text from the prophet Isaiah. God loves you, and He is for you. As His son or daughter, you are forever on His heart, mind, and His very hands.

....

Lord, thank You for Your nail-pierced hands, which have Your people's names inscribed upon them. Thank You for never leaving me nor forsaking me. Amen.

DR. DANNY FORSHEE, GREAT HILLS BAPTIST CHURCH, AUSTIN, TX

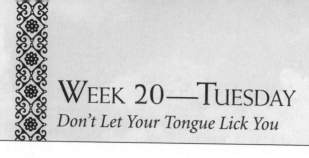

Week 20—Tuesday
Don't Let Your Tongue Lick You

The Lord God has given Me the tongue of the learned, that I should know how to speak a word in season to him who is weary. He awakens Me morning by morning, He awakens My ear to hear as the learned. The Lord God has opened My ear; and I was not rebellious, nor did I turn away.

ISAIAH 50:4–5

I saiah taught us that God grants His people the tongue of the learned, and the evidence of such a gift of speech is that we know how to speak a timely word to one in distress. Unfortunately, we are all too often guilty of just the opposite.

Don't let your tongue lick you! Ask God to help you never to harm others with hurtful speech, but to use your words to bless and edify. Proverbs 18:21 so wisely states, "Death and life are in the power of the tongue, and those who love it will eat its fruit." God loves you and He is for you. You are more than a conqueror by His great might. You can control the words you say!

....

Dear God, thank You for enabling me to know how to speak a timely word to those who are weary. Help me not to have a rebellious spirit and turn away from Your instructions. Grant me the wisdom to listen to Your voice and then to speak life to all those with whom I come in contact. And grant me the courage to listen to others, then speak a timely word. As Proverbs 25:11 reminds me, "A word fitly spoken is like apples of gold in settings of silver." In Jesus' name, amen.

WEEK 20—WEDNESDAY
Never Once

"For the mountains shall depart and the hills be removed, but My kindness shall not depart from you, nor shall My covenant of peace be removed," says the LORD, who has mercy on you.

ISAIAH 54:10

Mount Everest is quite the sight. A few years ago while on a mission trip to Nepal, I was on a chartered flight that took me close to Everest, which is the highest mountain peak in the world. Everest stands 29,029 feet tall, king of the mountains. Seeing this snow-covered peak from the cockpit of the airplane was breathtaking.

The God who created not only this mountain, but all the mountains and valleys, promises His children that though these massive masterpieces He has formed will one day be no more, His kindness will never depart from His people. And He promises that His peace will not be removed.

If you are doubting the goodness and power of God, glance at the mountains you can see with your physical eyes, and let them remind you of the power and presence of God that you can see only with your spiriutal eyes. Look at the verse again—God promises His kindness, peace, and mercy to you. Be encouraged, child of God. He will never leave or forsake you—not even once.

God, thank You for Your promise never to leave me. I believe. Help my unbelief. I reaffirm my trust in You and my love for You. I love You, knowing You first loved me. Amen.

DR. DANNY FORSHEE, GREAT HILLS BAPTIST CHURCH, AUSTIN, TX

WEEK 20—THURSDAY
God Is Smarter

"For My thoughts are not your thoughts, nor are your ways My ways," says the LORD. "For as the heavens are higher than the earth, so are My ways higher than your ways, and My thoughts than your thoughts."

ISAIAH 55:8–9

A pastor friend of mine likes to say, "God is just smarter than we are." God is omniscient, meaning He knows all things. He never has to learn anything because He simply knows it all. We, on the other hand, are limited in what we know. As followers of Christ, we should keep in mind that God is indeed smarter than we are. If His knowledge and wisdom were comparable to the height of the heavens above, then our understanding would be comparable to the height of a vertical domino.

The next time you are tempted to question God's wisdom or His timing, keep this in mind—He knows what He is doing. He has never lost a single thing or person, and He is not going to begin with you. Don't be offended if God does not do what you think He should do. Jesus said, "And blessed is he who is not offended because of Me" (Matthew 11:6). You must trust that God's plans are better than your plans.

....

Lord, please forgive me for my lack of faith, for not trusting in You, and for questioning Your power and wisdom. God, I need Your help. Restore to me the joy of Your salvation. Help me trust in You and remember that You have my best interests at heart and You will take care of me. Amen.

WEEK 20—FRIDAY
A Promise to Prosper

"For as the rain comes down, and the snow from heaven, and do not return there, but water the earth, and make it bring forth and bud, that it may give seed to the sower and bread to the eater, so shall My word be that goes forth from My mouth; it shall not return to Me void, but it shall accomplish what I please, and it shall prosper in the thing for which I sent it."

ISAIAH 55:10–11

The promise in our text for today is one of my favorites. God compares His word to the rains that fall to the earth. The rain from heaven waters the earth and causes seeds to grow and bring forth bread. God says the word that goes forth from His mouth shall accomplish exactly what He pleases, and it shall prosper.

God always fulfills His promises. But that does not mean He will always do it in the way or timing we would like! A pastor once shared the gospel with a young man numerous times, and each time the student said no to the offer of salvation. A guest preacher came and spoke, and the young man prayed to receive Christ, saying, "I have never heard this before!" The pastor was dumbfounded because he knew he had witnessed to this young man numerous times.

Yes, God remains true to His promises, but always in His way and in His time.

Thank You, Lord, that You are faithful and You always keep Your promises. I am especially grateful for this promise that Your word will never return void but will always accomplish what You please, and it will prosper. Amen.

DR. DANNY FORSHEE, GREAT HILLS BAPTIST CHURCH, AUSTIN, TX

Week 20—Weekend
A Simple Sandwich

"If you extend your soul to the hungry and satisfy the afflicted soul, then your light shall dawn in the darkness, and your darkness shall be as the noonday. The LORD will guide you continually, and satisfy your soul in drought, and strengthen your bones; you shall be like a watered garden, and like a spring of water, whose waters do not fail."

ISAIAH 58:10–11

Earlier this week I was driving to work and saw a homeless man at an intersection. I was running a little late due in part because I had made my lunch for the day. As I sat at the light, I felt compelled to give the man my sandwich. I thought I did not have enough time because the light would soon change, but I decided to go for it. I reached in my bag, took out my sandwich, and gave it to the very grateful homeless man. Later that day someone bought me a sandwich, and it was ten times better than the one I had given away!

If you feel down and discouraged, allow me to challenge you to go do a good deed for someone less fortunate than you. As you get out and help others, you will have a sense of peace and joy come over you, and you will experience the truth of our text today as God guides, satisfies, and strengthens you.

Dear God, help me to bless someone this very day who stands in need. Forgive me when I am too consumed with my wants and my needs. Help me to bless someone in Your name. Amen.

WEEK 21—MONDAY
I Will Rejoice in the Lord

I will greatly rejoice in the LORD, my soul shall be joyful in my God; for He has clothed me with the garments of salvation, He has covered me with the robe of righteousness, as a bridegroom decks himself with ornaments, and as a bride adorns herself with her jewels. For as the earth brings forth its bud, as the garden causes the things that are sown in it to spring forth, so the Lord GOD will cause righteousness and praise to spring forth before all the nations.

ISAIAH 61:10–11

You will probably agree that praising God is easy when your life is going well. What about during challenging times? Do you find it difficult to praise Him when life is hard? Today's verses reveal some very interesting truths about God's faithfulness that may help you during difficult times. First, notice that God has clothed you with salvation and adorned you in righteousness. Now look at God's promise of spring that comes after the weariness of winter. Though the ground appears barren, new life springs forth from what was previously planted.

God's promises are true. Whether you are skipping through good times or plodding through a difficult season, you can trust God's faithfulness will prevail. He is with you through it all, and He will make sure what He has sown within you will spring forth in its time.

Heavenly Father, thank You for your promises. Your presence with me, no matter what the season, brings comfort to my soul. I lift my heart and my hands in praise to you, Lord, and I declare Your goodness in my life, my family, and my situation. You are my Shield and my Strength, and in You I am safe and secure. Amen.

TIM DETELLIS, NEW MISSIONS, ORLANDO, FL

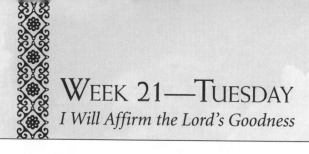

WEEK 21—TUESDAY
I Will Affirm the Lord's Goodness

I will mention the lovingkindnesses of the LORD and the praises of the LORD, according to all that the LORD has bestowed on us, and the great goodness toward the house of Israel, which He has bestowed on them according to His mercies, according to the multitude of His lovingkindnesses. For He said, "Surely they are My people, children who will not lie." So He became their Savior.

ISAIAH 63:7–8

When life slips into a seemingly unchanging routine, it can be easy to fall into the trap of thinking you have made no progress . . . until you look back and see how far you have come. The act of looking back does to the memory what a defibrillator does to a heart in cardiac arrest. Suddenly you see that what had seemed to be a stale routine was instead God's working out His plan in your life.

Today's verses serve as a reminder to look back and recall everything the Lord has done in your life to bring you to where you are. It is a call to immerse yourself in the memories of God's goodness, provision, lovingkindness, and faithfulness. As you consider all God has done in your life, both your faith and your resolve will strengthen. Then you, like the apostle Paul, truly can say you are content in what God provides (Philippians 4:11).

....

Heavenly Father, Your active presence in my life enables me to be content whatever the circumstances that surround me. Therefore, I will boldly proclaim Your name as I testify of Your goodness and lovingkindness. Thank You for providing me with opportunities to declare your provision and protection. Amen.

WEEK 21—WEDNESDAY
I Will Declare the Name of the Lord

Oh, that You would rend the heavens! That You would come down! That the mountains might shake at Your presence— as fire burns brushwood, as fire causes water to boil— to make Your name known to Your adversaries, that the nations may tremble at Your presence! When You did awesome things for which we did not look, You came down, the mountains shook at Your presence.

ISAIAH 64:1–3

D o you ever feel as if you are surrounded by people who are hostile toward God? With all the ways information is delivered today, it is not difficult to find comments made by people who simply do not believe God exists. Hostility against God is alive and well in American society.

Today's verses highlight the frustration of being surrounded by people who refuse to embrace the Lord. Like the prophet, you may ask God to showcase His mighty power in the lives of unbelievers, but why? Is it to prove to people you are right, or so that those people will believe in Him and turn to Him?

God showcases His mighty power in many ways, but often it is through the submitted life of a person who loves Him and is committed to serving Him. God reveals His power through the grace by which His people handle difficult situations. As you submit your life fully to God, He will show His power to other people through you.

Lord, I want You to show Your power through my life. Help me to grow in my confidence of Your ability to support me through challenging times. I commit my life to You, Lord. Help me to be an example to people who do not know You so they can be saved. Amen.

TIM DETELLIS, NEW MISSIONS, ORLANDO, FL

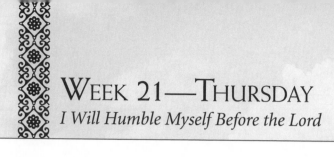

WEEK 21—THURSDAY
I Will Humble Myself Before the Lord

For since the beginning of the world men have not heard nor perceived by the ear, nor has the eye seen any God besides You, who acts for the one who waits for Him. You meet him who rejoices and does righteousness, who remembers You in Your ways. You are indeed angry, for we have sinned— in these ways we continue; and we need to be saved.

ISAIAH 64:4–5

Every person who has ever walked this earth needs to be saved because "all have sinned and fall short of the glory of God" (Romans 3:23). The Lord acts on behalf of those who wait for Him, but He is angry with those who continue in their rebellious ways. The difference between the two groups is their posture before Him: either they show humility or arrogance.

How about you? Do you like to choose your own way and follow your own path? Do you believe your strength is sufficient to overcome every obstacle in your way? If so, you may be missing out on some profound blessings God wants to give you.

Isaiah wrote how God stands ready to come alongside you and walk with you through anything you may face. But to receive His help, you must be willing to humble yourself before Him and stop trying to do things your own way. When you surrender to the Lord and submit to following His ways, you automatically move into position to receive His blessings. Then as you begin to rejoice in the Lord, He will join you on your life's journey.

Father, thank You for promising to meet me on my life's journey. I want to live in Your presence; therefore, I humble myself before You and ask You to walk with me each day. Amen.

WEEK 21—FRIDAY
I Will Trust in the Lord

"Blessed is the man who trusts in the LORD, and whose hope is the LORD. For he shall be like a tree planted by the waters, which spreads out its roots by the river, and will not fear when heat comes; but its leaf will be green, and will not be anxious in the year of drought, nor will cease from yielding fruit."

JEREMIAH 17:7–8

Uncertainty has been a nearly constant companion for many people for the past several years. Financial turmoil, employment woes, political unrest, wars, the threat of terrorism—all of this and more are reported daily in the news. Where should a person turn for rest from these troubles?

Today's verses make it very clear that one's only hope is to turn to the Lord and place his or her trust in Him. The picture in this passage is that of a tree planted by the waters that will withstand heat and drought and still bear fruit.

Trust, however, is not always easy to give. Are you the type of person who finds it difficult to trust someone else, especially someone you can't see? If so, God knows and understands your reluctance. This is one reason He sent the Holy Spirit to live inside of you. Now you have God with you every single moment of your life. As you learn to trust the Holy Spirit, you will discover a new closeness with the Father and trusting Him will become much easier. You will then become like a tree planted by the waters.

....

Lord, thank You for giving me the gift of Your Holy Spirit to dwell inside me. Your presence in my life brings peace and comfort within and gives me courage to proclaim Your fame boldly. Amen.

TIM DETELLIS, NEW MISSIONS, ORLANDO, FL

Week 21—Weekend
I Will Call Upon the Lord

For I know the thoughts that I think toward you, says the Lord, thoughts of peace and not of evil, to give you a future and a hope. Then you will call upon Me and go and pray to Me, and I will listen to you. And you will seek Me and find Me, when you search for Me with all your heart.

Jeremiah 29:11–13

To call upon the Lord is to reach out to the only One who can shape your future into the best possible outcome. God's thoughts are far above the thoughts of a human being, and far vaster. So when God says He has good thoughts toward you, your mind is unable to contain them (1 Corinthians 2:9).

Today many people feel as if God is out to get them. They believe God wants to punish them for some evil deed they have committed—either real or perceived—and that He will plague their lives until they have "paid the last penny." God, in their mind's eye, is a vindictive, angry God who takes pleasure in making their lives miserable.

Today's verses refute that idea. Instead, we see God wants the best for each person and will work with each person to help his or her best come true. All a person needs to do is call upon Him, for to seek Him is to find Him.

God's promise is very real. Apprehend it for your life now, and you will immediately begin to see changes occur. God wants to bring His peace into your life in a way you have never known; you just need to call upon Him.

....

Lord Jesus, I believe You, and I ask for Your presence to be tangible in my life every day. Thank You for thinking of me. Amen.

Week 22—Monday
Loving As He Loves

The Lord has appeared of old to me, saying: "Yes, I have loved you with an everlasting love; therefore with lovingkindness I have drawn you. Again I will build you, and you shall be rebuilt, O virgin of Israel! You shall again be adorned with your tambourines, and shall go forth in the dances of those who rejoice. You shall yet plant vines on the mountains of Samaria; the planters shall plant and eat them as ordinary food."

JEREMIAH 31:3–5

God loves us with an everlasting love! As Jeremiah said, God loves us before we first love Him. He loves us in spite of our sins. He draws us to Himself and He will never stop loving us. He will "rebuild" us as many times as we need. Nothing can separate us from the love of God in Christ Jesus as Paul asserted in Romans 8:31–39.

We are to love God with all our hearts, souls, and strength. We should love what He loves and hate what He hates. By this all people will know that we are His disciples, if we love one another (John 13:35). God's love builds others up instead of tearing others down.

We can't do anything to make God love us more, and we can't do anything to make God love us less. His love is not conditional. He does not say, "I will love you if. . . ." God loves us just because! Love does not need a reason. Love is the reason. He will never give up on us because He loves us.

....

Father, thank You for loving me unconditionally. Help me to love You with all my heart, soul, and strength. Amen.

DR. GRANT ETHRIDGE, LIBERTY BAPTIST CHURCH, HAMPTON, VA

WEEK 22—TUESDAY
Hoping in the Lord

"The LORD is my portion," says my soul, "Therefore I hope in Him!" The LORD is good to those who wait for Him, to the soul who seeks Him. It is good that one should hope and wait quietly for the salvation of the LORD.

LAMENTATIONS 3:24–26

As its title suggests, the book of Lamentations contains all kinds of laments from the prophet Jeremiah. Verse after verse expresses his sorrow, suffering, and grief. He used statements such as "My eye overflows with water" (1:16) and "My sighs are many, and my heart is faint" (1:22). Have you ever been there?

Tucked right in the middle of the book, however, is the passage for today. Lamentations 3:21–22 says, "This I recall to my mind, therefore I have hope. Through the LORD's mercies we are not consumed." What a powerful phrase in the midst of such all-consuming darkness! Even though Jeremiah felt overwhelmed by all that was going on around him, he still had hope in the Lord.

"The LORD is my portion," Jeremiah said. The Lord was enough for this prophet. The Lord is enough for you also. You have hope because of Him! He is good, and it is good for you to be reminded of that. Even when you are unfaithful to God, He is faithful to you.

Every day is a new beginning. Remember the Lord's love and hope in Him. Wait for His salvation. It is coming! Don't quit. He has not forgotten you. His compassions never fail! They are new every morning.

....

Lord, thank You for being my portion. You are more than enough for me. Thank You for being good to those who look to You. I hope in You today. Amen.

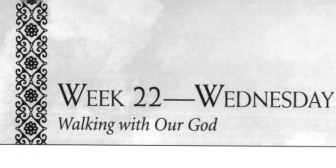

WEEK 22—WEDNESDAY
Walking with Our God

He has shown you, O man, what is good; and what does the LORD require of you but to do justly, to love mercy, and to walk humbly with your God?

MICAH 6:8

Every time I read today's text I think of one of the most-loved members in my second pastorate. She preached her own funeral by the way she lived. Even when she did not know her own name because of Alzheimer's, she would pray the sweetest prayers and cry tears of joy as she talked about the Lord. On the inside of her Bible cover was her favorite verse: Micah 6:8.

Micah was a prophet who preached primarily to the Southern Kingdom. In Micah 6:7, the people asked a question about what God required from His people. Micah 6:8 is the prophet's answer.

Outwardly, we are to do justly. This refers to being ethical in our dealings with others. Believers are to live by a higher standard. No hypocrisy. No double standard. We are to be the same in private as we are in public. Our goal every day should be to do right.

Inwardly, we are to love mercy. Showing mercy means freely and willingly showing kindness to others. It means being compassionate toward others. Our God is the Father of mercies.

Upwardly we are to walk humbly with God. Humility should encompass our lifestyles and daily walks with God. Humility is not a weakness; rather, it takes great character to exhibit humility.

"He has shown you, O man, what is good." Let's do these things today!

....

Father, please help me to do outwardly, inwardly, and upwardly what You have asked of me today. Amen.

DR. GRANT ETHRIDGE, LIBERTY BAPTIST CHURCH, HAMPTON, VA

WEEK 22—THURSDAY
Rejoicing in Our Creator

Yet I will rejoice in the LORD, I will joy in the God of my salvation. The LORD God is my strength; He will make my feet like deer's feet, and He will make me walk on my high hills.

HABAKKUK 3:18–19

Even when we cannot rejoice in our circumstances, we can rejoice in our Creator. The Christian life is not based on feelings but on faith. The Bible tells us God is always at work, even when we do not see it, and He works for the good of those who love Him (Romans 8:28). But what do we do when we are going through the valleys of life?

Revive! In Habakkuk 3:2, the prophet cried out to God for a fresh touch. We should ask God to do a new work in our lives. We should ask Him to make Himself known to us in the midst of our circumstances.

Remember! In verses 3–15, Habakkuk recalled the works of God in the past. Christians should look back on the ways God has been faithful to them before. The God of the past is the God of the present.

Rejoice! Although Habakkuk was in a valley, in verse 18 he chose to rejoice. The Lord enables us to walk through the valleys of life, and He keeps us from falling. He also lifts us up to new levels of faith. The struggle is not in vain!

Habakkuk 2:4 says, "The just shall live by his faith." Both the Old and New Testaments often remind us of this truth. What do we do when we have more questions than answers? We trust God.

....

Father, I'm thankful I can trust You. Please help my unbelief and increase my faith. Help me to rejoice in You today. Amen.

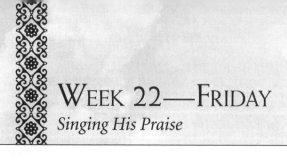

WEEK 22—FRIDAY
Singing His Praise

"The LORD your God in your midst, the Mighty One, will save; He will rejoice over you with gladness, He will quiet you with His love, He will rejoice over you with singing."

ZEPHANIAH 3:17

Did you know God sings? The God who is the Mighty One, Savior, Deliverer, King of kings, and Lord of lords also sings!

He made us in His image, and when He saved us, He gave us new identities, new lives, new beginnings, and new songs. Psalm 40:3 says, "He has put a new song in my mouth—praise to our God." It is the song of redemption for the glory of God. This is a song many will hear, and they will fear the Lord and place their trust in Him.

We sing because God sings. Music is a gift from God, and He has given us much about which to rejoice. Authenticity should mark our worship. It should involve a response from our hearts to praise Him for all He has done for us.

Paul wrote, "Let the word of Christ dwell in you richly in all wisdom, teaching and admonishing one another in psalms and hymns and spiritual songs, singing with grace in your hearts" (Colossians 3:16). Singing stirs ours hearts and hides God's Word in our hearts. It helps us remember all the Lord has done and helps us teach others. Worship and singing should be a way of life!

....

Father, thank You for salvation. Thank You for loving me and rejoicing over me. May my song to You bring You glory today. Amen.

DR. GRANT ETHRIDGE, LIBERTY BAPTIST CHURCH, HAMPTON, VA

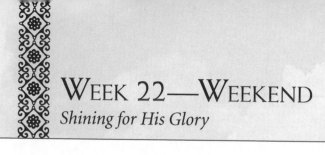

Week 22—Weekend
Shining for His Glory

"You are the light of the world. A city that is set on a hill cannot be hidden. Nor do they light a lamp and put it under a basket, but on a lampstand, and it gives light to all who are in the house. Let your light so shine before men, that they may see your good works and glorify your Father in heaven."

MATTHEW 5:14–16

I like salt! It seasons foods to make them taste better. It also creates thirst. Christians who live out what Jesus taught in Matthew 5 will do the same. Christians should flavor the culture around them and create a thirst for the gospel. They should not repel but attract. When Christians are tasteless, they turn off an unbelieving world to God and the gospel.

Jesus is the Light of the World, and He sent us to take that light to the nations. We cannot produce the light ourselves—we are just the lamps. Christ in us shines out to the world; He is the hope of glory. We do not perform good works to call attention to ourselves, but to bring glory to God. We are not to be on display, but Jesus should be on display, shining brightly for all to see.

Works do not save, but every saved person will do good works. What are some good works we can do today that will show others the light of Jesus and glorify our Father in heaven? As the classic song says, "This little light of mine / I'm gonna let it shine!"

....

Father, help me to be a light to those around me today. May they see my life and glorify You! In Jesus' name, amen.

WEEK 23—MONDAY
Treasure That Lasts

"Do not lay up for yourselves treasures on earth, where moth and rust destroy and where thieves break in and steal; but lay up for yourselves treasures in heaven, where neither moth nor rust destroys and where thieves do not break in and steal. For where your treasure is, there your heart will be also."

MATTHEW 6:19–21

God does not call us to poverty. He calls us to great wealth. But to be truly rich we need to open our eyes to where the real treasure is. Real treasure isn't found here on earth. Real treasure is not found in the abundance of possessions and accumulated cash. Real treasure is in heaven, and God invites us to lay up treasures there.

When followers of Christ embrace lives of generosity, they don't give wealth away; they invest it for a greater return. An investment is when someone sacrifices today for a greater return tomorrow, and that is exactly what Christ invites us to do here: to invest in heaven. Heavenly riches are a superior investment to earthly riches because earthly riches are temporary. Earthly treasures are always at risk. Jesus mentioned moths, rust, and thieves as some of the dangers that threaten material possessions, and we have our own list, probably longer, of things that can erase our possessions at any moment. But even if we dodge the moths, the rust, and the thieves, our earthly possessions are still temporary. We will die someday and all we have laid aside on earth will be gone. Only what we have sent ahead will remain.

God, teach me to see the lasting value of eternal treasure and to demonstrate a life of faithful generosity. Amen.

DR. WILLIAM RICE, CALVARY CHURCH, CLEARWATER, FL

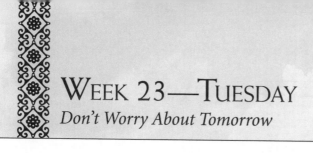

WEEK 23—TUESDAY
Don't Worry About Tomorrow

"But seek first the kingdom of God and His righteousness, and all these things shall be added to you. Therefore do not worry about tomorrow, for tomorrow will worry about its own things. Sufficient for the day is its own trouble."

MATTHEW 6:33–34

What are you worried about? When you wonder, *What if?* that simple question cracks open the door for anxiety and fear to haunt you. The antidote to worrying is to place your trust in God. Worrying is a practical atheism. Worrying assumes control for things you cannot control. Worrying never solves one problem. So how do you overcome worry? Jesus gave two ways to trade your worries for peace.

First, put God's kingdom first. When you focus on God's kingdom as your priority, the rest of life has a way of falling into place. If you try to pursue many things, you may end up with nothing. Pursue God, His will, His purpose, His glory, and you will end up with everything you really need. Once you let go of your priorities and your dreams, you will find He has more blessings in store for you than you ever could have planned.

Second, trust God with tomorrow. Worrying about tomorrow doesn't change tomorrow—it changes today. Worrying doesn't take the strain out of tomorrow; it just takes the strength out of today. God promises to provide what you need when tomorrow comes. If you knew everything in your future, you would be overwhelmed, but when you trust God day by day, then day by day He provides the grace and strength you need to obey Him.

....

Father, help me to seek Your kingdom and Your righteousness and to trust You with my tomorrows. Amen.

WEEK 23—WEDNESDAY
Just Ask

"Ask, and it will be given to you; seek, and you will find; knock, and it will be opened to you. For everyone who asks receives, and he who seeks finds, and to him who knocks it will be opened."

MATTHEW 7:7–8

A sk. Seek. Knock. God calls us to pray. Prayer itself is a bit of a mystery. Why should we inform God of something He already knows? And can prayer alter the plans of God, who already knows the end from the beginning?

Prayer does matter, or else why did Jesus so strongly and consistently implore us to pray? And for that matter, why was prayer such an important part of Jesus' life? Clearly God will not do some things in our lives except through prayer. Prayer is part of God's working in us to bring us to a place of humility and dependence on Him.

What is it we seek? What do we need God to do for us? Jesus said all we need to do is ask.

God is not some cosmic genie who bends His will toward ours to meet our selfish desires. But during prayer God bends our wills toward His. During prayer God conforms our hearts to see His will. God accomplishes this sanctifying work when we humble ourselves, acknowledge our dependency on Him, and pray.

Yes, we can plan. Yes, we can work. But until we stop and pray, some things will not happen. So let's pray.

Father, forgive me for my prideful sense of self-sufficiency and guide me to a humble dependence on You. Amen.

DR. WILLIAM RICE, CALVARY CHURCH, CLEARWATER, FL

Week 23—Thursday
The Sure Foundation

"Therefore whoever hears these sayings of Mine, and does them, I will liken him to a wise man who built his house on the rock: and the rain descended, the floods came, and the winds blew and beat on that house; and it did not fall, for it was founded on the rock."

Matthew 7:24–25

The day will eventually come: the day the wind blows; the day the rain falls; the day the floodwater rises. You will not go through life without difficult days and times of testing. The question is not if they will come. The question is: Will you be ready?

Jesus told you how to be ready. He told you how to build your life on a sure foundation, one that will stand the tests of life. Jesus challenged you to hear His words and put them into practice. The person who follows Christ builds his or her life on a sure foundation and will stand strong even in life's toughest moments.

Maybe you're facing a test right now. You wonder if you can make it—if you can endure. If you trust Christ, He will give you the strength you need. His truth endures. Never doubt in the darkness what God has shown you in the light of day. You may be tested in the night, but God promises He will help you through the darkest hours. You may be going through difficult days right now, but you do not walk alone.

Father, thank You for the promise that if I hear and obey Christ, my life will be built on a sure foundation that will last throughout eternity. Amen.

WEEK 23—FRIDAY
Find Rest

"Come to Me, all you who labor and are heavy laden, and I will give you rest. Take My yoke upon you and learn from Me, for I am gentle and lowly in heart, and you will find rest for your souls. For My yoke is easy and My burden is light."

MATTHEW 11:28–30

J esus promised rest to believers. This is a welcome promise in your world of trouble, turmoil, and stress. This is not the kind of rest where one ceases from activity. Sometimes you need to take a break, but this is far more than catching your breath or taking a few days off.

Jesus called you to His yoke, to accept His burden. But unlike the kind of labor that leads to stress, working for Jesus leads to rest in your soul—contentment. When you work for Jesus, you actually work with Jesus. You yoke yourself to Him. He does the heavy lifting, and you follow along in obedience.

You don't have to build the church; He does that. You can't save a person, but He can. All Jesus asks is for you to come and follow Him.

Do what He commands, and trust Him to do what He promises. The world isn't on your shoulders; it's on His. Resign from trying to rule the universe and let Him be God. Instead of worry and stress you will find rest for your weary soul.

....

Father, remind me that all I have to do today is follow You. Help me to walk in obedience and trust You with the big problems I cannot control. Amen.

DR. WILLIAM RICE, CALVARY CHURCH, CLEARWATER, FL

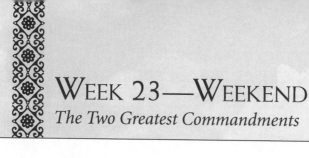

WEEK 23—WEEKEND
The Two Greatest Commandments

Jesus said to him, "'You shall love the LORD your God with all your heart, with all your soul, and with all your mind.' This is the first and great commandment. And the second is like it: 'You shall love your neighbor as yourself.' On these two commandments hang all the Law and the Prophets."

MATTHEW 22:37–40

Love God and love people. It's pretty simple really. Every biblical law and command ultimately comes down to one of those two. There were 613 laws in the Jewish law, but you can sum them all up with just two: you need to love God and you need to love people.

The famous Westminster Shorter Catechism says, "Man's chief end is to glorify God, and to enjoy Him forever." Thus Christians need to glorify God, which occurs when one loves God. Loving God transforms your life. Worship is the act of loving God. Christians use music to express their love to Him, but worship is more than music. Worship is about expressing your love to God.

The second command is as important as the first: love people. If you truly love God, you will also love people who bear the image of God. People who brag about their spiritual devotion but then mistreat others or use them for selfish gain deceive themselves. If you don't love people, you don't love God.

. . . .

Father, I love you. Help me to demonstrate that love to You not only in my worship, but also in my service, kindness, and generosity to others. Amen.

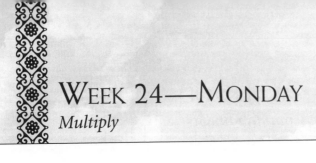

WEEK 24—MONDAY
Multiply

And Jesus came and spoke to them, saying, "All authority has been given to Me in heaven and on earth. Go therefore and make disciples of all the nations, baptizing them in the name of the Father and of the Son and of the Holy Spirit, teaching them to observe all things that I have commanded you; and lo, I am with you always, even to the end of the age." Amen.

MATTHEW 28:18–20

Suppose you were given a choice: take $10,000 each day for 30 days or take $1 on day one and have it doubled for 30 days. Which would you choose? If you chose option 1 you would have $300,000. That's not bad. But if you chose option 2, you would have $536,870, 912! Option 1 is good. Option 2 is a lot better! And what is true with money is equally true with the kingdom of God.

Jesus told us to go and make disciples of all nations. That's the definition of evangelism. He told us to share the gospel with and reach everyone we can. And we should. But if we stop there we will simply add to the kingdom, and Jesus didn't stop there. He told us to teach the new disciples to obey all things. This includes telling them to go and make disciples. Jesus commanded us to make disciples who make disciples! That's multiplication. If we would all do this, we could reach the world at an incredible rate. So why don't we?

....

Father, thank You for giving me a plan to accomplish Your mission. Give me both the desire and the power to do what You have commanded. Amen.

ROCKY PURVIS, NORTHSIDE BAPTIST CHURCH, LEXINGTON, SC

WEEK 24—TUESDAY
Priorities

"For whoever desires to save his life will lose it, but whoever loses his life for My sake and the gospel's will save it. For what will it profit a man if he gains the whole world, and loses his own soul? Or what will a man give in exchange for his soul?"

MARK 8:35–37

I heard about a lawyer who was driving his new BMW on a mountain road during a snowstorm. As he veered around a sharp turn, he lost control and began sliding off the road. At the last moment he was able to unbuckle himself and jump out of the car as it flew off a cliff, hit the bottom of the ravine, and burst into flames. Unfortunately, during the jump, the lawyer's arm got caught in the door and was ripped off at the shoulder. A passing trucker saw the accident and pulled over to help. When he got there, he found the lawyer looking down at his burning BMW, moaning, "My BMW! My new BMW!"

The trucker pointed at the lawyer's shoulder and said, "Listen, you've got bigger problems than that car. We've got to find your arm. Maybe the doctors can reattach it!"

The lawyer looked where his arm used to be, paused a moment, and groaned, "Oh no! My new Rolex!"

It's so easy to get caught up in the things this world has to offer—the pleasures, the riches, the status, and the fame. Yet Jesus said, "What will it profit a man if he gains the whole world, and loses his own soul?" The things of this world, no matter how good, are all temporary. Make sure your priorities are in order.

....

Father, today, help me to keep my priorities in order. Amen.

WEEK 24—WEDNESDAY
Who Can Be Saved?

But Jesus looked at them and said, "With men it is impossible, but not with God; for with God all things are possible."

MARK 10:27

This verse comes at the end of one of the most well-known stories in the Bible: the story of the rich young ruler. The young man approached Jesus and asked what he needed to do to be saved. Jesus responded by reminding the young man that he knew the commandments. Without hesitation, the young ruler said he had obeyed the commandments since he was a young boy. This response showed arrogance on his part because he believed he was good enough to earn his way to heaven.

The Bible makes it clear no one is ever made right with God by following the law. Romans 3:20 says, "Therefore by the deeds of the law no flesh will be justified in His sight, for by the law is the knowledge of sin." Jesus told the young man to sell his possessions and give the proceeds to the poor. The young man left very sad because he had many possessions. Jesus pointed out that it's very hard for rich people to enter the kingdom of heaven. The disciples then asked who could be saved if this rich man couldn't.

There's absolutely no way, on our own, we can be saved. There's nothing you or I can do to earn our place in heaven. But then Jesus said, "With God all things are possible." In other words, we can't save ourselves, but God can! And that's what Jesus did on the cross. He took our sins on Himself so we could have eternal life. We have only to trust Him.

....

Father, thank You for doing for me what I could never do on my own. In Jesus' name, amen.

ROCKY PURVIS, NORTHSIDE BAPTIST CHURCH, LEXINGTON, SC

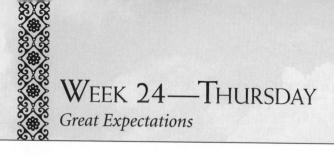

WEEK 24—THURSDAY
Great Expectations

And you, child, will be called the prophet of the Highest; for you will go before the face of the Lord to prepare His ways, to give knowledge of salvation to His people by the remission of their sins, through the tender mercy of our God, with which the Dayspring from on high has visited us; to give light to those who sit in darkness and the shadow of death, to guide our feet into the way of peace.

LUKE 1:76–79

All parents have great expectations for their children. I can remember the birth of each of our children and the hopes and dreams I had and still have for them. When our first was born, I held him up, thanked God for him, and then gave him back to the Lord. I asked God to use him to reach the world.

We all have hopes and dreams for our children. Maybe we want one to be a doctor, an athlete, or a teacher. Perhaps we want them to take over the family business, or maybe we want them just to love and serve the Lord with all their hearts. But when John was born, Zechariah had more than hopes and dreams. God had given him a prophecy regarding John's birth. John would be a prophet of the Most High. He would prepare the way for the Lord. And he would tell people how to find salvation and forgiveness from their sins. That was his God-given purpose in life.

Our children have purposes too, and our task as parents and grandparents is to help them discover and fulfill those purposes. Who knows? We may be raising the next John the Baptist!

....

Father, guide me as I seek to guide my children in fulfilling Your purpose for their lives. Amen.

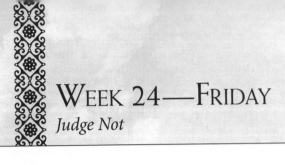

Week 24—Friday
Judge Not

"Judge not, and you shall not be judged. Condemn not, and you shall not be condemned. Forgive, and you will be forgiven. Give, and it will be given to you: good measure, pressed down, shaken together, and running over will be put into your bosom. For with the same measure that you use, it will be measured back to you."

Luke 6:37–38

Fewer sayings of our Lord are better known or more often quoted than the first part of these verses, yet they are often misunderstood. Some have interpreted this to mean that we cannot make an evaluation of a person's behavior, beliefs, or teachings. If we do this, we will be judging. Yet that is not true. What Jesus warned against is a critical, condemning, fault-finding, picky spirit. Further, Jesus warned against criticizing others for the same faults that we have. When Christians point out faults in others, they should do so in the hopes of helping others recognize their need for repentance.

Jesus wants His people to have a joyful spirit and not to complain. He doesn't want Christians condemning others without just cause. If we do need to point out someone's sin, we need to first make sure we are free from the sin ourselves and seek only spiritual restoration for this individual (Galatians 6:1).

Father, forgive me for the times I have a critical spirit. Help me to bring out the best in people rather than focus on the worst in them. Also, help me not to be hypocritical and find in others the same faults of which I am guilty. In Jesus' name, amen.

ROCKY PURVIS, NORTHSIDE BAPTIST CHURCH, LEXINGTON, SC

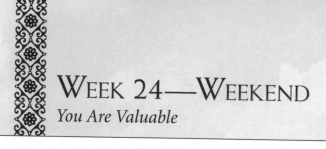

WEEK 24—WEEKEND
You Are Valuable

"Are not five sparrows sold for two copper coins? And not one of them is forgotten before God. But the very hairs of your head are all numbered. Do not fear therefore; you are of more value than many sparrows."

LUKE 12:6–7

I don't know about you, but there are times I feel unworthy, unimportant, and insignificant. We sometimes do our best in school, and we barely get by. We often try to eat healthily and exercise, but we still don't like what we see in the mirror. We sometimes work hard on our jobs and are still passed over for a promotion or raise. Or in my case, we hear other preachers or see how their churches are growing—only suddenly to feel like failures.

Now it may just be me, but I imagine most of us struggle with this. That's why this passage is so important. Luke 12:1 tells us that "an innumerable multitude of people had gathered" to hear Jesus. The rich. The poor. The married. The divorced. The single. The healthy. The sick. The misfits. The successful. That crowd mirrored the society back then and our society today. And Jesus' message to everyone was, "You are valuable to God." The same message applies to everyone today.

God loves you! He has a plan for you! He will never leave you, and He will never turn His back on you! You are fearfully and wonderfully made! You are His prized possession! So stop it. Stop letting the enemy fill your mind with thoughts that you are insignificant or unimportant. It's a lie. Today go out there and live as the prized possession of God you are!

....

Father, help me to find my value in You. Amen.

WEEK 25—MONDAY
Kneeling Tall for Jesus

"Also I say to you, whoever confesses Me before men, him the Son of Man also will confess before the angels of God. But he who denies Me before men will be denied before the angels of God. And anyone who speaks a word against the Son of Man, it will be forgiven him; but to him who blasphemes against the Holy Spirit, it will not be forgiven."

LUKE 12:8–10

I t was my first trip to Russia. Siberia was my mission assignment. All of my life I heard about the horrors of Siberia. But everywhere we went the people received the gospel and invited Christ into their lives.

One Sunday I preached at a small house church. A lady rushed in to tell the believers that a brother in Christ had died. She asked if I would come the next day and conduct the funeral, which I agreed to do. It was a wild scene as they laid the body in the road and I preached on the resurrection.

When I finished, I took in my surroundings. The deacons were some of the roughest-looking men I had ever seen. I learned from my interpreter that they had spent an average of nine years in prison because of their faith in Jesus. They could have been released if they would recant their faith and deny Jesus. Every time they were challenged to do so, they would kneel and put up praying hands and say, "Jesus is Lord!" The guards would then hurl an iron rod across their faces, breaking every bone.

For this American preacher who had never known persecution, these men instantly became beautiful trophies of God's grace. They had knelt tall for Jesus and confessed Him boldly. Could I do the same?

....

God, may I have such boldness to kneel tall and confess You as Lord. Amen.

DR. FRANK COX, NORTH METRO FIRST BAPTIST CHURCH, LAWRENCEVILLE, GA

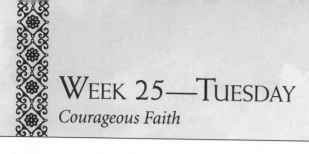

Week 25—Tuesday
Courageous Faith

"Life is more than food, and the body is more than clothing. Consider the ravens, for they neither sow nor reap, which have neither storehouse nor barn; and God feeds them. Of how much more value are you than the birds? And which of you by worrying can add one cubit to his stature?"

LUKE 12:23–25

How courageous is your faith? You might respond: "Very courageous!" Really? Do you trust God with everything in your life? Think it through. Now answer.

Jesus had just taught His disciples the parable of the rich fool. The rich fool, like so many others, was consumed with wealth. When a desire for more becomes your obsession, your focus shifts from God to temporary distractions.

Did you know Jesus had more to say about money than any other topic? Nowhere did Jesus condemn having possessions or money, but He challenged Christians to keep money in check so it does not rule their lives. Courageous faith in Jesus should mark your life instead of the wealth of this world.

Many seek wealth for security rather than seeking God, who is their real Provider. Here is what Jesus taught: Look at the ravens of the fields. They neither sow nor reap and they sure don't hoard supplies in a room or barn, yet God makes sure they have their needs met.

Seeking the treasures of this world can dominate one's life. Jesus desired for believers to have courageous faith that the One who saves them will provide for their every need. By trusting in Him they will have needs met, not only in this life, but for eternity.

....

Lord, thank You for being the Source for every need in my life. Amen.

WEEK 25—WEDNESDAY
God as Our Provider

"Consider the lilies, how they grow: they neither toil nor spin; and yet I say to you, even Solomon in all his glory was not arrayed like one of these. If then God so clothes the grass, which today is in the field and tomorrow is thrown into the oven, how much more will He clothe you, O you of little faith?"

LUKE 12:27–28

Believers can be paradoxical at times. We invite Christ into our lives and trust Him to take care of us for all eternity. Yet when it comes to our everyday needs here on earth, we spend a lot of time worrying! Strange, isn't it? We trust Him for the eternal, but in the temporal realm our faith struggles.

We all live with pressures: finances, family, work, relationships. In fact, these pressures can become all-consuming. When we focus on these pressures, they can lead us to worry and depression. But Jesus reminded us that worrying will not add one hour to our lives.

Jesus told us worrying about food and clothing should not be a part of our lives. We are the crown of God's creation. If God will feed the birds or clothe the lilies of the fields, do we not trust He will provide for us? It is a matter of taking God at His word. God is our resource and will provide for our every need. Knowing that, we need to make sure our primary concern is to glorify Him and trust Him.

....

Lord, as I progress in this life, help me trust You as my Provider. Let me glorify You through courageous faith. Amen.

WEEK 25—THURSDAY
What a Mighty God!

In the beginning was the Word, and the Word was with God, and the Word was God. He was in the beginning with God. All things were made through Him, and without Him nothing was made that was made. In Him was life, and the life was the light of men. And the light shines in the darkness, and the darkness did not comprehend it.

JOHN 1:1–5

We serve the mighty God who is the Creator of this world. What an awesome thought! It is hard for the finite mind to grasp the Trinity. God exists in three divine persons. Such a thought supersedes human comprehension.

John opened his gospel with a great declaration that God has always been and that Jesus was with God in the beginning. In fact, he told us Jesus played the key role as Creator of everything. When we study the vastness of this universe, we must allow the truth—that everything came into existence by the power of Jesus—to be firmly planted in the depths of our minds. We worship the mighty Creator.

In the creation, Jesus revealed God. Then Jesus came to this world to show us God in physical form. Later, after Philip had asked for Jesus to show the disciples the Father, Jesus said, "He who has seen Me has seen the Father" (John 14:9). In a sinful, dark world Jesus came to shine as light so we could know of God's love and respond to it through a relationship with Him. Thank God for the light that pierces the darkness and leads us to eternal life! What a mighty Savior we serve!

Jesus, thank You for coming to reveal the love of the heavenly Father. Thank You for being a mighty God! In Jesus' name, amen.

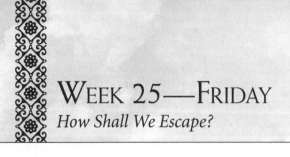

WEEK 25—FRIDAY
How Shall We Escape?

He came to His own, and His own did not receive Him. But as many as received Him, to them He gave the right to become children of God, to those who believe in His name: who were born, not of blood, nor of the will of the flesh, nor of the will of man, but of God.

JOHN 1:11–13

When John the Baptist preached of the coming Messiah, he had to be stunned anyone would reject Jesus and the life He came to offer. But they did in his day and still do in ours. Think about it for a moment. Throughout the Old Testament the Jews lived in anticipation of the coming Messiah. Then Jesus came to His own to free them from their adherence to the law and to give them new life. They decided to reject Him because Jesus was not the kind of Messiah they expected or wanted. To this day many still reject the Savior.

The writer of Hebrews asked, "How shall we escape if we neglect so great a salvation?" (Hebrews 2:3). The gospel is so simple. Jesus came to die upon the cross for our sins. He took our place and paid sin's debt that we owed. He arose again on the third day and offers salvation to all who will repent of their sins and place their trust in Him. It is the gift of God. He offers it to us, but we must receive Him. When we do, God gives us eternal life!

We can't be like those who rejected Him; we must receive Him as our Lord and Savior.

....

Lord, may Your gospel go forth and may many receive the gift of salvation! In Jesus' name, amen.

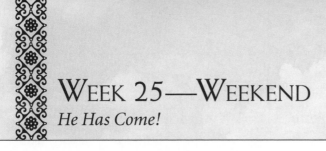

WEEK 25—WEEKEND
He Has Come!

And the Word became flesh and dwelt among us, and we beheld His glory, the glory as of the only begotten of the Father, full of grace and truth. John bore witness of Him and cried out, saying, "This was He of whom I said, 'He who comes after me is preferred before me, for He was before me.'"

JOHN 1:14–15

John, like a great preacher, could hardly contain his excitement as he spoke of Jesus. He shouted to the world that the Savior had come!

The promise had been fulfilled. The long-awaited Messiah had arrived. Yes, the One who has always been, who created everything, and who holds everything in the palm of His hand had left heaven's glory to come to earth. His purpose? He came to show God is not some abstract religious thought but real. Jesus came into this world of darkness to reveal the love of God. The reality of His coming was the good news the Jews needed to hear.

Here is even greater news for us in the twenty-first century: God, by coming to earth, demonstrated loudly and clearly how He desires to be involved in our lives. He is not only the Savior for those who believe, He is also their Sustainer. He identifies with all we experience in life, our gains and our pains, and He makes us more than conquerors. He adds meaning and value to our lives as we shine as His lights in darkness. He unconditionally offers to each of us His love, His forgiveness, and His unmerited grace.

Think about it. He could have allowed us to spend eternity in hell. Instead He came to reach out to us with His amazing love.

....

Lord, thank You for coming to earth to show the way to salvation. Thank You for Your amazing love. Amen.

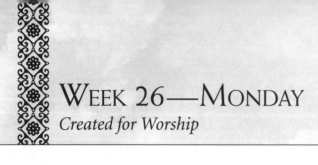

WEEK 26—MONDAY
Created for Worship

"But the hour is coming, and now is, when the true worshipers will worship the Father in spirit and truth; for the Father is seeking such to worship Him. God is Spirit, and those who worship Him must worship in spirit and truth."

JOHN 4:23–24

J esus went out of His way to meet this woman at the well to bring her a life-changing message. She was a sinful woman, and Jesus quickly directed their discussion to the details of her sin, but she tried to deflect the conversation to religious minutia. Jesus would have none of that! He immediately turned the discussion back to worship—true worship.

You see, true worship is not about a place or a practice. True worship is about a love relationship with our Creator. And why should we love Him? Because He saves us from our sin! When we realize our guilt before a holy God, we can choose either despair or forgiveness, and by choosing forgiveness, we enter a permanent love relationship with our God. He becomes our Savior and we His protected children. That truth alone gives us reason to worship.

No other religious leader offers what Jesus does. Jesus embodies the fullness of God (Colossians 2:9). He is the Truth (John 14:6). When we receive Him as Savior, His Spirit indwells us (Romans 8:9). Only then are we capable of worshipping Him in spirit and in truth.

Jesus told the woman at the well this news, and she became His follower. Have you become one? If so, then worship Him today!

......

Lord, help me today to worship You in spirit and truth. Amen.

WEEK 26—TUESDAY
The Light of His Will

"All that the Father gives Me will come to Me, and the one who comes to Me I will by no means cast out. For I have come down from heaven, not to do My own will, but the will of Him who sent Me."

JOHN 6:37–38

Starting a new day brings new challenges sometimes. On those days I always have to look back and remember why I do what I am doing in the ministry or at my job. Whether it is ministry, an exciting job, or a mundane one, I have to remember God put me here for a reason.

If I am submitting to His will in my life today, He is going to work through me as I humble myself and allow His Spirit to guide me. Looking back at the life of our Lord, I see His reason for living was doing the will of God. The key was going to the Father for strength. Jesus spent time with God regularly.

The people God uses today have one key practice in their lives, and it is fostering a close relationship with Jesus through prayer, repentance, and devotion to the Lord. Those who daily seek out the Father are the ones God uses to touch the world.

These folks draw closer to Him as they spend time with Him. As a result, God gives them light that enables them to touch their world wherever they go. For this is the will of God for us: to touch the world wherever we go (Matthew 28:18–20).

....

Lord, as I come to You, reveal Your will to me for my life today so I can touch my world! In Jesus' name, amen.

Week 26—Wednesday
Living Water

On the last day, that great day of the feast, Jesus stood and cried out, saying, "If anyone thirsts, let him come to Me and drink. He who believes in Me, as the Scripture has said, out of his heart will flow rivers of living water."

John 7:37–38

The Feast of Booths was an eight-day festival with a twofold purpose. It was to be a generational reminder of God's graciousness in bringing His people out of slavery and sustaining them before they entered the promised land. It was also a time to thank God for the preceding year's provision and to pray for rain for their crops. The central element in both celebrations? *Water.* It was water that sustained them then and water that would sustain them now.

As time passed, the festival became marked with a water-pouring ceremony. Each day, the priest would lead a parade to the Pool of Siloam where he would gather water using a golden pitcher. After returning to the temple, the priest would pour the water into a basin near the altar.

It was at this moment during the festival in His own day that Jesus proclaimed, "If anyone thirsts, let him come to Me and drink." Thus Jesus connected Himself to the salvation that the water ceremony represented.

To them and to us, Jesus is the ultimate fulfillment of God's promise to provide for His people. He has rescued us from slavery to sin and sustains us as we sojourn toward our heavenly home.

. . . .

Jesus, You are my Living Water! Help me to drink deeply from the well that never runs dry. Amen.

DALLAS WHITE, FIRST BAPTIST CHURCH WOODSTOCK, WOODSTOCK, GA

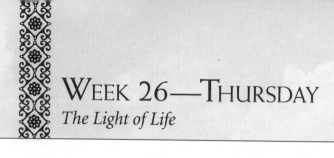

WEEK 26—THURSDAY
The Light of Life

Then Jesus spoke to them again, saying, "I am the light of the world. He who follows Me shall not walk in darkness, but have the light of life."

JOHN 8:12

All of us have attempted to find the way in a dark place before locating the light switch. I do that most mornings as I get out of bed to get my first cup of coffee. I do that primarily so I do not wake up my wife. On several occasions she has shifted a piece of furniture into a different position before she retired the night before. Well, I don't have to tell you what the result is because you can relate, can't you?

The purpose of light is to illuminate. Jesus said in this verse that He is the Light of this world and if we receive Him, our paths will be made clear and darkness will not rule us. Many today walk in darkness because they refuse to accept the free gift God offers to all who will reach out and take it.

Earlier in this chapter, Jesus forgave an adulterous woman who was walking in darkness. When she had an encounter with Him, she began to walk in the light. We can all experience that same light that will lead us to an eternity with Jesus. I pray you have done so.

· ·

Jesus, thank You for giving me light to guide my way in this life. I bless You for that. Help me today to share that light with others who are struggling to find their way as they stumble in darkness. Amen.

WEEK 26—FRIDAY
Freedom in Christ

Jesus answered them, "Most assuredly, I say to you, whoever commits sin is a slave of sin. And a slave does not abide in the house forever, but a son abides forever. Therefore if the Son makes you free, you shall be free indeed."

JOHN 8:34–36

Slavery was very common in biblical times, and Jesus often spoke in language that His audience could relate to. Jesus said if a person participates in sin, then sin legally owns him or her. Jesus wanted to make the point that a person who is a slave to sin needs to find the freedom that only He can offer.

Jesus went on to say that a slave does not abide in the house forever, but a son abides forever. Remember Abraham's two sons, Ishmael and Isaac? Isaac, the son of promise, was Abraham's preferred son and, therefore, remained in the house. But Ishmael, the son of the flesh, was removed. Thus, Isaac symbolized righteousness and Ishmael symbolized sin.

In the New Testament Jesus is the true Son and seed of Abraham (Galatians 3:16), and He not only remains in the house, but He rules over it (Hebrews 3:6). As a result, people can experience true freedom only by becoming sons of God by faith in Christ (Galatians 3:26). They must cast the sin out and remain in the house with the Son.

Lord Jesus, I was a slave to sin, but thank You for paying the penalty for my sin and conquering death through Your resurrection! Because I have trusted in You, I am now truly free indeed! Amen.

JJ WASHINGTON, FIRST BAPTIST CHURCH WOODSTOCK, WOODSTOCK, GA

Week 26—Weekend
In the World with Purpose

"I must work the works of Him who sent Me while it is day; the night is coming when no one can work. As long as I am in the world, I am the light of the world." When He had said these things, He spat on the ground and made clay with the saliva; and He anointed the eyes of the blind man with the clay.

JOHN 9:4–6

Our lives are busy, and often our chaotic schedules cause us to overlook those around us. As followers of Jesus, we are placed where we can recognize brokenness and to do something about it. We must slow down because people cannot be ignored.

One day Jesus saw a man who was born blind. At that time, people believed that if someone had a physical ailment, the person's parents must have committed some sin to bring forth such a punishment for their child. Yet Jesus stated that neither the man nor his parents had done anything to deserve blindness. Jesus then healed the man of this malady that had afflicted him since birth.

In this instance, Jesus revealed His heart for people. In the midst of His busy day, Jesus stopped to care for the blind man. Jesus showed His disciples what it looks like to be light. He saw a need and He stepped up to help.

What does it look like for Christians today to do the same?

> *Father, help me to see the brokenness all around me. Give me the heart of Jesus that cares for people, even in the midst of my busy day. Let me be a light to the world everywhere I go. Amen.*

TJ JOY, FIRST BAPTIST CHURCH WOODSTOCK, WOODSTOCK, GA

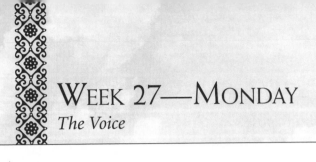

WEEK 27—MONDAY
The Voice

"But he who enters by the door is the shepherd of the sheep. To him the doorkeeper opens, and the sheep hear his voice; and he calls his own sheep by name and leads them out. And when he brings out his own sheep, he goes before them; and the sheep follow him, for they know his voice."

JOHN 10:2–4

*T*he Voice is one of the most popular TV shows of its kind. As the contestants sing, the judges have their backs to the contestants, eliminating the possibility of judging them based on anything except their vocal skills.

We have not had a face-to-face encounter with Jesus, our Shepherd. But if we are His sheep, we know His voice and have responded to it. In our world of constant noise and activity, we always are listening for our Shepherd's voice. Though we cannot see Him, we can hear Him if we have "ears to hear" (Mark 4:9). Most everyone has ears, but not all ears are tuned in to the Shepherd's voice.

Most who are reading this probably are not as familiar with shepherding as were Jesus' first-century listeners. We need to know sheep are very skittish creatures; their first response to danger is to flee. Also, the sheep knows the sound of the shepherd's voice and respond to it. Finally, the sheep trusts the shepherd, even when he cannot see the shepherd. In like manner, Jesus is our Good Shepherd, and we must heed His voice.

....

Jesus, help me to hear Your voice today and to respond to Your leading in my life. Amen.

ROY MACK, GRACE FELLOWSHIP CHURCH, WARREN, OH

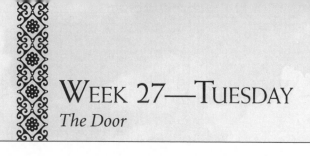

WEEK 27—TUESDAY
The Door

"I am the door. If anyone enters by Me, he will be saved, and will go in and out and find pasture. The thief does not come except to steal, and to kill, and to destroy. I have come that they may have life, and that they may have it more abundantly."

JOHN 10:9–10

Shepherding, in many ways, is a dirty and dangerous occupation. The shepherd stays continually with his sheep. A shepherd is expected to fight off wild animals that would harm the sheep as well as ward off any thieves who would want to steal the sheep. The shepherd values the sheep as much as his own life.

The shepherd also takes his sheep where he desires them to go. As Psalm 23:2 tells us, the shepherd leads his sheep "to lie down in green pastures" or "beside the still waters." In Jesus' day, at night the shepherd would often construct a makeshift pen, with only one way in and out. The shepherd himself would lie down in the opening of the pen; thus, the shepherd became the door to the sheep. A thief could not come through the door to harm the sheep without going through the watchful shepherd who literally laid down his life for the welfare of the sheep.

In Jesus' day, the Pharisees were the self-appointed, self-righteous shepherds who were more interested in sacrificing the sheep than caring for them. These thieves had turned God's living Word into dead rules and regulations that stole from God's people and killed the joy God desired them. In contrast, Jesus said He was the Door, not just to life, but to abundant life. He offers a life worth living!

....

Jesus, I acknowledge You as the Door. Lead me to Your abundant life. Amen.

WEEK 27—WEDNESDAY
The Good Shepherd

"I am the good shepherd; and I know My sheep, and am known by My own. As the Father knows Me, even so I know the Father; and I lay down My life for the sheep. And other sheep I have which are not of this fold; them also I must bring, and they will hear My voice; and there will be one flock and one shepherd."

JOHN 10:14–16

I f there are good shepherds, one can surmise there are also bad shepherds. We noted a few in yesterday's devotion: thieves and false shepherds who intend only harm for the sheep. Conversely, the Good Shepherd is the one willing to lay down His life for His sheep.

Jesus spoke mainly to a Jewish audience. The Jews were His sheep, but there were other sheep He wanted to be a part of His flock. These were sheep from other nations that He wanted to bring into His fold. This was a reference to the Gentiles who would one day receive God's salvation.

How will the Good Shepherd bring new sheep into His fold? By His Word, His own voice, calling them to Himself. His sheep hear His voice and follow Him. All Christians are united in this way—we have one Shepherd. We have heard His voice and responded. We are one flock, His church. We follow His voice and He leads us. Where are we going? We are going on a mission with the Good Shepherd to bring other sheep into His fold.

....

Father, may I be about Your business today, finding lost sheep for whom You have died. Amen.

ROY MACK, GRACE FELLOWSHIP CHURCH, WARREN, OH

WEEK 27—THURSDAY
The Grip of Grace

"My sheep hear My voice, and I know them, and they follow Me. And I give them eternal life, and they shall never perish; neither shall anyone snatch them out of My hand. My Father, who has given them to Me, is greater than all; and no one is able to snatch them out of My Father's hand. I and My Father are one."

JOHN 10:27–30

In a world where everything is dying, it seems so touching to hear Jesus' words, "I give them eternal life, and they shall never perish." Our world is filled with clichés about death: "the circle of life," "all things must end," and "only death and taxes are certain in this world." The statistics on dying reveal that one in every one person dies. And because of our sinful natures, relationships also sometimes die, marriages fail, friendships fall apart. As James reminded us: "When desire has conceived, it gives birth to sin; and sin, when it is full-grown, brings forth death" (1:15). Death seems to be the master of our current world.

Yet the Good Shepherd tells us even death cannot snatch us out of His hand. When we come to know Jesus as our Savior and Shepherd, the Father provides us with eternal salvation. Our Good Shepherd will ultimately lead us through the "valley of the shadow of death" (Psalm 23:4), but death has no grip on His sheep. We are in His grip. We don't have to worry about holding on to Him, for He holds onto us.

....

Father, thank You that nothing I face today will rival Your grip of grace. Amen.

WEEK 27—FRIDAY
Only Believe

Jesus said to her, "Did I not say to you that if you would believe you would see the glory of God?" Then they took away the stone from the place where the dead man was lying. And Jesus lifted up His eyes and said, "Father, I thank You that You have heard Me. And I know that You always hear Me, but because of the people who are standing by I said this, that they may believe that You sent Me."

JOHN 11:40–42

Toccoa Falls College, located in the Blue Ridge Mountains, has a very humble history. The Christian Missionary Alliance held its annual delegation meeting there in 1919. The delegates were housed in army tents supplied by Fort McPherson in Atlanta. Rev. Paul Rader was elected president of the council that same year. After listening to the struggles Toccoa Falls College had experienced, Rev. Rader wrote a hymn in 1920 to encourage them about God's faithfulness. I grew up singing the chorus of this hymn in church: "Only believe, only believe; / All things are possible, only believe."

This simple chorus captures the words Jesus spoke in what seemed to be a hopeless situation: His friend, Lazarus, had been dead four days. Jesus' prayer on that day is also for those who are going through life's difficult circumstances. Our Father hears the prayers of our intercessory High Priest, Jesus. Then God answers our prayers so we may lift up our eyes and see His glory in all things.

If you face something impossible, perhaps Jesus' words in Rev. Rader's chorus will comfort you today.

....

Dear Jesus, help me only to believe. All things are possible when I believe. Amen.

ROY MACK, GRACE FELLOWSHIP CHURCH, WARREN, OH

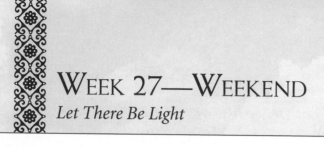

WEEK 27—WEEKEND
Let There Be Light

Then Jesus cried out and said, "He who believes in Me, believes not in Me but in Him who sent Me. And he who sees Me sees Him who sent Me. I have come as a light into the world, that whoever believes in Me should not abide in darkness."

JOHN 12:44–46

As a boy growing up in Arkansas, I liked to hunt with my dad. But I had a heightened fear of the dark. More accurately stated, I had a healthy fear of what could be in the dark: poisonous snakes, wild animals, and, of course, the various monsters of my vivid imagination. Two things comforted me while in the dark of night: my dad's presence and what we called a "wheat light." A wheat light is a very bright light we used to light our path and to see high up into a tree after our dogs treed a raccoon.

Genesis 1 describes our world in its early state as being "without form, and void; and darkness was on the face of the deep" (v. 2). That is what our lives are like before we become Christians: dark and without form, void of purpose, order, or direction. Then in Genesis 1:3 God said, "Let there be light," and light came into existence.

Light by definition divides and dispels darkness. No wonder Jesus declared Himself a light in the world. When we invite Jesus into our lives, we no longer have to live or dwell in the fear of darkness. His light and the comfort of His presence flood us. Our duty is then to share that light with others.

....

Father, guide me out of the darkness that I may walk in Your light. Amen.

WEEK 28—MONDAY
The Moments That Defy Answers

"Let not your heart be troubled; you believe in God, believe also in Me. In My Father's house are many mansions; if it were not so, I would have told you. I go to prepare a place for you. And if I go and prepare a place for you, I will come again and receive you to Myself; that where I am, there you may be also."

JOHN 14:1–3

The disciples loved Jesus, and they put their trust in Him. When He initially told them He would die and return to His Father, they were confused, filled with grief and disbelief, and deeply troubled. Realizing they were overwhelmed with misunderstanding, the Lord Jesus made a move that He had used many times: He made Himself the issue rather than their circumstances or emotions. In so many words He said to them, "Don't get caught up in all the emotions of the moment and the things you don't understand. Believe Me!" He told His disciples they could continue to trust Him even without His bodily presence on earth.

That challenge of the Lord Jesus is still applicable today. Many times confusing things happen. These times have the potential to steal our faith and cause our hearts to be troubled. Sometimes all we need is information—a few facts, a little understanding, and then things are resolved. But other moments defy answers. Perhaps it is the doctor's report, the loss of a loved one, a troubled child, or times of disappointment that seem beyond explanation. During those moments we must listen to Jesus saying, "Believe in Me. I'm doing something that is beyond you."

....

Dear Lord, help me to hear Your voice and not be troubled by my circumstances. Amen.

DR. DAVID EDWARDS, CHURCH PROJECT, THE WOODLANDS, TX

WEEK 28—TUESDAY
When It's Above You and Beyond You

Thomas said to Him, "Lord, we do not know where You are going, and how can we know the way?" Jesus said to him, "I am the way, the truth, and the life. No one comes to the Father except through Me."

JOHN 14:5–6

The gospel seems obvious to us. We have heard the story of Jesus dying on the cross, rising from the dead, and ascending into heaven. It is good news to us!

But it did not sound like good news to the disciples. The idea completely overwhelmed them. The Lord Jesus said He was preparing a place for them to be with Him, and He concluded by telling the disciples they knew where He was going. Thomas, thoroughly confused, challenged Him: "Lord, we do not know where You are going. How can we know the way?" The disciples didn't know what Jesus was talking about.

Jesus was not upset or caught off guard by the challenge; instead He turned to Thomas and stated very succinctly, "I am the way, the truth, and the life." At that moment, it was not essential that Thomas have exact knowledge of every detail, but it was critical for Thomas to have confidence that Jesus was doing something good. It was a difficult moment filled with great doubt and confusion. Yet Jesus said the disciples must trust Him and yield to His will.

The will of the Lord Jesus is often beyond us. Many times it demands we go forward without perfect sight or complete knowledge. It challenges us to believe and act with no other confidence than the assurance that it is His will.

....

Lord Jesus, I don't need to have all the answers to trust You. You alone are trustworthy. Amen.

WEEK 28—WEDNESDAY
The Truth Remains

"If you love Me, keep My commandments. And I will pray the Father, and He will give you another Helper, that He may abide with you forever—the Spirit of truth, whom the world cannot receive, because it neither sees Him nor knows Him; but you know Him, for He dwells with you and will be in you."

JOHN 14:15–17

J esus had just told His disciples that He would be leaving them soon, and the disciples were greatly troubled. To counter the negativity and despair, Jesus led them into a new truth that would become a very important aspect of their lives. Jesus assured them, "I will pray the Father, and He will give you another Helper, that He may abide with you forever." That new Helper was the Holy Spirit. The disciples would quickly learn that one of the greatest blessings of their lives as Christians would be the presence of the Holy Spirit. The Holy Spirit would guide them and give them comfort in the days ahead.

The truth remains for Christians today. If you have received Jesus as Lord and Savior, the Holy Spirit is alive in you. Jesus told the disciples the world would not receive the Spirit or see Him or know Him, but Jesus assured them the Spirit would be inside each of them. Jesus expects those who follow Him as Lord to allow the Spirit to empower them, lead them, and help them fully to succeed. This truth should bring comfort to all of Jesus' disciples.

> *Lord Jesus, I admit I'm completely dependent on You. I can't accomplish Your will on my own, but I can with the help of the Holy Spirit. Amen.*

DR. DAVID EDWARDS, CHURCH PROJECT, THE WOODLANDS, TX

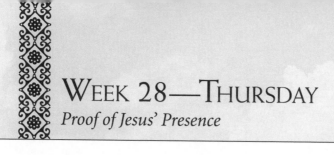

Week 28—Thursday
Proof of Jesus' Presence

"A little while longer and the world will see Me no more, but you will see Me. Because I live, you will live also. At that day you will know that I am in My Father, and you in Me, and I in you. He who has My commandments and keeps them, it is he who loves Me. And he who loves Me will be loved by My Father, and I will love him and manifest Myself to him."

JOHN 14:19–21

The news of His upcoming death had shattered Jesus' disciples. What would they do, where would they go, how would they continue without the Lord? These and a thousand other questions filled their thoughts. To help assuage their fears, Jesus had told them of the resurrection: "A little while longer and the world will see Me no more, but you will see Me. Because I live, you will live also." While on earth, the disciples would still have the presence of Jesus in their lives. This would be possible by the indwelling of the Holy Spirit.

When an individual receives Jesus as Lord and Savior, that person is born again and his or her dead spirit is resurrected! All of this is based upon the resurrection of Jesus. The Lord insisted, "Because I live, you will live also. At that day you will know that I am in My Father, and you in Me, and I in you." Believers can be comforted knowing they have the power of Jesus' presence indwelling them at all times and leading them in the way to go.

Jesus, You are the Leader and Lord of my life. I take comfort in knowing that Your presence dwells within me in the person of the Holy Spirit. Amen.

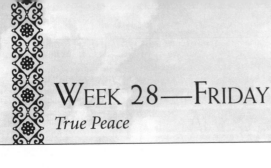

WEEK 28—FRIDAY
True Peace

"These things I have spoken to you while being present with you. But the Helper, the Holy Spirit, whom the Father will send in My name, He will teach you all things, and bring to your remembrance all things that I said to you. Peace I leave with you, My peace I give to you; not as the world gives do I give to you. Let not your heart be troubled, neither let it be afraid."

JOHN 14:25–27

Jesus wanted to bring comfort to His disciples by explaining the work of the Holy Spirit. To encourage the disciples, Jesus defined one of the critical works of the Spirit. "He will teach you all things, and bring to your remembrance all things that I said to you."

Jesus obviously believed we cannot know many things without the ministry of the Holy Spirit. Can it be that many Christians stumble from bad decision to bad decision because they refuse to accept the work of the Holy Spirit in giving them the truth they require? Yes, it is absolutely true! Jesus went further: "Peace I leave with you, My peace I give to you." The Lord tied the truths revealed by the Holy Spirit to genuine peace. Jesus promised the peace of the Holy Spirit is not the type of peace the world gives. This is not a peace that comes and goes; it is peace that stays and builds. It is a peace that led Jesus to insist, "Let not your heart be troubled, neither be afraid." True peace in this world comes from Jesus.

....

Dear Jesus, I choose this day for my faith in You to be greater than my fear. Your Spirit is powerfully at work in my life. Amen.

DR. DAVID EDWARDS, CHURCH PROJECT, THE WOODLANDS, TX

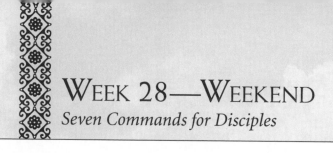

WEEK 28—WEEKEND
Seven Commands for Disciples

"Peace I leave with you, My peace I give to you; not as the world gives do I give to you. Let not your heart be troubled, neither let it be afraid. You have heard Me say to you, 'I am going away and coming back to you.' If you loved Me, you would rejoice because I said, 'I am going to the Father,' for My Father is greater than I."

JOHN 14:27–28

The apostle John spent the fourteenth chapter of his gospel documenting the actions and teachings of the Lord Jesus as He prepared His disciples to lead His church to success. Jesus completed His instructions by reiterating seven important commands for His disciples. The Lord's commands to His disciples are the same commands He gives Christians today.

First, remember your entire relationship with Jesus is based upon Jesus. He is the way. Stay close to Him, focused on Him, and don't be drawn away by things you do not understand. Second, receive the work of the Holy Spirit and His ministry. Third, expect the Holy Spirit to teach and bring you into all truth. Fourth, revel in the peace Jesus gives and expect it to be a lasting aspect of your life. Fifth, reject thoughts that keep you full of anxiety. Sixth, reject fear! Then the Lord Jesus gave one final command: "If you loved Me, you would rejoice because I said, 'I am going to the Father,' for My Father is greater than I." Christianity is not about accomplishing the personal desires of Christians; it is about the will of the Lord Jesus and His glorious purpose and ministry. You are to follow God's will for your life.

....

Jesus, You have given me Your peace and courage. I will not shrink back from doing Your will. Amen.

WEEK 29—MONDAY
Stay Close!

"I am the vine, you are the branches. He who abides in Me, and I in him, bears much fruit; for without Me you can do nothing. . . . If you abide in Me, and My words abide in you, you will ask what you desire, and it shall be done for you. By this My Father is glorified, that you bear much fruit; so you will be My disciples."

JOHN 15:5, 7–8

Jesus' use of "I am" was certainly intentional and purposeful. The use of the biblical phrase "I AM" as the name of God goes all the way back to Moses (Exodus 3:14). Thus Jesus showed His divinity in His "I am" statements. In John 15, Jesus made it clear that the branches should never be confused with the Vine, that the Creator should never be confused with the creation.

In this text Jesus mentioned the importance of abiding in Him, which means to have close fellowship with Him. That is the entirety of our responsibility as branches in relationship to the true Vine. In simple terms, our role in the kingdom of God is to stay close to God. Jesus, who was and is God, made clear that when we abide in Him, His Word will abide in us. When we abide in Jesus, His desires will guide our desires—including what we pray for. This constant abiding in Jesus will allow Christians to produce fruit that is beneficial for the kingdom of God.

Will you abide in Jesus today? Will you make the focus of your spiritual journey abiding in the Son of God?

Jesus, help me abide in You today. Amen.

DR. ALEX HIMAYA, THECHURCH.AT, BROKEN ARROW, OK

WEEK 29—TUESDAY
How to Stay Close

"If you keep My commandments, you will abide in My love, just as I have kept My Father's commandments and abide in His love. These things I have spoken to you, that My joy may remain in you, and that your joy may be full."

JOHN 15:10–11

The little word *if* has such big implications, and the enemy has been ferocious in confusing the if/then correlation presented here by Jesus. Your enemy would have you believe that being loved by God is contingent on your keeping His commandments and being a rule follower. Nothing could be further from the good news of the gospel. The most famous verse in the whole Gospel of John is: "For God so loved the world that He gave His only begotten Son, that whoever believes in Him should not perish but have everlasting life" (John 3:16). Make no mistake that God loves you unconditionally, and when you believe on Him, He fills your life with His presence.

From that point on, His goal is for you to abide in Him—not so you can be loved by Him, but because you are loved by Him. In John 15, *abiding* implies you will not just be the recipient of His love, you will be protected by His love. In other words, if you keep His commandments because you love Him and are close to Him, it is for your good. This is similar to a loving father who says to his child, "Son, don't run out in front of that car!" Your loving heavenly Father gives you commandments to follow in order to protect you. When you walk closely with your heavenly Father, your joy will be full!

. . . .

God, because You love me, will You help me see that Your ways are higher and better than my ways? Will You please open my eyes to see Your rules as Your protection for me? In Jesus' name, amen.

WEEK 29—WEDNESDAY
The Greatest Love

"Greater love has no one than this, than to lay down one's life for his friends. You are My friends if you do whatever I command you. No longer do I call you servants, for a servant does not know what his master is doing; but I have called you friends, for all things that I heard from My Father I have made known to you."

JOHN 15:13–15

There is no greater love than the love of the Father, expressed in the incarnation, crucifixion, and resurrection of the Son, Jesus Christ. He did this to show His amazing grace and love to the whole world. The "if you do whatever I command" part of this passage is not placing a conditional statement on the love of God. Rather, it offers the believer not a distant relationship but the path to an abiding one.

Jesus does not want us just to be saved; He wants us to be His friends! His desire is not that we do whatever He says because of some sort of master-servant relationship. His desire is that we would know Him so well that we would do what He says because we love and trust Him.

Can you believe the same God who spoke this whole universe into existence with a word wants to be your friend? This is the great mystery of the gospel. His grace is not just good; it is amazing!

God, help me to develop a close relationship with You so I can recognize just how deeply You love me. Help me to walk in that love today. Amen.

DR. ALEX HIMAYA, THECHURCH.AT, BROKEN ARROW, OK

WEEK 29—THURSDAY
What Came First: The Fruit or the Tree?

"You did not choose Me, but I chose you and appointed you that you should go and bear fruit, and that your fruit should remain, that whatever you ask the Father in My name He may give you. These things I command you, that you love one another."

JOHN 15:16–17

I t was mutual." Do you remember saying that as a teenager about a breakup? It was usually followed up with someone saying, "No! I broke up with him [or her]!" It seemed so important to clarify who was the initiator. In today's text, Jesus made it very clear that in your relationship with Him that He alone was the initiator. He chose you, and not only that, He appointed you. Being appointed is a much bigger deal than simply being chosen. He has set appointments for you. For what? To go and bear fruit.

What does that mean? There are several applications. In Galatians 5:22–23, Paul listed the fruit of the Spirit. They are love, joy, peace, patience, kindness, goodness, faithfulness, gentleness, and self-control. Clearly God has appointed you to bear and demonstrate this fruit in your life.

Fruit can also be the production of new believers as a result of your life. Are you leading people to Christ? Can people see the evidence of the fruit of the Spirit in your life? With whom have you have been appointed to share Christ in this season of your life?

....

God, will You show me my appointments for this season in my life? In Jesus' name, amen.

Week 29—Friday
Sin and Righteousness

"Nevertheless I tell you the truth. It is to your advantage that I go away; for if I do not go away, the Helper will not come to you; but if I depart, I will send Him to you. And when He has come, He will convict the world of sin, and of righteousness, and of judgment."

JOHN 16:7–8

In today's passage, Jesus told both the disciples and us that His going back to the Father would be better for them and us. It would be advantageous because Jesus would send a Helper to be with us. Do we think of the Holy Spirit as a Helper? He is!

One of the ways the Holy Spirit helps us is through conviction. Jesus said, "He will convict the world of sin." We get this one. If conviction is associated with any other word at all, it is the word *sin*. It is crucial that we understand the distinction between conviction and condemnation. Conviction is feeling the guilt of what we've done. Condemnation is feeling bad for who we are.

Conviction will motivate us to live a good life, to correct our problems, to ask forgiveness for sin, and to become a better follower of Christ. Condemnation is feeling as though we can't do anything to please God.

Conviction is from God. Condemnation is from the enemy.

Jesus also said the Holy Spirit would convict of righteousness. What does that mean? It means the Holy Spirit convicts us of the righteousness that is ours in Christ. We are new creations, and righteousness is one of our new attributes. So, we should live righteously in accordance with who we already are before God.

....

Holy Spirit, convict me if there is any sin in my life that keeps me from being the righteous child of God that I am. In Jesus' name, amen.

DR. ALEX HIMAYA, THECHURCH.AT, BROKEN ARROW, OK

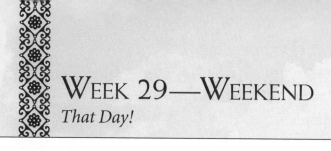

WEEK 29—WEEKEND
That Day!

"A woman, when she is in labor, has sorrow because her hour has come; but as soon as she has given birth to the child, she no longer remembers the anguish, for joy that a human being has been born into the world. Therefore, you now have sorrow; but I will see you again and your heart will rejoice, and your joy no one will take from you."

JOHN 16:21–22

Much of the Bible is written in the future tense. Today's passage is no different. John used a universal illustration: childbirth. Even though we all understand childbirth, one cannot fully comprehend the intensity and pain of childbirth until labor pains come. Only a woman who has given birth can understand the pain involved, and only a mother can explain how, in an instant, the labor pains give way to sheer joy!

Labor pains come quickly and unexpectedly. This is how the second coming of Christ will occur. While we are exposed to momentary sorrow and pain here on this earth, a day is coming when our joy will be complete and permanent. On the day we see Jesus face-to-face, our hearts will rejoice. In addition, no one and nothing will be able to take that joy from us.

....

Lord, will You remind me today that these light and momentary troubles are achieving for me an eternal glory that far outweighs them all? In Jesus' name, amen.

Week 30—Monday
We Are Never Alone

Jesus answered them, "Do you now believe? Indeed the hour is coming, yes, has now come, that you will be scattered, each to his own, and will leave Me alone. And yet I am not alone, because the Father is with Me. These things I have spoken to you, that in Me you may have peace. In the world you will have tribulation; but be of good cheer, I have overcome the world."

JOHN 16:31–33

What thoughts possibly rushed through the minds of the disciples when Jesus told them He would soon be leaving? This was devastating news!

Is this our last meal with Jesus?

How will we make it without our constant companion for more than three years?

Does He want to leave us?

Are we going to die?

You may also struggle with similar anxious thoughts. Everyone experiences questions, doubts, disappointments, and fear. Yet in John 16 Jesus spoke words of assurance right to His disciples' hearts. He said to them, "In Me you may have peace. . . . Be of good cheer."

The Lord's peace is your peace. His peace is present even in the midst of trouble. It's not the absence of trouble that Jesus promised. It's the presence of His peace. Now for the good news: His words were for all of His disciples. So be of good cheer today, Jesus follower! Whatever you deal with, you have His presence; you are never alone. And to have His presence is to have His peace.

....

Dear Father, thank You for the promise of Your presence. In Jesus' name, amen.

JEFF CROOK, BLACKSHEAR PLACE BAPTIST CHURCH, FLOWERY BRANCH, GA

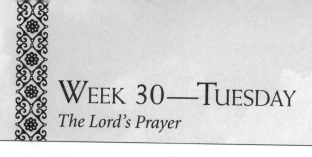

WEEK 30—TUESDAY
The Lord's Prayer

Jesus spoke these words, lifted up His eyes to heaven, and said: "Father, the hour has come. Glorify Your Son, that Your Son also may glorify You, as You have given Him authority over all flesh, that He should give eternal life to as many as You have given Him. And this is eternal life, that they may know You, the only true God, and Jesus Christ whom You have sent."

JOHN 17:1–3

I f someone asked you to recite the Lord's Prayer, you would probably begin by saying, "Our Father in heaven" (Matthew 6:9). But actually this prayer is perhaps not best called the Lord's Prayer—a better title is the Disciples' Prayer because Jesus gave the prayer as a model for disciples to pray.

On the other hand, the Lord's prayer in John 17 is one of the greatest prayers ever prayed. In it we see the heart of our Lord and discover His purpose for us. In verses 1–5, Jesus prayed for Himself. He prayed for His disciples in verses 6–19. And in verses 20–26, Jesus prayed for you and me!

We are part of the greatest prayer Jesus ever prayed. He prayed for us because He loves us deeply and wants us to know Him personally. Jesus prayed "that they may know You, the only true God, and Jesus Christ whom You have sent." To know Him is to talk to Him in prayer. How wonderful it is to be known by Jesus and to know Him in prayer.

....

Dear Jesus, nothing is greater than knowing You. I'm glad You prayed for me, and I'm so glad I can pray to You. I'm always assured of Your love and that You hear my prayers. I love You, Jesus. Amen.

WEEK 30—WEDNESDAY
Jesus Thought of Us

"I do not pray for these alone, but also for those who will believe in Me through their word; that they all may be one, as You, Father, are in Me, and I in You; that they also may be one in Us, that the world may believe that You sent Me. And the glory which You gave Me I have given them, that they may be one just as We are one."

JOHN 17:20–22

Thoughtfulness characterizes those who consider others first, even putting others' needs before their own. When we do this, we act like Jesus. When the Lord began His ministry, He announced His purpose was to serve others—even to the point of giving His life. Jesus thought of others throughout His time on earth.

This is exactly what Jesus did in the famous prayer in John 17. Jesus would experience the suffering and agony of the cross shortly after praying this powerful prayer to the Father. Yet hours before being crucified, Jesus thought of us. He included us in His prayer! Jesus prayed: "I do not pray for these alone, but also for those who will believe in Me though their word." He prayed for us to experience the unity He and the Father enjoy, and He asked that God would enable us to show His glory to others.

Thoughtfulness should be a trait of a Jesus follower. Jesus showcases His power and glory through us so others may believe on Him. Jesus prayed for us, and His prayers were heard and answered. We also should pray for others.

....

I love You, Lord. Use my life today to show others Your power, glory, and love. Amen.

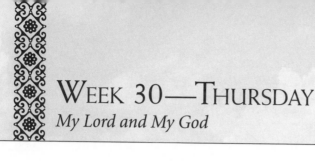

WEEK 30—THURSDAY
My Lord and My God

*Jesus came, the doors being shut, and stood in the midst, and said, "Peace to you!"
Then He said to Thomas, "Reach your finger here, and look at My hands; and reach
your hand here, and put it into My side. Do not be unbelieving, but believing." And
Thomas answered and said to Him, "My Lord and my God!" Jesus said to him,
"Thomas, because you have seen Me, you have believed. Blessed are those who have not
seen and yet have believed."*

JOHN 20:26–29

Have you noticed how a nickname given by a family member or school-mate can stick with someone throughout the years? People know one of the twelve disciples by his nickname: Doubting Thomas. The name is a mischaracterization of Thomas; he actually was a strong believer. The confession he made standing before the risen Jesus Christ was powerful. Thomas looked into Jesus' eyes and said, "You are my Lord and my God." Thomas had no doubts at that point.

After the ascension, Thomas became a bold Jesus follower who took the gospel, as some accounts suggest, even as far as India. Tradition teaches that Thomas died from a spear wound. As his own body was pierced to death, his heart's confession remained: "My Lord and my God." Thomas didn't waver in his faith after he saw Jesus' resurrected body.

Have you made the confession Thomas made? Do others know? Don't let today pass without making it known that you love and serve the Lord God.

....

*Jesus, I believe in You. I know You live, for You live within my heart. Help me to
be a bold believer and to tell others of You, my risen Savior. Amen.*

Week 30—Friday
Search and Rescue

"So that they should seek the Lord, in the hope that they might grope for Him and find Him, though He is not far from each one of us; for in Him we live and move and have our being, as also some of your own poets have said, 'For we are also His offspring.'"

Acts 17:27–28

In Acts 17, the apostle Paul was on a search-and-rescue mission in ancient Athens. The number of lost souls in that city was overwhelming. Yet Paul did not shrink from the assignment; he boldly engaged others with the gospel, even quoting one of the Greeks' famous poets to communicate the gospel in their context.

Let's look at his message to them. First, he pointed out the Creator has revealed Himself to us, and He is closer than we realize. Actually, we live, move, and exist because of Him. Then he said this Creator not only made us, He wants a relationship with us, even going so far as to seek us out. When we open our hearts to God, we find Him. We find His forgiveness and peace. We find joy and purpose. We find redeeming grace. So God finds us, and we find Him.

Further, we find others as we join Him on the search-and-rescue mission. It's an old saying yet still true: "The act of evangelism is one beggar telling another beggar where to find bread."

Will you share today what you have found in Him? Will you pray for others whom the Lord is seeking? Will you report for duty today?

. . . .

Dear Father, I never want to forget that I once was lost before You found me. Thank You for Your saving grace. There is no other word for it but amazing. Use me today as a witness for You and Your saving grace. Amen.

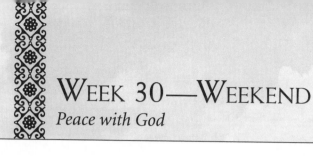

Week 30—Weekend
Peace with God

Therefore, having been justified by faith, we have peace with God through our Lord Jesus Christ, through whom also we have access by faith into this grace in which we stand, and rejoice in hope of the glory of God.

ROMANS 5:1–2

Having pastored now for more than two decades, I have received many requests to pray for the dying. I still remember a phone call to my home several years ago. A woman asked me to come quickly to speak with her husband who was near the end of his battle with cancer. "He is not ready to meet God," she said.

I wasted no time as I made my way to their home, praying fervently on the way. I am thankful to share that God answered those prayers. When I talked to him, the man was alert and responsive to the gospel. He was overwhelmed with guilt from his past and had great uncertainty about his future in eternity. He said these exact words: "Preacher, I want to be at peace with God."

I shared the gospel right from the pages of God's Word. God had prepared his heart, and the dying man put his faith in Jesus Christ. In an instant, he was at peace with God. He was ready to meet God and did so just a few hours later. Cancer took his life, but he received eternal life through our Lord Jesus Christ.

We can rejoice in the hope of heaven because of the peace Jesus brings when we put our trust in Him for salvation.

Dear Father, thank You for giving Your Son to die for me. I praise You for salvation, for grace, and for the joy of having peace with You, my Lord and my God. Amen.

WEEK 31—MONDAY
The Hope of Christ

And not only that, but we also glory in tribulations, knowing that tribulation produces perseverance; and perseverance, character; and character, hope. Now hope does not disappoint, because the love of God has been poured out in our hearts by the Holy Spirit who was given to us.

ROMANS 5:3–5

There is nothing like a cool glass of fresh lemonade on a hot summer day. But have you ever given much thought to the work that goes into preparing the lemonade before you can enjoy it? The fresh, ripe lemon must be cut, placed into a lemon press, and squeezed until every drop of juice is extracted from its pulp. Only then can you mix the lemon juice, sugar, and water, which results in a most enjoyable summer drink.

While considering Paul's words of encouragement here in Romans 5:3–5, we understand the tribulations in our lives have a way of squeezing the life right out of us. These afflictions should not come as a surprise to believers. Jesus said, "In the world you will have tribulation" (John 16:33). The pressures of a world that does not know Christ often become overbearing for those following Him. But we have a choice! We can choose to allow these trials to squeeze us, leaving our lives a useless pulp, or we can do as Paul wrote, and allow these moments of testing to bring about perseverance, character, and hope in our lives.

Hope in this life is found in Jesus! Remember His words, "But be of good cheer; I have overcome the world" (John 16:33).

Father, help me to persevere as You use my moments of suffering to build my character, and let me find my hope in the love of Christ. Amen.

DR. KELLY BULLARD, TEMPLE BAPTIST CHURCH, FAYETTEVILLE, NC

WEEK 31—TUESDAY
Stand Free

There is therefore now no condemnation to those who are in Christ Jesus, who do not walk according to the flesh, but according to the Spirit. For the law of the Spirit of life in Christ Jesus has made me free from the law of sin and death.

ROMANS 8:1–2

The effects of salvation for the believer are many, and one of the most powerful is found here in Romans 8:1—no condemnation! To be condemned is to receive a verdict of guilt and the accompanying penalty. The Bible renders a verdict of guilt for humanity: "All have sinned and fall short of the glory of God" (Romans 3:23). Furthermore, death stands as a justifiable penalty (Romans 6:23). We all stand condemned before a holy and righteous God. Paul explained, "O wretched man that I am! Who will deliver me from this body of death? I thank God—through Jesus Christ our Lord!" (Romans 7:24–25). The beauty of the gospel is not only the forgiveness of our sin, but the pardon of our guilty verdict and its penalty. In Christ, we stand free!

Unfortunately, many believers still carry the condemnation of others and sometimes themselves. Today let the verdict of heaven's court stand in your heart! Find rest in knowing that no sin—past, present, or future—can or will be held against you! When the light of Christ shines in your heart, the darkness is dispelled forever and you are set free from sin, guilt, and shame.

Father, thank You for Your forgiveness and mercy! Let me walk in the light of Your love and grace today! In Jesus' name, amen.

Week 31—Wednesday
Children of God

The Spirit Himself bears witness with our spirit that we are children of God, and if children, then heirs—heirs of God and joint heirs with Christ, if indeed we suffer with Him, that we may also be glorified together.

Romans 8:16–17

As a pastor, I am often asked a pointed question: "How can I know that I'm a Christian?" When we are adopted into God's family, through faith in Christ we receive the Holy Spirit as a promise of God (Romans 8:15; Ephesians 1:13–14). It is the Holy Spirit's responsibility to testify of our faith in Christ. Just as the Roman law required witnesses to confirm the validity of adoption, God gives believers the Holy Spirit to confirm the validity of their adoption in Christ.

My wife and I adopted our son in 2012. I will never forget the day we received the final adoption decree. One paragraph of this document stood out among the rest: "Now therefore, it is hereby ordered, adjudged, and decreed by the Court that from the date of the entry of this Decree herein, the said minor is declared adopted for life by the petitioners . . . and has the same legal status, including all legal rights and obligations of any kind whatsoever, as a child born the legitimate child of the adoptive parents." On the bottom of the decree were the signature and seal of the court county clerk.

Documents such as these legalize earthly adoptions; heaven's decree has been issued by the blood of Christ and stamped on our hearts by the Holy Spirit. Forever we are known as children of God, having all the rights and responsibilities as His children!

....

Father, thank You for adopting me into Your family. Amen.

DR. KELLY BULLARD, TEMPLE BAPTIST CHURCH, FAYETTEVILLE, NC

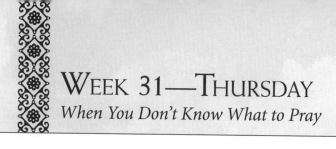

WEEK 31—THURSDAY
When You Don't Know What to Pray

Likewise the Spirit also helps in our weaknesses. For we do not know what we should pray for as we ought, but the Spirit Himself makes intercession for us with groanings which cannot be uttered. Now He who searches the hearts knows what the mind of the Spirit is, because He makes intercession for the saints according to the will of God.

ROMANS 8:26–27

Have you ever found yourself in a situation where you did not know what to pray? The Bible describes this as a moment of weakness. Sometimes the overwhelming circumstances of life leave one helpless and without direction. This is not an indictment on the believer, but rather a reality of life. But the promise of God is the help of the Holy Spirit. In fact, this is His primary role in the believer's life—to come alongside and help. This intercession of the Holy Spirit involves divine words that cannot be expressed in human language.

When you do not know what to pray, the Holy Spirit intercedes to the Father on your behalf, and He always works in accordance to the will of God! Oswald Chambers writes in *My Utmost for His Highest* that God seeks out the prayers of the Spirit in your heart.

Today, if you do not know what to pray, rest in the truth and work of the Holy Spirit. Know that He is praying for you, interceding to the Father on your behalf. Here is the best part—God always answers the Holy Spirit's prayers!

....

Father, thank You for the wonderful gift of the Holy Spirit who intercedes for me! In Jesus' name, amen.

Week 31—Friday
Our Good, His Glory

And we know that all things work together for good to those who love God, to those who are the called according to His purpose. For whom He foreknew, He also predestined to be conformed to the image of His Son, that He might be the firstborn among many brethren. Moreover whom He predestined, these He also called; whom He called, these He also justified; and whom He justified, these He also glorified.

ROMANS 8:28–30

Why do bad things happen to good people? This question gets asked many times and in many ways! But these words from Paul bring encouragement to our hearts amid difficult circumstances. Notice what Paul said and what he didn't say. Paul did not say, "All things are good!" Rather, he said, "All thing work together for good." A lot of things in life are not good—cancer, the death of a child, domestic violence, and so on. But the promise of this passage is that God can take all the bad things of life and orchestrate them for our good and for His glory!

While God never promised to answer your questions of suffering or pain, He did promise His presence (Isaiah 43:2; 1 Peter 5:7). Rest in the truth that your circumstances do not take God by surprise. God knows every day of your life before you experience them (Psalm 139:16). He has a plan for your life, which includes a process to conform you more into the image of His Son, Jesus Christ. Sometimes the process of being conformed is painful, yet you have the promise of a future joy and of all things being made new.

....

Father, thank You for the promise of Your presence in my life, even during the darkest of days. May I find my hope in You! In Jesus' name, amen.

DR. KELLY BULLARD, TEMPLE BAPTIST CHURCH, FAYETTEVILLE, NC

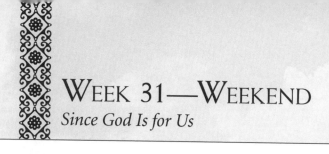

WEEK 31—WEEKEND
Since God Is for Us

What then shall we say to these things? If God is for us, who can be against us? He who did not spare His own Son, but delivered Him up for us all, how shall He not with Him also freely give us all things?

ROMANS 8:31–32

In his book *When People Are Big and God Is Small*, Ed Welch explains we often fear people more than we fear God. This plays out in our seeking approval, recognition, and acceptance from other people. But Christians are called to fear God, not people. When we fear people, we cross the line of idolatry and make God insignificant in our lives. But when we fear God, we make the fear of people insignificant in our lives. Whom are we afraid of today? Who is standing against us? What enemy is staring us down? With God on our side, we have nothing and no one to fear.

Once again, Paul encouraged us to consider Christ. Paul's argument is from greater to lesser. Since God willingly gave up His Son for humankind, how much more will He give us everything we need in Christ?

Peter reminded us: "His divine power has given to us all things that pertain to life and godliness" (2 Peter 1:3). All we need for eternal life has been granted through Jesus Christ. All we need to be like Jesus in this life has been given to us as well.

....

Father, forgive me for allowing the opinions of people to dictate my life. Help me to make You big in my life today! In Jesus' name, amen.

Week 32—Monday
We Are Persuaded!

For I am persuaded that neither death nor life, nor angels nor principalities nor powers, nor things present nor things to come, nor height nor depth, nor any other created thing, shall be able to separate us from the love of God which is in Christ Jesus our Lord.

ROMANS 8:38–39

Did you know that more than three hundred Christians will die for their faith this month and more than seven hundred Christians will suffer imprisonment, assault, abduction, or something worse? Paul's admonition to the Christians in Rome was written in the face of growing persecution and suffering with no immediate end in sight. He wanted them to remember that nothing would separate them from God's love or circumvent their relationship with Jesus Christ.

When you face adversity in life, remember you're not alone. Give thanks to God that He won't let anything come between you and His wonderful love. For a Christian to become separated from the love of God is impossible. Every Christian has been spiritually placed in Christ. Therefore, God's love for them is unassailable.

God cares for you more than you know. His love for you is both unconditional and unending. Although you may face hardships, sorrows, sickness, and even persecution for your faith, nothing can come between you and His love. Thank Him, and determine to love Him with all of your heart, mind, soul, and strength. Remember God loved you first and He proved it by dying for you on the cross.

Lord, help me never to take Your love for granted. Amen.

DR. BRYAN E. SMITH, FIRST ROANOKE BAPTIST CHURCH, ROANOKE, VA

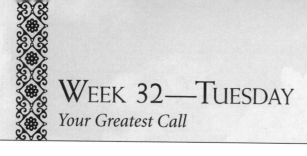

WEEK 32—TUESDAY
Your Greatest Call

For the Scripture says, "Whoever believes on Him will not be put to shame." For there is no distinction between Jew and Greek, for the same Lord over all is rich to all who call upon Him. For "whoever calls on the name of the LORD shall be saved."

ROMANS 10:11–13

I remember watching as a kid the daredevil motorcyclist Evel Knievel. He was the most famous motorcycle rider in the world. As boys we all wanted to be like him, daring each other to attempt jumps on our bicycles, which our mothers never would've approved of. But Knievel's fame and fortune came at a high price. Forty bone fractures and a seven-times-broken back left him physically crippled. In his later years the American hero whose motorcycle is displayed in the Smithsonian and who had performed so many death-defying stunts could barely walk across a room by himself.

Over the course of his life, Knievel had missed his mark in front of a national TV viewing audience numerous times. His successes and failures were a fixture on ABC's *Wide World of Sports* program. But in April 2007, Knievel made the greatest leap of faith of his entire life when he called upon God to save him. Evel Knievel had achieved great fortune and fame, but he gained infinitely more when he believed in Christ and was saved.

··

Lord, thank You for saving me. I praise You for all the blessings that come from knowing You. Help me to tell others about Your wonderful salvation. Amen.

WEEK 32—WEDNESDAY
The Real Transformers

I beseech you therefore, brethren, by the mercies of God, that you present your bodies a living sacrifice, holy, acceptable to God, which is your reasonable service. And do not be conformed to this world, but be transformed by the renewing of your mind, that you may prove what is that good and acceptable and perfect will of God.

ROMANS 12:1–2

When my son was little he liked Transformers, toy robots that transformed into cars, planes, trucks, and just about anything else one could think of. The idea carried over into comic books, a cartoon series, and even multimillion-dollar movies. I guess there's something exciting about transforming from one thing into something else.

Paul talked about the exciting transformation that a Christian experiences as a "living sacrifice" who refuses to be "conformed to this world." A living sacrifice gives everything to God. As Christians, we're to resist being conformed and squeezed into the world's mold. As Paul also said elsewhere: "Therefore, if anyone is in Christ, he is a new creation; old things have passed away; behold, all things have become new" (2 Corinthians 5:17). When we surrender our wills to God, He transforms us into being more like His Son.

This transformation occurs in our minds. Since our bodies are temples for the Holy Spirit (1 Corinthians 6:19–20), our minds are the launch pads for our attitudes, thoughts, words, and desires. When we give ourselves to meditating on God's Word, praying, and worshipping with our church family, we can experience the joy of living as true transformers!

....

Lord, I don't want to be conformed to this world but transformed into Your image. Renew my mind with the light of your Word. Amen.

DR. BRYAN E. SMITH, FIRST ROANOKE BAPTIST CHURCH, ROANOKE, VA

Week 32—Thursday
Dressed for the Occasion

The night is far spent, the day is at hand. Therefore let us cast off the works of darkness, and let us put on the armor of light. Let us walk properly, as in the day, not in revelry and drunkenness, not in lewdness and lust, not in strife and envy. But put on the Lord Jesus Christ, and make no provision for the flesh, to fulfill its lusts.

ROMANS 13:12–14

It's Sunday morning and Mom has already gotten little Johnny dressed in his brand-new Easter outfit. But while she and Dad are getting ready, Johnny decides not to waste a chance for playtime, so out he goes into the backyard. By the time Mom discovers what's happened, Johnny's covered in dirt from head to toe!

One of the ways the Bible describes the concept of holiness is putting on a new self in the likeness of Christ (Ephesians 4:24; Colossians 3:10; Galatians 3:27). The apostle Paul said that we should "put on the Lord Jesus Christ" (Romans 13:14). In other words, we should seek to live lifestyles befitting those who have "cast off the works of darkness." Followers of Christ should strive to "make no provision for the flesh, to fulfill its lusts."

Paul's admonition was urgent because our Lord's return is closer than ever! "The night is far spent, the day is at hand." The time for fighting the good fight of faith is now and not later. And of this we can be certain—whether Jesus returns in our lifetime or not, all of us are closer to seeing Him then ever before!

....

Lord, I don't want to waste my faith. Help me to live my life with holiness and in the anticipation of seeing You face-to-face. Amen.

WEEK 32—FRIDAY
What a Fellowship!

Therefore receive one another, just as Christ also received us, to the glory of God. Now I say that Jesus Christ has become a servant to the circumcision for the truth of God, to confirm the promises made to the fathers, and that the Gentiles might glorify God for His mercy, as it is written: "For this reason I will confess to You among the Gentiles, and sing to Your name."

ROMANS 15:7–9

I can still remember those awkward, intimidating, and uncomfortable feelings of that first day of class in a brand-new school. One of the thoughts that raced through my mind was whether the other kids would accept me. Would I find a friend among so many unfamiliar faces?

Paul instructed the believers in Rome to accept each other despite their many differences. Their motivation to do so was that Jesus had already accepted them. They must not turn their backs on their brothers and sisters in Christ. After all, Jesus taught His disciples that the world would know they belonged to Him by the way they loved each other (John 13:35).

The ultimate outcome of our receiving each other is that "the Gentiles might glorify God for His mercy." Receiving each other in love as Christ has received us, no matter how great our differences might be, is a wonderful witness of God's grace to anyone who knows us but doesn't yet know Him.

> *Lord, thank You for accepting and loving me. Fill me with Your love as I seek the well-being of others in my church and serve them in Your name. In Jesus' name, amen.*

DR. BRYAN E. SMITH, FIRST ROANOKE BAPTIST CHURCH, ROANOKE, VA

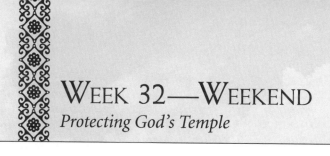

WEEK 32—WEEKEND
Protecting God's Temple

Do you not know that you are the temple of God and that the Spirit of God dwells in you? If anyone defiles the temple of God, God will destroy him. For the temple of God is holy, which temple you are.

1 CORINTHIANS 3:16–17

In today's text Paul referred both to the believer's physical body and a body of believers as the temple of God's Holy Spirit. The very moment we accepted Him, the Holy Spirit came to dwell within us. His entrance into our lives wasn't a delayed, multi-staged process but an instantaneous miracle of redemption!

In verse 16, the word "you" is plural, referring to a body of believers—the church. Unholy conduct, dissension between Christians, and carnal conversations are tools of the enemy designed to destroy a church's witness and work. Because the Holy Spirit dwells within us personally and corporately, we should take great care in how we speak about and treat the church. After all, Jesus bought His church with His own blood and He calls the church His bride!

No matter where we go or what we do, the Holy Spirit is always with God's people. Can others see Him at work in our lives? His presence ought to have changed our attitudes toward sin. Do we desire to obey God and live separately from the sins of the world? Whether we're at church, at work, or at home, we should seek to protect His temple.

....

Lord, through your Spirit who dwells within me, use what I say and do to help build up the faith of others in my church family and to encourage them. Amen.

WEEK 33—MONDAY
Are Some Sins Worse Than Other Sins?

Do you not know that your body is the temple of the Holy Spirit who is in you, whom you have from God, and you are not your own? For you were bought at a price; therefore glorify God in your body and in your spirit, which are God's.

1 CORINTHIANS 6:19–20

To read Paul's letter to the church at Corinth almost brings amazement at all the wickedness going on in the church. From dividing factions at odds with each other, to condoning sexual immorality, to suing one another, to getting drunk at the Lord's Supper, to misusing spiritual gifts, the Corinthians were guilty of many sins.

Yet among all of these sins, Paul singled out sexual immorality as different. Why? Because sexual immorality is a sin against the believer's own body—it is particularly grievous.

When we trusted in the Lord Jesus Christ, the Father sent the Holy Spirit to live inside us. Though these earthly bodies are temporary, they nonetheless are the dwelling places of the Holy Spirit. So when a person commits sexual sin, it dishonors God, who has purchased us with the blood of Jesus Christ.

Also, a word for those who may not struggle greatly with sexual immorality: How are you doing with overeating? How are you doing with exercising? How about getting enough sleep and rest? Because the body is the temple of the Holy Spirit, sinning against the body also includes these sins. You should seek to honor God with your body in every way you can.

....

Heavenly Father, thank You so much for choosing to live inside of me. I want to honor You with my body today and every day. Amen.

WEEK 33—TUESDAY
Is Experience the Best Teacher?

Now all these things happened to them as examples, and they were written for our admonition, upon whom the ends of the ages have come. Therefore let him who thinks he stands take heed lest he fall. No temptation has overtaken you except such as is common to man; but God is faithful, who will not allow you to be tempted beyond what you are able, but with the temptation will also make the way of escape, that you may be able to bear it.

1 CORINTHIANS 10:11–13

In the opening verses of chapter ten, Paul talked about various events that happened to the Israelites when they were wandering in the desert. He talked about the Israelites in relationship to their worshipping idols, committing sexual immorality, grumbling—and the painful, sometimes deadly, consequences of these sins.

Then Paul said the judgments that came upon the Israelites were to be examples for Christians and to warn them of the consequences of sin. You may have heard the adage, "Experience is the best teacher." This passage makes it clear: "Someone else's experience is the best teacher!" Try to learn from their pain so you don't experience the pain yourself.

Perhaps you are thinking, *I don't struggle with any of these sins.* You may not, but you struggle with something else. Don't be arrogant, because pride goes before a fall. Regardless of what temptation you may face, God is always faithful. He will always make a way to escape. Too often Christians try to resist temptation through their own power. Rather, they should depend on God to enable them to escape from temptation and the tricks of the devil.

Father, help me to avoid temptation. Amen.

WEEK 33—WEDNESDAY
Loving Others

Love suffers long and is kind; love does not envy; love does not parade itself, is not puffed up; does not behave rudely, does not seek its own, is not provoked, thinks no evil; does not rejoice in iniquity, but rejoices in the truth; bears all things, believes all things, hopes all things, endures all things.

1 CORINTHIANS 13:4–7

Most people equate love with how they feel toward someone and how they can fall in or out of love. Love, however, is also an action verb, not just a noun. We know this because Paul told the Romans, "God demonstrates His own love toward us, in that while we were still sinners, Christ died for us" (Romans 5:8). God put His love in action.

A summary of the characteristics of love in 1 Corinthians 13:4–7 could be, "Love puts the interests of someone else ahead of its own." A person who loves doesn't think his or her opinion is always best or he or she is most important. Love doesn't insist on having its way. Just think how many arguments, hurts, and heartaches people avoid when they show love.

Frankly, these verses are the most convicting to me as a follower of Jesus of all the verses in the Bible. I have these verses written on a three-by-five card that I keep in my car and often in my pocket. I encourage you to do this, or even better, to memorize 1 Corinthians 13:1–7.

....

Heavenly Father, help me to show love to others through my actions today. Amen.

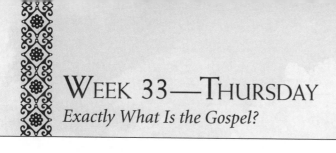

WEEK 33—THURSDAY
Exactly What Is the Gospel?

Moreover, brethren, I declare to you the gospel. . . . For I delivered to you first of all that which I also received: that Christ died for our sins according to the Scriptures, and that He was buried, and that He rose again the third day according to the Scriptures.

1 CORINTHIANS 15:1, 3–4

As we probably are aware, the word *gospel* means "good news." Numerous authors have written volumes of books about the depth and breadth of the gospel. Here in 1 Corinthians 15, Paul defined the gospel in a nutshell. The gospel is the message that Christ died for our sins, He was buried, and He rose from the grave on the third day, all according to the Scriptures.

Jesus commanded Christians to share the gospel with others. Using our personal testimony is the easiest way to share the gospel. Often a person will refer to his or her salvation in a general way, such as "I received Jesus." When we do so, we remove the effectiveness of sharing our testimony because the gospel message is where the power of God is—not in our story.

The gospel is not just that Jesus died for our sins but that He also rose from the dead. Around the world, people give their lives for causes in which they believe. Jesus also had a cause—He came to pay for our sins. How do we know His death on the cross was really payment enough for our sins? Because Jesus did not stay dead! He rose from the dead! That is the essence of the gospel message.

. . . .

Father, help me always to make the gospel clear. Amen.

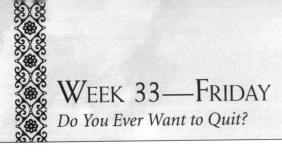

WEEK 33—FRIDAY
Do You Ever Want to Quit?

The sting of death is sin, and the strength of sin is the law. But thanks be to God, who gives us the victory through our Lord Jesus Christ. Therefore, my beloved brethren, be steadfast, immovable, always abounding in the work of the Lord, knowing that your labor is not in vain in the Lord.

1 CORINTHIANS 15:56–58

P aul concluded the book of 1 Corinthians with an exhortation to believers. Paul did not want Christians to lose heart in their service for the Lord.

If you are a faithful servant of the Lord Jesus, you will get tired in your service for Him. Whether your ministry at church is greeting people, working with children, leading a small group, helping the homeless, pastoring, or participating in any other ministry, do you occasionally find yourself thinking that what you're doing is not very profitable? I certainly feel this way occasionally, and most believers struggle with this from time to time. Times arise when Christians just want to give up!

Yet, Paul gave a personal exhortation for believers to be steadfast and immovable, and even to abound, to overflow, to be highly productive. Rather than give up, Christians are to increase!

Why? Since Jesus was victorious over death, we also will be victorious over death. When we see our Savior one day, all our struggles on earth will seem so slight! Whether or not we see evidence of success now, we will see it when we dwell with Jesus in heaven.

Lord, when I am weary, help me remember I want to hear You say one day, "Well done, My good and faithful servant." In Jesus' name, amen.

DENNIS NUNN, EVERY BELIEVER A WITNESS MINISTRIES, DALLAS, GA

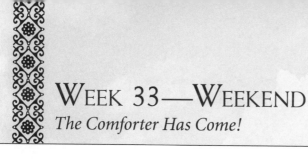

WEEK 33—WEEKEND
The Comforter Has Come!

Blessed be the God and Father of our Lord Jesus Christ, the Father of mercies and God of all comfort, who comforts us in all our tribulation, that we may be able to comfort those who are in any trouble, with the comfort with which we ourselves are comforted by God.

2 CORINTHIANS 1:3–4

One of the names of the Holy Spirit is "the Comforter," and it refers to one who comes alongside and consoles and encourages. That is how He deals with us when we have troubles. The Holy Spirit does this not only to help us but to show us how we are to treat others who are experiencing pain in their lives.

God's comfort involves a peace that can come only from Him. People try to find comfort in this world through various avenues: substance abuse, relationships, material possessions, and so on. True peace and help can come only from an intimate relationship with our heavenly Father.

In my forty years of following Jesus, I have experienced God's comfort in almost every possible kind of life situation. I try to remember that because God comforts me, I am to comfort others in "any trouble" they experience. What a blessing it is to offer support to those in need!

Whether it is comforting someone who is struggling with the death of a loved one, a health problem, a crisis with his or her children, or "any trouble," we can reassure them because we have personally experienced God's encouragement.

Father, help me always to share the comfort You have given me. In Jesus' name, amen.

WEEK 34—MONDAY
Tamper-Proof

Now He who establishes us with you in Christ and has anointed us is God, who also has sealed us and given us the Spirit in our hearts as a guarantee.

2 CORINTHIANS 1:21–22

Some time back, I came across what "sealing" meant in the Roman world. Two facts stood out to me in particular. First, when a government affixed its seal on anything, tampering with it was viewed as an attack on the government itself. An example would be Pilate's sealing of Jesus' tomb. Second, a government seal was an official reassurance that a container held exactly what it claimed.

Now consider those two things in regard to your relationship with God. Belonging to Him means you are so secure that to "tamper" with you would be to take on all the powers of heaven! I love this second one. When I read the Scriptures, God says that I am loved, blessed, forgiven, gifted, a child of God, and I have an eternity with Him. Often, I don't *feel* all those things. But His seal guarantees that my "vessel" contains exactly what His Word says. I can take comfort in knowing that I belong to God. He has sealed me for all of eternity, and nothing can remove His seal!

....

Dear Father, being sealed by You is awesome. Whatever I face today, it's good to know that I'm protected and blessed for all of eternity! In Jesus' name, amen.

MARK HOOVER, NEWSPRING CHURCH, WICHITA, KS

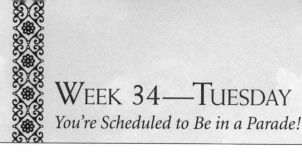

Week 34—Tuesday
You're Scheduled to Be in a Parade!

Now thanks be to God who always leads us in triumph in Christ, and through us diffuses the fragrance of His knowledge in every place. For we are to God the fragrance of Christ among those who are being saved and among those who are perishing.

2 Corinthians 2:14–15

When a professional sports team wins a championship, a parade often takes place in the hometown. It seems as if the whole city shows up to experience the euphoric feeling of winning. In biblical days something similar occurred. If a Roman general won a meaningful battle, a parade was given in his honor. It must have been a spectacle! Everywhere were the sights and sounds of victory as people rejoiced with beautiful displays and music. But if we were transported back to one of those parades, it might have been the scents that captured our attention. Wreaths of fragrant flowers were strung about, and wafting through the air was the delicious aroma of incense.

Our verses tell us God schedules a fragrant parade for his Son, Jesus, every day. He has won. The outcome was settled long ago. He never loses. And as God's children, we're not just part of the crowd—we're in the parade too!

. . . .

Dear Father, I love being in Your family. You've adopted me as Your child and told me that I am Your friend. And because of Jesus, I get to be in Your parade today. I can't wait to see what You have for me! In Jesus' name, amen.

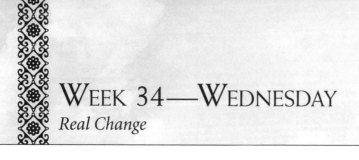

WEEK 34—WEDNESDAY
Real Change

Now the Lord is the Spirit; and where the Spirit of the Lord is, there is liberty. But we all, with unveiled face, beholding as in a mirror the glory of the Lord, are being transformed into the same image from glory to glory, just as by the Spirit of the Lord.

2 CORINTHIANS 3:17–18

I think one of the most frustrating things about being human is our failed attempts at change. Stubborn habits and patterns keep cropping up like indestructible weeds. What makes today's passage one of my favorites is the assurance that real change is not only possible, it's readily available. Let's see how it works.

First, the "veil" refers to something that happened long ago in the life of Moses. When he came off the mountain, having received the Law, his face shone because he'd been in the presence of God. The radiance of the glow frightened the people, so Moses covered his face with a veil. Thus Paul reminded us that having grace is so much more awesome than being under the Law.

Unlike Moses, we stand before Jesus with faces uncovered. And just as a person looks into a mirror, we get to gaze at the glory of Jesus. Now here's the exciting part. As we focus on Jesus, God's glory actually transforms us! He makes us into the image of His Son every day.

Try this exercise today. Block out all the competing noise. Open the Gospels and read about Jesus. Think about Him for a while. You won't walk away unchanged.

....

Dear Father, as I open the Scriptures today, let me see Jesus. Really see Him! I want your Holy Spirit to bring real change to my life. In Jesus' name, amen.

MARK HOOVER, NEWSPRING CHURCH, WICHITA, KS

WEEK 34—THURSDAY
It's Not About Us

For we do not preach ourselves, but Christ Jesus the Lord, and ourselves your bondservants for Jesus' sake. For it is the God who commanded light to shine out of darkness, who has shone in our hearts to give the light of the knowledge of the glory of God in the face of Jesus Christ.

2 CORINTHIANS 4:5–6

Paul was perhaps the most effective communicator of his time, and the Corinthians were perhaps his most sophisticated audience. Sometimes when I research Corinth, I get the idea they were more like Americans than any first-century group. Located at a trade crossroads, they picked up a sampling from multiple cultures. Roman muscle, Greek philosophy, along with their own brand of materialism thrown in, made them feel as if they were the smartest kids on the block. Paul would have felt pressure to impress them. Corinth was looking for "rock stars" to speak to them.

Paul, however, told the people of this "enlightened" city that he intentionally did not talk about himself. His only message was Jesus. He gave the perfect reason why his ministry was not about himself. In both creation and salvation, only God could command the "light to shine out of the darkness." And this same God is the One who gives true knowledge about His glory and His Son.

Today we'll face scores of decisions, some huge. They'll either be about us, revolving around what we think or feel, or Jesus will be the subject. The temptation to focus on ourselves is strong. But before we act, we should ask the question, "How can I keep the focus on Jesus Christ?"

. . . .

Dear Father, I want Jesus to rule in my life today. Help me to keep my focus solely on Him. In Jesus' name, amen.

Week 34—Friday
Stronger Every Day

Therefore we do not lose heart. Even though our outward man is perishing, yet the inward man is being renewed day by day. For our light affliction, which is but for a moment, is working for us a far more exceeding and eternal weight of glory.

2 Corinthians 4:16–17

For those who live in an affluent culture, aging is often seen as the enemy. People go to amazing lengths to try to look and feel younger. But ultimately, as we know, it's a losing proposition. As Paul wrote these words, he also no doubt felt the weight of years.

It's clear from our text, however, that he had a different perspective. He saw the process of aging as God's way of signaling that the bodies we live in are temporary and ultimately disposable. But unlike our bodies, our inner persons aren't disposable. In fact, while our bodies will eventually weaken, our inner persons grow stronger every day!

Think about this. How often does the condition of our bodies drive the narrative of our days? How we feel, concerns about our health, and worries about the future often drown out the reality that we are completely and eternally secure in Jesus.

Maybe the most encouraging news from our text is the last part. The problems of our lives, which are small compared to eternal blessings, actually are working for us. Whatever hurts we experience here, God will more than make up them for when we see Him.

....

Dear Father, help me to remember that regardless of what's happening in my body, my inner person in Jesus Christ grows stronger every day. In Jesus' name, amen.

MARK HOOVER, NEWSPRING CHURCH, WICHITA, KS

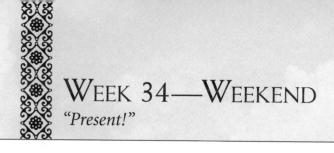

Week 34—Weekend
"Present!"

So we are always confident, knowing that while we are at home in the body we are absent from the Lord. For we walk by faith, not by sight. We are confident, yes, well pleased rather to be absent from the body and to be present with the Lord.

2 Corinthians 5:6–8

On a road trip to Florida with my family, I stopped in Vicksburg, Mississippi. Touring a major cemetery, I came across a couple of aged headstones marking the graves of two children who had died in 1861—a little girl of three and her six-year-old brother. I don't remember the girl's headstone, but the message on her brother's shocked me: "No kisses fall upon the cheek, / Those lips are sealed to me. / Dear God, how could we give him up?"

As I read those words, my imagination transported me back to being with the grieving parents. They had lost two children in the same year! I could see why they would want their pain carved into stone: "Dear God, how could we give him up?"

For some reason I fell to my knees in front of the headstone, and when I did, my knees pulled down grass that concealed a fourth line—words that changed the way I look at death. The whole inscription read: "No kisses fall upon the cheek, / Those lips are sealed to me. / Dear God, how could we give him up / To anyone but thee?"

God wants Christians to know death isn't the end. It's only the beginning of eternity with Him.

....

Dear Father, how great to know that when I leave this life, the first touch I'll feel is the hand of Jesus. In Jesus' name, amen.

WEEK 35—MONDAY
All-In!

For the love of Christ compels us, because we judge thus: that if One died for all, then all died; and He died for all, that those who live should live no longer for themselves, but for Him who died for them and rose again.

2 CORINTHIANS 5:14–15

*A*ll-in describes being fully committed, sold-out. Being all-in with Jesus is practical evidence that there has been a supernatural change. Many Christians describe drastic alterations that take place after they establish a relationship with Jesus.

After someone is born again, a change always takes place. Justification is the finished work at Calvary, the death, burial, and resurrection of Jesus. After personally accepting this finished work, we are saved. Then the process of sanctification comes. That is when one transforms into being more like Jesus.

One's love for Christ drives this commitment to being spiritually transformed. Many athletes practice, work, and sacrifice for the sports they love. Many parents do without or go far beyond the call of duty for the children they love. In marriage, we plan, prepare, and often change ourselves to please our spouses. Love motivates all of this hard work and discipline—the love of the game, love for a child, or love for a spouse. In like manner, our love for Jesus should compel us to be all-in for Him with our time, talents, and treasures. Our desire to be more like Him should be a daily delight and not a duty!

....

Dear Lord Jesus, help me from this day forward to be all-in for You! Amen.

REV. BRIAN FOSSETT, FOSSETT EVANGELISTIC MINISTRIES, DALTON, GA

WEEK 35—TUESDAY
The Ministry of Reconciliation

Therefore, if anyone is in Christ, he is a new creation; old things have passed away;
behold, all things have become new. Now all things are of God, who has reconciled us
to Himself through Jesus Christ, and has given us the ministry of reconciliation.

2 CORINTHIANS 5:17–18

We have been reconciled, converted, and changed by Christ Jesus, and our relationship with God has been restored through our salvation. As a result, God gives Christians the mighty, awesome, and sometimes overwhelming ministry of reconciliation. Christians need to be in the restoration business!

We need to help others to restore, rebuild, and mend broken families and relationships. This is a personal assignment in a team effort. The church is called to the ministry of reconciliation. We should do our part!

We can offer an encouraging word, pray, or give a financial gift, but our goal is to make whole, restore, and bring together as many as possible. In other words, God instructs us to add value to others. My life goal, while I fail often, is for everyone I come in contact with to say, "I am better for having Brian Fossett in my life."

We should inspire, encourage, and uplift others every chance we have. Each new day provides a host of new opportunities. We should be blessings, not burdens.

....

Lord Jesus, help me recognize the divine appointments You present to me this
day. Give me boldness and urgency to inspire, encourage, and uplift all those You
put in my path. Help me to be a blessing, not a burden. Amen.

WEEK 35—WEDNESDAY
We Are Ambassadors

Now then, we are ambassadors for Christ, as though God were pleading through us: we implore you on Christ's behalf, be reconciled to God. For He made Him who knew no sin to be sin for us, that we might become the righteousness of God in Him.

2 CORINTHIANS 5:20–21

During revival events around the country, I often say the most important thing you can do is to know that you are saved. Not be 98 percent sure, but know with confidence that there was a time in your life that you repented of your sins and asked the Lord to come into your heart. The second most important thing is to know all of those around you are saved: your family, friends, coworkers, and even casual contacts.

We are His ambassadors! We are His representation here on earth. We should intentionally and enthusiastically share His story and His love with a lost and dying world. When lost people hear the gospel, they understand hope and redemption are possible. What would we think of an ambassador who was appointed to represent our country to another nation, but he was lazy, selfish, and ineffective in his representation for the nation? In the same way, we don't want to let God down as His ambassadors.

If you are not 100 percent sure of your salvation, you will never be an effective ambassador for Christ. You cannot compel others with confidence to a relationship with a Savior you are not sure you have. In order to be a good ambassador for God, you also have to be intentional. You must be sensitive to the opportunities the Lord puts in front of you.

....

Lord, help me today to be Your representative. Help me to recognize when I should share Your story with others. Amen.

REV. BRIAN FOSSETT, FOSSETT EVANGELISTIC MINISTRIES, DALTON, GA

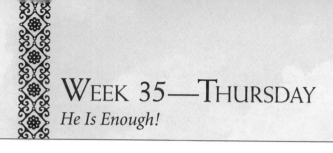

Week 35—Thursday
He Is Enough!

By the word of truth, by the power of God, by the armor of righteousness on the
right hand and on the left, by honor and dishonor, by evil report and good report; as
deceivers, and yet true; as unknown, and yet well known; as dying, and behold we live;
as chastened, and yet not killed; as sorrowful, yet always rejoicing; as poor, yet making
many rich; as having nothing, and yet possessing all things.

2 Corinthians 6:7–10

One of the greatest aspects of one's relationship with Jesus is having confidence in Him. He will provide, protect, guide, and love us. We always need to remain steadfast in believing He has the best for us. We cannot let the world, circumstances, or conditions overwhelm us.

No matter our struggles, problems, or situations, the Lord can handle them. He cares for us. When we are in a valley, He is right there with us. Learning to be content, happy, and full of joy in all circumstances is having full trust in the Lord for all things; this kind of mindset comes with a mature faith.

Our commitment, devotion, belief, and trust in Him are anchored in our love for Him. There are many fans when their teams are in the championship, but few that are committed fully when their teams are in a slump. Sometimes we can have a personal slump when we face vocational, relational, or financial difficulties. But no matter the situation, He is enough. He is all we need.

....

Lord Jesus, thank You for all You do. Thank You for Your protection, provision,
and love. Thank You for peace, favor, and all the blessings You bestow on me.
Most of all, thank You for my salvation. Today lead me, guide me, and help me
to be content and full of Your joy in all things. Amen.

Week 35—Friday
Oh, It's On Now!

For the weapons of our warfare are not carnal but mighty in God for pulling down strongholds, casting down arguments and every high thing that exalts itself against the knowledge of God, bringing every thought into captivity to the obedience of Christ.

2 Corinthians 10:4–5

You have probably heard people say, "Oh, it's on now!" when they realize someone has waged war against them. But some fights are spiritual fights. There is a war waging every day! I have heard people say they believe in angels, but not demons. You cannot believe in one without the other. Pretending spiritual conflict is not happening all around you does not make it any less real. It just leaves you ill-prepared.

The best preparation is prayer and knowing your Bible. Pray that the Lord gives you spiritual insight, timing, and wisdom. Pray that He gives you the words to say and the proper attitude to have while facing each day. Before barnstorming a situation you should ask: "How would the Lord have me handle this? What would the Lord have me say?" Always pray for the strongholds and walls Satan has built to be torn down. You should pray specifically and without ceasing.

If you will utilize these suggestions, then you will be better prepared for battle.

Lord, use me as Your instrument to strengthen others. Help me to resolve conflict. Help me live a life that brings glory to You. Give me wisdom and insight. Tear down the walls Satan has built between my family members, church members, and friends. In Jesus' name, amen.

REV. BRIAN FOSSETT, FOSSETT EVANGELISTIC MINISTRIES, DALTON, GA

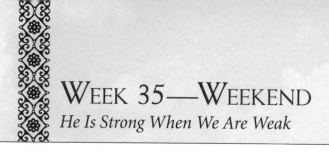

Week 35—Weekend
He Is Strong When We Are Weak

And He said to me, "My grace is sufficient for you, for My strength is made perfect in weakness." Therefore most gladly I will rather boast in my infirmities, that the power of Christ may rest upon me. Therefore I take pleasure in infirmities, in reproaches, in needs, in persecutions, in distresses, for Christ's sake. For when I am weak, then I am strong.

2 Corinthians 12:9–10

We need to understand our constant need for God. One of the biggest mistakes we can make is to think we are self-sufficient. We need God's love, wisdom, instruction, and fellowship every day. When we are at our weakest, lowest, or most broken, that is when the Lord's grace and power can shine through our lives the brightest.

We should never be embarrassed to need God. Rather, we should be embarrassed when we think we do not need God.

One of the most common excuses people give for not coming to church is, "I don't want to be with all those hypocrites." I respond by saying, "You go to the ballfield with us and grocery store with us. You might as well come to church with us." I usually get a laugh at that point, but it's true. No one is living 100 percent of what they know 100 percent of the time, which qualifies us all as hypocrites occasionally.

We need to have total dependence on the Lord. Being too proud to admit our need for Him in our lives is really to be ashamed of Him. Denying the need for His power in our lives works only to our peril.

Lord, today I recognize my deep need for You in every area of my life. Amen.

WEEK 36—MONDAY
The Perfect Recipe

Now I pray to God that you do no evil, not that we should appear approved, but that you should do what is honorable, though we may seem disqualified. For we can do nothing against the truth, but for the truth. For we are glad when we are weak and you are strong. And this also we pray, that you may be made complete.

2 CORINTHIANS 13:7–9

Paul challenged the church of Corinth never to forget the *why* when dealing with the *what*. He wanted the church to have the perfect recipe for growth. A growing relationship with Christ has a precise recipe! It reminds us that devotion can't endure without discipline . . . and discipline is empty without devotion.

A daily relationship with God requires discipline (praying, reading the Scriptures, and so forth) to help you endure difficult seasons. When the valleys of life come, these disciplines will help you sustain your connection with Him. But you must be careful not to forget the heart behind the discipline. In other words, always remember *why* you started the discipline in the first place. Then be purposeful and invest your heart, mind, and body in it.

Great faith requires a strong combination of devotion and discipline. Too much discipline won't allow you to experience the sweet, heartfelt moments with God, while devotion without discipline could lead to unhappiness.

....

Father, help me to find the right routine and discipline that will keep me growing closer to You. Allow me always to remember why I need to spend time with You every day. You have my best intentions in mind, and You always seek to work in and through me. Thank You that I can come to You every day and share my heart. In Jesus' name, amen.

WEEK 36—TUESDAY
Anchored

I have been crucified with Christ; it is no longer I who live, but Christ lives in me; and the life which I now live in the flesh I live by faith in the Son of God, who loved me and gave Himself for me. I do not set aside the grace of God; for if righteousness comes through the law, then Christ died in vain.

GALATIANS 2:20–21

After completing a closet renovation in my house, I took all my clothes and hung them up on my newly installed masterpiece. A few moments later, I heard a loud crash, and I found that my triumph had collapsed! The new closet system had hung on two anchor brackets that gave way under the weight. The whole system was destroyed when the support brackets failed.

This illustration can be applied to our faith in Jesus Christ. The apostle Paul reminded the church of Galatia that their relationship with God depended on their faith in Jesus Christ. The faith of the Jewish people once hung upon the Law of Moses, but now because of Christ, that faith rested upon Jesus, who Himself had fulfilled the Law.

Our faith anchors upon two important commands from Jesus: to love God and to love people. The rest of the Law hangs on these two commands. If we focus on fulfilling these two commands, we will fulfill all the laws God has given us, and then show that it is no longer we who live, but Christ who lives within us. If not, our relationships with God will collapse because they are not anchored to the correct support.

Father, help me each day to love You and Your people more. Keep me anchored to Your Son. Amen.

WEEK 36—WEDNESDAY
Interdependent

For you are all sons of God through faith in Christ Jesus. For as many of you as were baptized into Christ have put on Christ. There is neither Jew nor Greek, there is neither slave nor free, there is neither male nor female; for you are all one in Christ Jesus. And if you are Christ's, then you are Abraham's seed, and heirs according to the promise.

GALATIANS 3:26–29

I grew up playing team sports, and I was known as a very competitive, driven person. I was pretty independent, priding myself on being prepared and not wanting to depend on anyone else. As the teams I was on became more competitive, I soon realized that independence on a team was lonely and unsuccessful.

The apostle Paul reminded each of us that God doesn't want us to be independent. He wants us to be interdependent. God designed each of us to lean on Him and one another. By breaking down the walls of denomination and class, Paul reminded us that we were never meant to do life alone.

In fact, if you find yourself struggling today, ask yourself the question, "Whom am I depending upon to help me through?" If the answer is no one, then you are not living the interdependent life God desires of you. If you don't have a church to call home, or if you are acting independently of it, then maybe it's time to break down the walls of pride and take your first step today.

Remember, a great team is never lonely. By banding together with other believers, you can do immeasurably more than you ever thought possible.

....

God, may I remember today that I'm not alone and can depend both on You and others to accomplish Your will. Amen.

Week 36—Thursday
Imprint

For you, brethren, have been called to liberty; only do not use liberty as an opportunity for the flesh, but through love serve one another. For all the law is fulfilled in one word, even in this: "You shall love your neighbor as yourself." But if you bite and devour one another, beware lest you be consumed by one another!

GALATIANS 5:13–15

The fingerprint is one of God's smallest yet most amazing creations. Did you know that even identical twins have different sets of fingerprints? These unique signatures don't ever change, and they leave an imprint on all they touch.

It could be that God gave us fingerprints to remind us of how special we are. They could also be reminders of how we leave an imprint of ourselves on others. What kinds of impression are we leaving on others? When we reach out to people, what do they experience? Jesus commanded us to love our neighbors as ourselves. If Christ is the definition of unconditional love, then we are to be examples of Christ to others. In other words, we are to leave behind imprints of Christ wherever we go!

As you go about your day, ask yourself: "What kind of impression am I leaving behind? Do the people with whom I interact see Jesus?" Remember, you have the privilege of leaving an imprint of Jesus wherever you go.

Jesus, may I leave an impression of Your love every day on others. Help me to inspire people to the kind of love You show me. Amen.

WEEK 36—FRIDAY
We Can't Do It Alone

I say then: Walk in the Spirit, and you shall not fulfill the lust of the flesh. For the flesh lusts against the Spirit, and the Spirit against the flesh; and these are contrary to one another, so that you do not do the things that you wish. But if you are led by the Spirit, you are not under the law.

GALATIANS 5:16–18

One of the greatest moments of my life came when I was my son's Little League baseball coach. I had spent countless hours with Connor, helping him learn to hit a baseball. Then, with the game on the line, my son stepped up to the plate and hit a game-winning single! After the game, someone told him how well he had hit that ball. Without hesitating, my son said, "I didn't do it alone. My dad helped me hit it."

In our lives, we sometimes fall into the "I" mode: "I did this" or "I accomplished that." In reality, apart from Christ, we can't do anything. The Holy Spirit is Christ inside of us, and He desires to work through us to do amazing works for the kingdom of God. The Holy Spirit gives us the wisdom and confidence to succeed in all we do. When we take control of our lives away from the Spirit, we quickly get off track. It's time to stop battling the Spirit so He can accomplish great things through us.

Father, I want to listen to Your Spirit today so You may complete stunning feats for Your kingdom. Help me to stop battling You so others can see You through me. Amen.

REV. TERRY SCALZITTI, OCEAN VIEW BAPTIST CHURCH, MYRTLE BEACH, SC

WEEK 36—WEEKEND
Huggers

But the fruit of the Spirit is love, joy, peace, longsuffering, kindness, goodness, faithfulness, gentleness, self-control. Against such there is no law. And those who are Christ's have crucified the flesh with its passions and desires. If we live in the Spirit, let us also walk in the Spirit.

GALATIANS 5:22–25

In both churches I have pastored, I have been blessed with a designated hugger. These individuals would hug everyone who came to our church, and every Sunday they would look to give me a "holy hug." I often noticed their hugs brought smiles to everyone they touched—even those who found it hard to smile at all! Those holy hugs would break through anyone's bad day, showering the fruit of the Spirit to all they touched.

Many look at these huggers and can't imagine doing what they do. They might think it's kind of odd. But I think these huggers actually get it: they live and walk in the Spirit each day, showing love, peace, joy, and goodness to everyone they meet. Maybe we could learn a lesson from these huggers.

Too often we hear more negative comments than positive ones. Maybe we could start changing our family, church, and community if we started walking more in the Spirit. Maybe we need to start hugging a little more. Maybe we need to start with kind words; a kind word or smile might just change the lives of those around us.

··

God, help me to stand out. I want people to see You in me each day and to experience the fruit of the Spirit every time they see me. Amen.

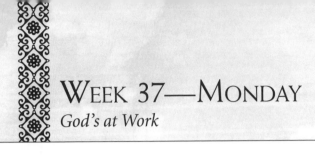

Week 37—Monday
God's at Work

Blessed be the God and Father of our Lord Jesus Christ, who has blessed us with every spiritual blessing in the heavenly places in Christ, just as He chose us in Him before the foundation of the world, that we should be holy and without blame before Him in love.

EPHESIANS 1:3–4

As followers of Christ, we are a package deal. In other words, we are tied together spiritually, mentally, and physically. Nothing happens in one area that doesn't impact the others. Paul here declared that even before time began, God already saw what we were capable of becoming for His glory. Like the father of a newborn who stands at the nursery window, our heavenly Father envisions great plans for us as He looks down from glory upon us.

Our spiritual rebirth launched us into that divine plan for the ages. Every single one of us has the Spirit-driven ability to follow God's original plans. Though we stumble at times, the Father's plans are still in place and each of us can discover and fulfill those heavenly blueprints.

Everything we are capable of becoming starts and stops with God. He believes in us and is at work in us. We are wonderfully blessed and highly favored of the Lord. Let's never forget it.

....

Heavenly Father, help me realize that You are at work and I will be under construction continually until I am at home in glory. Amen.

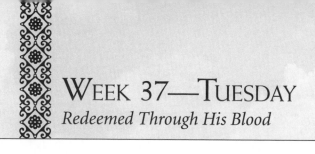

WEEK 37—TUESDAY
Redeemed Through His Blood

In Him we have redemption through His blood, the forgiveness of sins, according to the riches of His grace which He made to abound toward us in all wisdom and prudence, having made known to us the mystery of His will, according to His good pleasure which He purposed in Himself, that in the dispensation of the fullness of the times He might gather together in one all things in Christ, both which are in heaven and which are on earth—in Him.

EPHESIANS 1:7–10

Fanny Crosby wrote one of my favorite hymns of all time. It begins with these words: "Redeemed, how I love to proclaim it! / Redeemed by the blood of the Lamb; / Redeemed through His infinite mercy, / His child and forever I am."

Every now and then I get those words and the tune of the hymn in my mind and sing out for all it's worth. To think God would take me as I am and then "according to the riches of His grace" see me as though I've never sinned a day in my life just overwhelms my soul. These verses in Ephesians declare that God forgives purely out of His love and compassion for us. None of us deserves it. That's what grace is about, and that makes me want to shout!

Our forgiveness, however, came at a great cost to the Father. We should never take that declaration lightly. Whenever we enter a worship service and the preacher or song leader emphasizes the significance of the blood of Christ, something inside us ought to react in heartfelt praise to God. We must never take for granted what was required of Jesus to redeem us.

··

Father, please help me daily not to take the blood of Christ for granted. Amen.

WEEK 37—WEDNESDAY
Deposit Guaranteed

In Him you also trusted, after you heard the word of truth, the gospel of your salvation; in whom also, having believed, you were sealed with the Holy Spirit of promise, who is the guarantee of our inheritance until the redemption of the purchased possession, to the praise of His glory.

EPHESIANS 1:13–14

When my family moved to Mississippi when I was young, my mother went to work for a bank called Deposit Guaranty National Bank. Though that bank does not exist any longer, I believe its name summarized what current banks proclaim. If we place an investment in a bank, the bank guarantees that the investment is safe.

To this day I think about my mother's bank when I come across these verses in my Bible. When Christ saves us, He seals that salvation decision with the same Holy Spirit that was present when God created the world. In other words, Christ secures and guarantees our salvation. His power is unmatched by any and all threats—even our own sin.

There will always be those who struggle with the doctrine of eternal security, but I am not one of them. When God says in His Word that He will do what He says, I can take it to the bank. I am committed to the FDIC (Forever Depending In Christ).

Father, thank You that my salvation is all about Your holding on to me and not the other way around. Amen.

WEEK 37—THURSDAY
A Picture of Grace

But God, who is rich in mercy, because of His great love with which He loved us, even when we were dead in trespasses, made us alive together with Christ (by grace you have been saved), and raised us up together, and made us sit together in the heavenly places in Christ Jesus.

EPHESIANS 2:4–6

The resurrection of Lazarus in John 11 intrigues me greatly. John did not record what caused his death. All the Bible tells us is that he was sick. After being informed of Lazarus' sickness, Jesus purposely delayed going to His friend's side, for He knew the Father had a plan. Jesus knew a miracle would take place so the Son of God would receive glory.

In our passage from Ephesians 2, Paul declared that "we were dead in trespasses." Metaphorically speaking, we were like Lazarus when our sins separated us from God—we were wrapped up and put away in death. Prior to our salvation, our sins drove us away from the presence of God until He did something to rescue us.

That, dear friends, is the story of grace. Before coming to the saving knowledge of Christ, we were completely helpless to do anything about our condition. Similar to Lazarus, we were helpless. But praise be to God! When we responded to the gospel, Jesus set us free from spiritual death and bondage.

....

Thank You, Father, for raising me to new life in You. Amen.

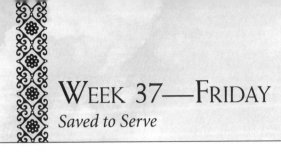

WEEK 37—FRIDAY
Saved to Serve

For by grace you have been saved through faith, and that not of yourselves; it is the gift of God, not of works, lest anyone should boast. For we are His workmanship, created in Christ Jesus for good works, which God prepared beforehand that we should walk in them.

EPHESIANS 2:8–10

It has been a while since I have visited our local swimming pool. But I fondly remember the last time I was there. While at the pool, I saw two brothers competing against one another on the diving board. One would get more daring than the other in what he tried to accomplish, only to have his brother improve on the dive. The competition escalated when their mom came looking for them. Then all I could hear was, "Look at me!" or "Watch me!" The mother seemed more nervous than entertained.

God didn't save us so we could sit around; He wants us to serve. If Christians are not careful, some might be tempted to boast, "Look at me!" when they serve in the church. At the same time, those who are more gifted to serve behind the scenes might be tempted not to do anything since no one notices.

All of us are to be workers for Him. God also intends for us to carry out our ministry of good works without regard for what others may think. God notices our service for His kingdom, and that is all that matters.

Lord, thank You for calling me into service. Help me to work hard for Your kingdom and not care about what others might think. Amen.

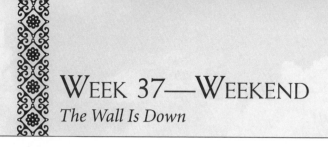

WEEK 37—WEEKEND
The Wall Is Down

For He Himself is our peace, who has made both one, and has broken down the middle wall of separation, having abolished in His flesh the enmity, that is, the law of commandments contained in ordinances, so as to create in Himself one new man from the two, thus making peace.

EPHESIANS 2:14–15

I have several dear Jewish friends. Two of them believe Christ to be the much-awaited Messiah. The others do not. My Jewish friends who are believers share in the hope of what a mutual faith in Christ offers. They live in Israel, where we visited them recently and plan to again in the future. Our friendship and love for one another are on a very deep level.

My other Jewish friends and I share stories of our families and we love each other, but not with the same bond. The apostle Paul, in today's passage, made it clear that Christ has in fact joined both Gentiles and Jews through satisfying the requirements of the law by His death, burial, and resurrection. Peace now exists between the Father and a believer when Christ becomes his or her Savior and Lord—regardless of whether he or she is a Jew or Gentile.

With God's help, I hope one day to be able to reach my unbelieving Jewish friends with the gospel message. Then we can share the same love that believers in Christ share.

....

Father, I know Christ is the great Reconciler. Help me to reach those who don't believe in You. Amen.

WEEK 38—MONDAY
The Greatest Gift

For this reason I bow my knees to the Father of our Lord Jesus Christ, from whom the whole family in heaven and earth is named, that He would grant you, according to the riches of His glory, to be strengthened with might through His Spirit in the inner man.

EPHESIANS 3:14–16

What is the greatest gift you've ever received? Most followers of Jesus would be quick to say their salvation. I would certainly agree with this answer, but let's dig a bit deeper and see why it is the greatest gift.

An amazing benefit of salvation is the indwelling of God's own Spirit in the life of one who has trusted Jesus as Savior. Jesus told His disciples He did not want to leave them without a Helper to guide them. He told them to wait on the Holy Spirit and they would be His witnesses throughout the world. Before the indwelling of the Holy Spirit, Jesus' disciples were afraid. After they received the Holy Spirit, the same disciples changed the world through the power of the gospel.

God does not ask us to follow Him in our own strength but through His Spirit working in us. We do not face the challenges of this world all alone. The same Spirit who indwelt the disciples as they turned the world upside down is the same Spirit who indwells Jesus' followers today. We must stop trying to fight our battles in our own strength and instead rely upon the greatest gift ever given to the world. Through God's forgiveness, we have His Spirit within us.

....

Father in heaven, forgive me when I seek to live in my own power and fail to remember that Your Spirit dwells within me. Thank You for this marvelous gift. Amen.

DR. MARTY JACUMIN, BAY LEAF BAPTIST CHURCH, RALEIGH, NC

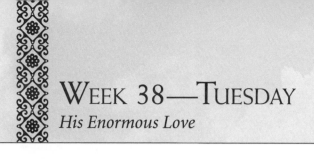

Week 38—Tuesday
His Enormous Love

That Christ may dwell in your hearts through faith; that you, being rooted and grounded in love, may be able to comprehend with all the saints what is the width and length and depth and height—to know the love of Christ which passes knowledge; that you may be filled with all the fullness of God.

EPHESIANS 3:17–19

We have a fairly large church facility that has gone through numerous additions over the past forty years. As new people come into our church, I often hear them say it's hard to remember how to get to and from the various locations. Perhaps they try to get to the worship center but they end up in the fellowship hall or gymnasium. I always tell them that I remember facing the same challenges when my family first arrived here. I also tell them to be encouraged, knowing the more time they spend here the easier it will be to find their way. I sometimes follow up with people to remind them of their comments. They usually laugh and tell me they now know where everything is.

How can we understand the love God has for us? The Bible describes that love as something that passes human understanding. Our text for today reminds us we are to be rooted and grounded in love so we may come to an understanding of the enormous love God has for us. Just as people become more familiar with our church facility as they spend more time there, we become more rooted in God's love as we spend time in fellowship with Him. We do that by studying His Word and talking with Him in prayer. If we abide with Him daily, we will come to understand the love of God more fully.

....

Father, thank You for Your amazing love. Amen.

WEEK 38—WEDNESDAY
The Wrong Mirror

Now to Him who is able to do exceedingly abundantly above all that we ask or think, according to the power that works in us, to Him be glory in the church by Christ Jesus to all generations, forever and ever. Amen.

EPHESIANS 3:20–21

When I was a young boy, I loved going to the carnival. One of my favorite attractions was the fun house. I loved the room that contained the different mirrors that distorted the way I looked. There was a mirror that made me look tall and thin and another that made me look short and wide. Regardless of how many mirrors distorted my reflection, I knew that's not how I really looked.

I meet Christians who have a distorted reflection of who they are in Christ. When they look in the mirror, they don't see people God can use to do something amazing. Our text for today reminds us we serve a Savior who is able to do exceedingly and abundantly more than we could ask or think. He is able to do this because of His limitless power.

The beautiful fact is God displays His power through His followers. We may look in the mirror and see people who look too young or too old to be used by God, but we must never doubt what God can do through us if we desire to follow Him.

As we remember this wonderful promise of God, let's make sure we praise God for the work He desires to do through us. He chooses to work through our lives because of His wonderful grace.

....

Lord, I praise You for Your power and might. Help me to trust what You are able to do if I surrender to You. Amen.

DR. MARTY JACUMIN, BAY LEAF BAPTIST CHURCH, RALEIGH, NC

WEEK 38—THURSDAY
The Little Troublemaker

Let no corrupt word proceed out of your mouth, but what is good for necessary edification, that it may impart grace to the hearers. And do not grieve the Holy Spirit of God, by whom you were sealed for the day of redemption.

EPHESIANS 4:29–30

I named today's devotion "The Little Troublemaker" because it speaks about the tongue. Our tongues certainly are not large parts of our body, but they tend to get us in trouble. Worse than that, our text reminds us, we can grieve the Spirit of God. This is a sobering thought.

We can use our words to share the gospel, so our tongues can be great tools for the kingdom of God. Yet today's passage reminds us that our tongues can also be used in a negative way. Oftentimes we use our tongues to tear one another down or to say words that do not build up God's kingdom.

The book of James says the tongue is like a wild horse that needs to be bridled (James 3:3). If we tend to speak when we are angry, we need to learn to control the words coming out of our mouths. It's not impossible to speak edifying words when we are angry, but we must be disciplined to do so.

I have found that it's much better to walk away and not say anything at all than to use the tongue in a way that dishonors the Lord. In our lives we will confront people who hurt us, but let's always do so in a way that honors our Savior and does not tear down His kingdom.

··

Father, remind me today of the power of the tongue. Lord, I pray that nothing corrupt would come out of my mouth but only words that reflect You and build up Your kingdom. Amen.

WEEK 38—FRIDAY
Don't Forget the Light

For you were once darkness, but now you are light in the Lord. Walk as children of light (for the fruit of the Spirit is in all goodness, righteousness, and truth), finding out what is acceptable to the Lord. And have no fellowship with the unfruitful works of darkness, but rather expose them.

EPHESIANS 5:8–11

I was recently reminded of how important light can be in a dark place. Woods surround our home and a pond is directly behind us. Because of where we are located, we are blessed to see an abundance of wild animals. One night I was taking our dogs outside before turning in for the evening. As I walked out our back door, one of the dogs stopped right in front of me. A small amount of light came from a window, and I was able to look past the dog and see why she had stopped. Right in front of her were three copperhead snakes. Had she not stopped, I would have stepped right on top of them.

Our text today reminds us that as Christ followers, we are no longer stuck in darkness, but we are actually reflections of God's light in the world. Thus we are no longer to have darkness as part of our lives; rather, we are to expose it, repent of it, and walk in a way that pleases the Lord.

Are there things in our lives that God would see as darkness? Are there sins in our lives that we need to repent of? Let's ask God to strengthen us and help us walk worthy of the sacrifice He has made for each of us.

....

Lord, thank You that I no longer have to walk in darkness but that I am blessed to be able to walk in Your light. Help me to reflect Your light in this dark world. I know that darkness is dangerous both physically and spiritually. Help me to impact the darkness by walking in Your light. Amen.

DR. MARTY JACUMIN, BAY LEAF BAPTIST CHURCH, RALEIGH, NC

Week 38—Weekend
Raise Your Voice

See then that you walk circumspectly, not as fools but as wise, redeeming the time, because the days are evil. Therefore do not be unwise, but understand what the will of the Lord is. And do not be drunk with wine, in which is dissipation; but be filled with the Spirit.

EPHESIANS 5:15–18

Recently I was traveling home from a conference on the West Coast. I settled into my seat and quickly began talking with the gentleman sitting beside me. Before the plane took off, the man ordered a mixed drink. During the flight back to the East Coast, we continued to converse and he continued to order cocktails. I noticed the more alcohol he consumed, the louder he spoke. When we first sat down together, he had been speaking rather quietly, but by the time we landed, he almost seemed to be shouting. He was not angry—he just seemed to have lost his volume control.

We live in a sinful world, but we are to redeem the time we have in this world. Paul exhorted us not to be drunk with wine but to be filled with the Spirit. We can certainly understand Paul's warning about being drunk with alcohol. It not only hurts our witness, it inhibits our effectiveness in sharing the gospel with others. Instead, if we are filled with God's Spirit, the message of His kingdom will naturally overflow. The more the Spirit fills us, the more we will share what Christ has done in our lives.

Just as the man sitting beside me spoke louder and louder the more he was filled with alcohol, so we will speak louder and louder the more we are filled with God's Spirit.

....

Father, give me the boldness to proclaim Your name. Amen.

Week 39—Monday
The Joy of Love and Marriage

Husbands, love your wives, just as Christ also loved the church and gave Himself for her, that He might sanctify and cleanse her with the washing of water by the word, that He might present her to Himself a glorious church, not having spot or wrinkle or any such thing, but that she should be holy and without blemish. So husbands ought to love their own wives as their own bodies; he who loves his wife loves himself.

EPHESIANS 5:25–28

Conflict is nowhere more inevitable than in marriage. The oldest and most intense battle in the world is the one between the sexes. In today's text Paul explained how to exhibit true love in order to nurture a healthy marriage.

Never has there been a word that needs an explanation as much as does the word *love*. Our culture so often misuses it. Love is used to describe everything from sexual passion to affinity for our favorite coffee. In Ephesians 5, Paul did not merely say, "Love your wives, just as Christ loved the church," but he actually explained what that love involves: "and [He] gave Himself for her." That is what biblical love is! It is sacrificial!

No husband plays his proper role in marriage until he learns to give sacrificially for his wife, to open his heart to her, to share his emotions and dreams, his thoughts and disappointments, and his joys. He must put her needs above his own. Moreover, nothing makes a woman happier than knowing she means something in her husband's life. That fulfills her, and it fulfills him.

Dear Jesus, please help me to love my spouse in a way that honors You as well. In Jesus' name, amen!

TIM ANDERSON, CLEMENTS BAPTIST CHURCH, ATHENS, AL

Week 39—Tuesday
Be Strong in the Lord

Finally, my brethren, be strong in the Lord and in the power of His might. Put on the whole armor of God, that you may be able to stand against the wiles of the devil.

Ephesians 6:10–11

From the womb to the tomb, life is hard. Our souls, our minds, our families, and our careers are all grounds for conflict. Not until God casts the devil into the eternal lake of fire will the world be at peace.

Maybe we are strong individuals, and maybe we can handle lots of pressure and keep up demanding hours, on and off the job. But we all become weary at times and need strength. The most important strength we need is that of the Lord. True Christian strength is not found in the body; it is found in the Spirit.

Paul also talked about how we need to gird ourselves in the armor of God so we can defeat the devil. The armor of God comprises the belt of truth, the breastplate of righteousness, shoes shod with the gospel of peace, the shield of faith, the helmet of salvation, and the sword of the Spirit, which is the Word of God. This armor is invincible because we receive the equipment from Christ Himself.

We must realize that part of Satan's plan for believers is to make us weary. But God wants us to be encouraged and realize we are more than conquerors in Jesus Christ.

Dear Jesus, I refuse to allow Satan to make me a weary Christian. I will dress in the armor of God each day. Amen.

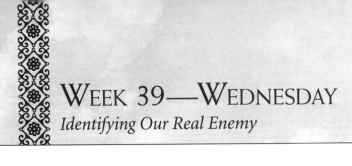

WEEK 39—WEDNESDAY
Identifying Our Real Enemy

For we do not wrestle against flesh and blood, but against principalities, against powers, against the rulers of the darkness of this age, against spiritual hosts of wickedness in the heavenly places. Therefore take up the whole armor of God, that you may be able to withstand in the evil day, and having done all, to stand.

EPHESIANS 6:12–13

All of us face challenges, battles, and various circumstances. We are all in need of help in different areas of our lives, and we are not always sure from whence it will come.

Many believers today deal with serious hardships. We all know people who have lost their jobs, their health, their wealth, and their loved ones. Many senior adults struggle with constant concern about how to cover the cost of medicine and doctor visits in addition to simple things such as food and shelter. Many dangers in the world threaten us daily, but our biggest enemy is unseen. In fact Paul said we are not at war with flesh and blood, but with the enemy of our souls. We must not be confused about who the real enemy is.

If we are Christians, we are in a real battle. No neutrality exists in this area. We must never underestimate the devil. He is as real as the God who saved us. But he is not as strong!

I believe as we get closer to the end of time the heat of the battle will increase for all believers. Yet James 4:7 says, "Therefore submit to God. Resist the devil and he will flee from you." We don't have to fight the devil on our own! God is with us every step of the way if we submit to Him.

....

Dear Jesus, my deep desire is to walk faithfully in Your sight. Amen.

TIM ANDERSON, CLEMENTS BAPTIST CHURCH, ATHENS, AL

WEEK 39—THURSDAY
Stand in Truth

Stand therefore, having girded your waist with truth, having put on the breastplate of righteousness, and having shod your feet with the preparation of the gospel of peace.

EPHESIANS 6:14–15

As Christians, we must learn that when we stay in the Word of God and spend time with the Holy Spirit, we begin to act like David when he faced Goliath. We begin to take a stand against the enemy. As soldiers of the cross, you and I are not supposed to be afraid of our enemy, the devil. He must be treated as a defeated foe. Yet all of us are afraid at times, and we occasionally battle with the spirit of fear. But rather than running away to hide, we can choose to be as bold as a lion in Jesus Christ.

"Having girded your waist with truth" in Paul's day referred to the section of Roman armor that usually housed the sword; therefore, it was essential. The belt also helped keep the other parts of the armor secure. If the belt was lost, a soldier was in big trouble. The truth of the Scriptures will protect us and enable us to defeat our foes. Paul also talked about wearing the "breastplate of righteousness" and "the gospel of peace" on our shoes. Both of these objects also protect the Christian soldier in battle, just as they did a Roman soldier in Paul's day.

. . . .

Dear Jesus, please help me to keep my eyes on You. I desire to fight the enemy with the proper tools You have given me. Amen.

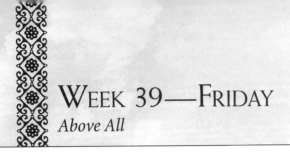

WEEK 39—FRIDAY
Above All

Above all, [take] the shield of faith with which you will be able to quench all the fiery darts of the wicked one. And take the helmet of salvation, and the sword of the Spirit, which is the word of God; praying always with all prayer and supplication in the Spirit, being watchful to this end with all perseverance and supplication for all the saints.

EPHESIANS 6:16–18

"Above all" introduces the last three pieces of armor. Disciples of Jesus Christ are often laughed at or made fun of. This is exactly why the shield of faith is so important. What are some of the objects the shield of faith has to guard us from? Certainly doubt and fear are among the largest. They can create uncertainty for all of us, and the shield of faith protects us from them.

The very fact the helmet is related to salvation indicates that Satan's blows are directed at the believer's security and assurance in Jesus Christ. Satan often points out past failures and sins to the believer. The helmet of salvation is important because it keeps the Christian safe from doubts.

Paul next mentioned the sword of the Spirit, which is the Word of God. Pastor and writer Thomas Guthrie said, "The Bible is an armory of heavenly weapons, a laboratory of infallible medicines, and a mine of exhaustless wealth. It is a guidebook for every road, a chart for every sea, a medicine for every malady, and a balm for every wound." Thus the Bible is an essential weapon for Christians as it performs a variety of functions.

All of these weapons are strengthened by prayer. When a Christian has the shield of faith, the helmet of salvation, the sword of the Spirit, and the weapon of prayer, he or she is ready for spiritual battle.

....

Dear Jesus, I pray I become and remain a good soldier in Your army. Amen.

TIM ANDERSON, CLEMENTS BAPTIST CHURCH, ATHENS, AL

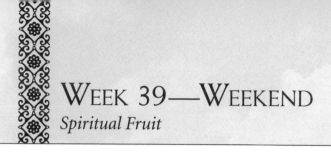

WEEK 39—WEEKEND
Spiritual Fruit

And this I pray, that your love may abound still more and more in knowledge and all discernment, that you may approve the things that are excellent, that you may be sincere and without offense till the day of Christ, being filled with the fruits of righteousness which are by Jesus Christ, to the glory and praise of God.

PHILIPPIANS 1:9–11

One of the primary reasons God saved us was so we might become fruitful and productive disciples. He did not save us just so we could go to heaven when we die; rather, He wanted the character of Jesus Christ reproduced in us. We are to live *in* the flesh but not *of* the flesh. We are to let our lights shine before others so they may see our good works and glorify our Father.

Our Lord has saved us by grace, He has a plan for our lives, and He has ordained that we walk in good works while waiting on His return. God is somewhat like a father who is raising a large family. He is pleased to have the family, and He is delighted we are members of it. But He is not satisfied with our only being in His family. He also wants us to grow up to be good citizens. Spiritually speaking, He wants productive children who accomplish great works for His kingdom.

Paul's deep desire was to walk in a manner worthy of the Lord, and he wanted to bear fruit that would always remain—even after his life on earth was over. We should have the same desire as Paul.

Dear Jesus, my deep desire is to bring You joy and to produce spiritual fruit that grows from my walk with You. Amen.

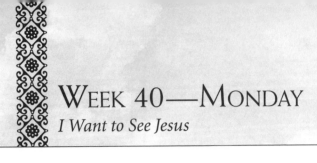

WEEK 40—MONDAY
I Want to See Jesus

For to me, to live is Christ, and to die is gain. But if I live on in the flesh, this will mean fruit from my labor; yet what I shall choose I cannot tell. For I am hard-pressed between the two, having a desire to depart and be with Christ, which is far better.

PHILIPPIANS 1:21–23

My wife and I have the same conversation on a regular basis: she often tells me she is ready to see Jesus. It's not that she doesn't want to be around me (I hope), around her family and friends, or even to deal with the pressures of life. Rather, our conversations always conclude with a reminder that the Scriptures tell of the joys that will be in heaven as we worship God.

As Christians who know what lies ahead for us, we can long for that time with God. But we must understand His timing is perfect and we have been given the task to tell the gospel with our lives and words. Thus we can use this passage in Philippians as a reminder to keep about the Father's business while keeping the promise of heaven in the backs of our minds.

Father, I pray You will continue to use me in spreading the gospel. Though life can be hard, the promise of spending eternity with You encourages me to press on. I want to see how many people I can point to You in the time You have given me to be a mirror of Your grace, love, and mercy. Thank You for Jesus and for loving me. Amen.

REV. DAVID RICHARDSON, FIRST BAPTIST CHURCH, CREEDMOOR, NC

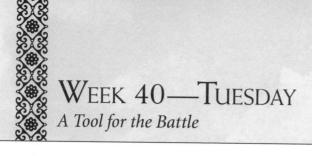

WEEK 40—TUESDAY
A Tool for the Battle

Only let your conduct be worthy of the gospel of Christ, so that whether I come and see you or am absent, I may hear of your affairs, that you stand fast in one spirit, with one mind striving together for the faith of the gospel, and not in any way terrified by your adversaries, which is to them a proof of perdition, but to you of salvation, and that from God.

PHILIPPIANS 1:27–28

I recently read an article that explained how Japanese sword makers produce the finest and strongest swords in the world. They have perfected a technique that uses more than thirty thousand layers of both hard and soft steel. If they were to use just one type of steel, the sword would either shatter when used or become dull very quickly. This is similar to how God uses the "hard steel" of His Word combined with the "soft steel" of our dependence on God to form us into strong tools of the gospel.

Paul reminded us that as tools of the gospel we are on display to the world as a gauge of the effectiveness of the gospel. We should strive to use our lives as practical applications of what God is doing in and through us. We always should speak the truth of the gospel. We should make sure our conduct and our lives point to the Christ who died for us.

Father, help me be strong and conduct myself in such a way that the world sees, not my love for You, but Your love for me because You are always faithful—even when I am not. Thank You for crafting me into a tool You will use to further the gospel. Amen.

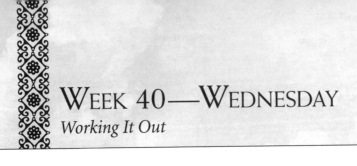

WEEK 40—WEDNESDAY
Working It Out

Therefore, my beloved, as you have always obeyed, not as in my presence only, but now much more in my absence, work out your own salvation with fear and trembling; for it is God who works in you both to will and to do for His good pleasure.

PHILIPPIANS 2:12–13

D o you remember being in school when your teacher was absent and a substitute was there? Often chaos ensued and the students forgot they were supposed to be learning. If this scenario played out, more than likely the returning teacher would talk to the class about his or her disappointment in the way the class acted while he or she was away.

In today's text, Paul did the opposite of what the teacher probably did in your class. Paul commended the Philippians for their faithfulness, not just when he was there leading them, but even when he was not there. The Philippians' faith, and ultimately their behavior, was not tied to Paul but to God, which is how it should be.

Brothers and sisters, I encourage you to work out your own salvation, not tied to any person, but to God. You will experience God more fully as you grow, learn, and encourage others through the testimony you build. Each day God will give you the opportunity to apply biblical truth to your life and situations. As you gain knowledge of truth, you will understand and see God's will for your life.

....

Father, help me to obey You even when others are not looking. Help me be a beacon of light, pointing others to the hope I have found in Jesus Christ. Amen.

REV. DAVID RICHARDSON, FIRST BAPTIST CHURCH, CREEDMOOR, NC

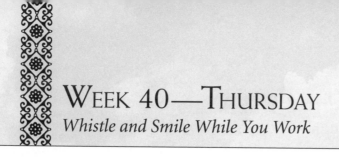

WEEK 40—THURSDAY
Whistle and Smile While You Work

*Do all things without complaining and disputing, that you may become blameless
and harmless, children of God without fault in the midst of a crooked and perverse
generation, among whom you shine as lights in the world.*

PHILIPPIANS 2:14–15

Do you remember complaining about doing chores? It may have taken
only five minutes to take out the trash, but to hear you tell it you had to
carry the trash uphill for five miles.

The Israelites had this attitude at times as well. God gave them specific
instructions, time and time again, that were ultimately for their own good.
But when they decided their ways were better, or that God was being unfair,
they suffered. Can you imagine how much your family would have suffered
if you had not taken the trash out just because you were lazy or did not think
it was a good idea?

Paul encouraged the Philippians to work for the Lord without complaining.
If they did this, they would exemplify the love of God to others. In like manner, you point to the faithfulness of God when you have a servant's heart.
When you love someone enough to lower yourself to a point of service, you
honor God and serve as an example of His love.

Wouldn't you work readily if Jesus were standing in front of you? Serve
those around you with gladness and joy.

*Father, I pray You will provide opportunities to serve others. Let me have a good
attitude and joy in my heart as I work. Amen.*

Week 40—Friday
Don't Sit on Laurel

Not that I have already attained, or am already perfected; but I press on, that I may lay hold of that for which Christ Jesus has also laid hold of me. Brethren, I do not count myself to have apprehended; but one thing I do, forgetting those things which are behind and reaching forward to those things which are ahead, I press toward the goal for the prize of the upward call of God in Christ Jesus.

PHILIPPIANS 3:12–14

As a kid, I could never figure why we were resting on Laurel. The adults said not to rest on Laurel, and that sounded like a good plan, but why would anyone want to do that? Years later I figured out what that phrase meant and was really embarrassed at all those times I was thinking we were sitting on this poor girl named Laurel.

Paul told the Philippians that even though he had achieved much through the grace of God, he had not perfected living the Christian life. If a giant like Paul understood that he would not achieve perfection in this life, it should come as no surprise to us that we will not achieve it either.

Paul often used imagery of athletics in his writing, and this passage speaks of winning the prize. The prize for the Christian is eternity with Christ and living a life that points to Him. This should be one's constant motivation.

It is often easy to look at past accomplishments and the number of people we have led to the Lord. But what we are doing to win the next person to the Lord is more important. Thus we should never sit on our laurels. We should always be looking to what lies ahead.

Lord, help me stay focused on the work to which You have called me, and let me not get blinded by my perceived past achievements. Amen.

REV. DAVID RICHARDSON, FIRST BAPTIST CHURCH, CREEDMOOR, NC

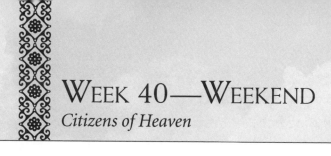

Week 40—Weekend
Citizens of Heaven

For our citizenship is in heaven, from which we also eagerly wait for the Savior, the Lord Jesus Christ, who will transform our lowly body that it may be conformed to His glorious body, according to the working by which He is able even to subdue all things to Himself.

Philippians 3:20–21

I cannot wait until we get to heaven! It flat-out excites me that we will spend eternity worshipping the Creator of the universe. Until then we must endure life on this earth—a life filled with heartache, disappointment, and tragedy because of sin. Life has its ups and downs, its relationship problems, and its frustrations.

But the Scriptures promise that if we call upon the name of Jesus and believe in Him as our Savior, we will be saved and will spend eternity in heaven. This promise guarantees that one day all of our sufferings will end, our bodies will no longer be diseased, and we will be transformed into the perfect image of God.

In this text Paul reminded his brothers and sisters that although they may have been geographical citizens of Philippi, their citizenship was ultimately in heaven. The same truth applies to all Christians today.

This news should excite you, and I hope it encourages you in your walk.

....

Father, thank You for loving me even to the point of death on a cross. Thank You for guaranteeing my citizenship in heaven, where one day I will stand before Your throne and shout, "Hosanna to the Lord!" In Jesus' name, amen.

Week 41—Monday
The Best Seat in the House

Be anxious for nothing, but in everything by prayer and supplication, with thanksgiving, let your requests be made known to God; and the peace of God, which surpasses all understanding, will guard your hearts and minds through Christ Jesus.

PHILIPPIANS 4:6–7

When my adult nephew was just a little boy, I use to carry him everywhere on my shoulders. Wherever we went, people would smile and wave at him and often ask: "How are you doing up there?"

He would always answer by saying: "I'm doing great! I have the best seat in the house!"

If Philippians 4:4 ("Rejoice in the Lord always. Again I will say rejoice") is the thesis statement of this wonderful book of joy, then today's passage has to be "the best seat in the house"!

Remember, Paul's seat as he wrote this precious letter was in a Roman prison. From that location he encouraged us to reside in the best seat in the house, the peace of our Lord Jesus Christ. Because we have this peace as Christians, we need not worry about anything.

Had he been sitting by the poolside sipping lemonade at a luxury beach resort, it would have been easy for us to say, "Look at his location! What did he have to worry about?" But Paul didn't have what the world would consider the best seat—he had the worst seat, the floor of a prison cell.

When we give everything to our Lord in prayer, the result will be the peace of God. His peace is so great it surpasses all that we could ever know or understand! His peace gives us the best seat in the house.

....

Dear Lord, I give You every concern that would tempt me to worry. Amen.

WEEK 41—TUESDAY
Not Fake News!

Finally, brethren, whatever things are true, whatever things are noble, whatever things are just, whatever things are pure, whatever things are lovely, whatever things are of good report, if there is any virtue and if there is anything praiseworthy—meditate on these things. The things which you learned and received and heard and saw in me, these do, and the God of peace will be with you.

PHILIPPIANS 4:8–9

I don't know about you, but the 2016 presidential election absolutely exhausted me. During that time we began to hear about "fake news" media outlets, which would simply frame the political narratives in order to fit their agendas. Knowing this, I often read a story or listened to a report and asked, "Is this true? Or was it drawn up and mapped out in a production meeting?"

But the accurate reporter, the apostle Paul, gave us nothing but the absolute facts. The Word of God is the genuine article!

Paul reported that it is imperative that our minds be clean before our Lord. That is a sobering report. This world throws everything at us, from every source and medium possible, in order to capture our attention, our hearts and our minds. Whatever is programmed into us is exactly what will come forth from our lives.

On the other hand, Paul said we should constantly be filling our minds with truth, justice, purity, loveliness, and goodness. The pundits and politicians may be enslaved to their "alternative facts" and "fake news," but I am grateful for the good news that Jesus saves!

. . . .

Thank You, Lord, that I can trust Your Word. I pray to surrender all of me to You! In Jesus' name, amen.

WEEK 41—WEDNESDAY
True Contentment

Not that I speak in regard to need, for I have learned in whatever state I am, to be content: I know how to be abased, and I know how to abound. Everywhere and in all things I have learned both to be full and to be hungry, both to abound and to suffer need. I can do all things through Christ who strengthens me.

PHILIPPIANS 4:11–13

I was recently in a store picking up some things for a children's camp, and I overheard a young mother's conversation with her young daughter. As they passed every aisle, regardless of the merchandise on the shelves, the little girl would say to her mother, "Go down here! There's stuff I need!"

To the young mother's credit, each time her young daughter said this, the mother replied, "There's nothing down there you need."

Unfortunately, aren't we often like that young girl? We often think we need everything, and we forget that God supplies all of our needs.

At the core of each of us is an intrinsic desire for true contentment. While the world would have us "Look over here!" or "Try this!" or "Go there!" the apostle Paul gave us the assurance that true contentment comes from Christ. Whether we are in a prison or a palace, whether free or in chains, whether starving or full, whether sick or suffering, everything we ever need in this life or the life to come we can find in our Lord Jesus!

Dear Lord, today I give all of me to You. I pray that You give me true contentment as I go about my world today. Amen.

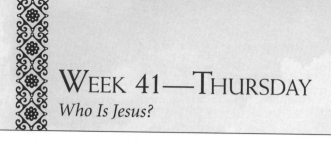

Week 41—Thursday
Who Is Jesus?

He is the image of the invisible God, the firstborn over all creation. For by Him all things were created that are in heaven and that are on earth, visible and invisible, whether thrones or dominions or principalities or powers. All things were created through Him and for Him. And He is before all things, and in Him all things consist.

COLOSSIANS 1:15–17

Several years ago I decided to go to one of the largest office buildings in downtown Jacksonville. I took a friend with me. Armed with nothing more than clipboards, legal pads, and pens, we stood at the opposite sides of the exit. As the employees left work in pursuit of the weekend, we asked each person who passed by, "May I ask you, in your opinion, who is Jesus?"

The opinions varied, and some people would not acknowledge us. Others replied they were too busy or that they never discussed religion and politics. Some took the time to stop for a second and give an answer.

Unfortunately, most of the answers had no scriptural foundation and could not be further from the truth. But my favorite answer came from an older lady who stopped, raised her hands to the sky, and shouted at the top of her lungs, "I will tell you who Jesus Christ is! He is my Savior and Lord! He is God!"

We had asked a very important question on that day. That sweet woman had given the only correct answer. Jesus Christ is Savior and Lord! Jesus Christ is God!

Paul wrote Colossians in order to combat false teachings. Paul wanted to explain Jesus' identity. Can we do the same today?

....

Dear Lord, please give me an opportunity to speak the truth and share with some precious soul that You are Savior, Lord, and God. Amen.

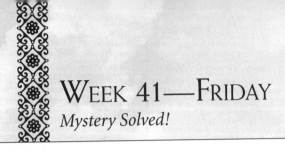

Week 41—Friday
Mystery Solved!

That their hearts may be encouraged, being knit together in love, and attaining to all riches of the full assurance of understanding, to the knowledge of the mystery of God, both of the Father and of Christ, in whom are hidden all the treasures of wisdom and knowledge.

COLOSSIANS 2:2–3

Throughout my lifetime I have been interested in mysteries. Some of the mysteries have been solved, and some have not. We still do not know what really happened to Amelia Earhart or whether Bigfoot and the Loch Ness Monster are real or fake.

When I was a boy, like many others I wanted to know who the source was for Woodward and Bernstein as they investigated the Nixon administration's cover-up of the Watergate debacle. Those two *Washington Post* reporters referred to their source as Deep Throat. Finally, just a few years ago that mystery was solved when former FBI official Mark Felt outed himself as Woodward and Bernstein's source. Felt had encouraged the two reporters to follow the money. They did and shortly thereafter solved the mystery.

Many at the church of Colossae faced a mystery. False teachings were rampant regarding Jesus Christ. In the New Testament, a mystery is often something that at one time had been hidden but now has been revealed. And as Paul pointed out, the mystery of Jesus Christ has been revealed!

Paul encouraged the church as well as each of us to follow the Scriptures. In them we find "the way, the truth, and the life" (John 14:6) in Jesus Christ alone. Mystery solved!

Dear Lord, thank You for revealing the truth of Jesus. Amen.

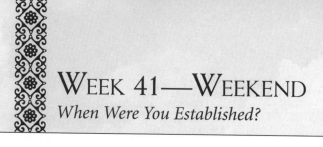

WEEK 41—WEEKEND
When Were You Established?

As you therefore have received Christ Jesus the Lord, so walk in Him, rooted and built up in Him and established in the faith, as you have been taught, abounding in it with thanksgiving.

COLOSSIANS 2:6–7

I am often interested in when particular businesses were established. I recently looked up five companies. You will likely recognize them: Chick-fil-A, established in 1946; Callaway Golf, established in 1982; Porsche, established in 1931; Shinola, established in 2011; and the New England Patriots, established in 1960. These organizations are diverse in what they produce, but they have one thing in common: there was a moment in time that each came into being.

I wonder if that is true for you as well. Have you been established? Spiritually speaking, I was established on September 8, 1982. For it was on that day I received the Lord as my personal Savior. At that moment, I was "established in the faith."

In our passage, Paul exhorted us after having received Christ to follow our Lord in three ways. First of all, we are to "walk in Him." As we walk in Him, our feet will not be led astray. Second, we are to be "rooted and built up in Him." It is a transformation that takes place as we read and follow His Word. As we do this, our roots grow stronger and deeper. Last of all, as a result of our obedience we will be "established in the faith." The result will be a life abounding in thanksgiving to our wonderful Lord Jesus.

Dear Lord, I pray that I may walk in You, be rooted in You, and forever be thankful to You for establishing me in the faith. Amen.

WEEK 42—MONDAY
Stay Away from Stinkin' Thinkin'

Beware lest anyone cheat you through philosophy and empty deceit, according to the tradition of men, according to the basic principles of the world, and not according to Christ. For in Him dwells all the fullness of the Godhead bodily; and you are complete in Him, who is the head of all principality and power.

COLOSSIANS 2:8–10

What's on your mind? That's always a good question to ask. God's Word regularly commands that you give careful thought to your thought life. In fact, the Bible even encourages you to take every thought captive (2 Corinthians 10:5).

The apostle Paul began Colossians by reminding Christ followers to "walk worthy of the Lord" (1:10). Here he challenged us to watch out for those things that hinder our Christian walk. A walk or lifestyle inconsistent with God's Word usually begins with thinking that is unsupported by God's Word. Have you allowed any wrong thinking to slip into your life?

Zig Ziglar used to put it this way: "We all need a daily checkup from the neck up to avoid stinkin' thinkin'." Are you being deceived by any stinkin' thinkin'?

The key to right thinking begins with the pursuit of Jesus. God's Word makes it clear: the traditions of men and the principles of the world will always leave you empty and longing for more, whereas a mind focused on Christ will always be complete. Jesus plus nothing equals everything. Ask God to give you the mind of Christ this week.

....

Heavenly Father, I recognize that all truth is Your truth. Help me to live this day with the mind of Christ, grounded in Your Word. Amen.

WEEK 42—TUESDAY
Designed by Grace

Therefore, as the elect of God, holy and beloved, put on tender mercies, kindness, humility, meekness, longsuffering; bearing with one another, and forgiving one another, if anyone has a complaint against another; even as Christ forgave you, so you also must do. But above all these things put on love, which is the bond of perfection.

COLOSSIANS 3:12–14

Think about this: God chose you, set you apart, and deeply loves you. These truths should make a difference in how you live. Your life should reflect the characteristics of the One who so richly invests in you.

We live in a society that is fashion conscious. People identify the rich and famous by what they wear and who designed it. In these verses, the apostle Paul reminded us that we are identified in the same way. We belong to our Designer, and He expects us to put on His garments.

This may seem easier said than done. You can't look like Jesus in your own strength. Only the truth and the power of the gospel and the gift of God's forgiveness make this lifestyle possible. But it is possible—by His grace.

This list closely resembles the fruit of the Spirit found in Galatians 5:22–23. Determine to be merciful, kind, humble, meek, longsuffering, forbearing, forgiving, and loving today; after all, that's how your Designer designed you to be.

You have been given the ultimate wardrobe that was crafted by a heavenly Tailor. Put on His garments today.

Dear Jesus, thank You for Your loving forgiveness. Please give me grace this day to reflect Your glory. Amen.

WEEK 42—WEDNESDAY
Peace in the Storm

And let the peace of God rule in your hearts, to which also you were called in one body; and be thankful. Let the word of Christ dwell in you richly in all wisdom, teaching and admonishing one another in psalms and hymns and spiritual songs, singing with grace in your hearts to the Lord. And whatever you do in word or deed, do all in the name of the Lord Jesus, giving thanks to God the Father through Him.

COLOSSIANS 3:15–17

How do you find peace in the midst of life's storms? You must allow God's peace to rule in your heart. If you want tranquility through life's difficult, disappointing, and discouraging times, you must allow God's supernatural peace to exercise authority over your natural self.

How do you do this? You let the Word of Christ dwell in you. You gain God's peace as you dwell on God's living and written Word. But be warned: God's Word will never dwell in you until you make a conscious decision to focus on it.

As Dwight L. Moody once said, "The Bible will keep you from sin, or sin will keep you from the Bible." Read God's Word, remember God's Word, and rely on God's Word today!

Let peace rule, let the Word of Christ dwell, and let everything you do be done in the name of the Lord Jesus. When you invite Jesus into the center of life's storms, He may or may not change the weather, but He will definitely change you.

God, with a grateful heart I submit to the rule of Your peace today. I commit to dwelling on the Word of Christ. May the name of Jesus Christ be glorified in me. Amen.

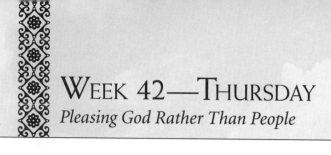

WEEK 42—THURSDAY
Pleasing God Rather Than People

Bondservants, obey in all things your masters according to the flesh, not with eyeservice, as men-pleasers, but in sincerity of heart, fearing God. And whatever you do, do it heartily, as to the Lord and not to men, knowing that from the Lord you will receive the reward of the inheritance; for you serve the Lord Christ.

COLOSSIANS 3:22–24

You have to decide whom you are going to please. Christ followers should live to please only one Master, but in pleasing Him, you should serve those around you as well. When you do what you do "heartily, as to the Lord," you will please God and you will stand out in a crowd. The world should know Christians to be the most effective, most efficient, and most energetic workers around.

This does not mean everything will go your way. It simply means that you focus on the things that matter most. You may find yourself in a difficult situation, and if you do, pause and remember your motivation. You cannot and will not please everyone. Stop trying. Instead, make it your goal to please Him (Matthew 6:24; Galatians 1:10).

This is important not just because He will reward you—according to His Word He will. It is important because you will one day stand before the One who really matters. Determine to live this day for that day!

Lord, help me to live this day with Your pleasure in mind. Forgive me for putting my wants and desires before You. Thank You for Your grace that meets my needs when I fall short. Allow me to do everything I do with all my heart for Your glory. Amen.

Week 42—Friday
Maximize the Moment

Walk in wisdom toward those who are outside, redeeming the time. Let your speech always be with grace, seasoned with salt, that you may know how you ought to answer each one.

Colossians 4:5–6

Are you making the most of the time God gives you? Are you maximizing the moments? The Scriptures teach that Christ redeems you, and then He expects you to redeem your time for His glory.

How do you redeem time? Isn't it interesting that Paul immediately addressed the importance of your speech? If you want every minute of your life to bring glory and honor to Jesus, you must pay careful attention to what you say. Your words have great power.

Determine to make your speech gracious. You may have heard as a child, "If you can't say something nice, don't say anything at all." Although common, this is great advice. Remember, you will never have grace-filled speech until you first have a grace-filled heart.

Let your words add value to every conversation. Salt preserves and purifies what it touches. Make the decision that what you say will do the same. Avoid idle and unnecessary speech (Matthew 12:36; Proverbs 10:19).

Make sure your speech is grounded in truth. The apostle Paul put it this way: "Know how you ought to answer each one." The apostle Peter referred to this as being "ready to give a defense" (1 Peter 3:15). Immerse yourself in God's Word so you will know what to say and when to say it.

Dear Jesus, may the words of my mouth please You today so I might redeem the time You've given me. Amen.

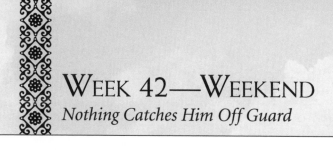

WEEK 42—WEEKEND
Nothing Catches Him Off Guard

But let us who are of the day be sober, putting on the breastplate of faith and love, and as a helmet the hope of salvation. For God did not appoint us to wrath, but to obtain salvation through our Lord Jesus Christ, who died for us, that whether we wake or sleep, we should live together with Him.

1 THESSALONIANS 5:8–10

As you conclude this week, why don't you end where you began? Ask God to guard your mind for His glory. Ask Him to give you clarity of thought so you can live with confident assurance.

You live in difficult days. In addition to the challenges of your personal life, chaos and crisis fill this world, and it is easy to become discouraged and sink into despair. But take heart—God has given you all you need in Jesus Christ. He is your "living hope" (1 Peter 1:3). Be sober; don't allow your senses to be dulled. Hold on to the hope of the gospel. God has already done everything necessary to save you from the penalty of sin.

Remember this today: nothing you face will ever catch God off guard. Regardless of your circumstances, He sees everything coming and He will see you through. Determine to let your mind be fixed on Him (Isaiah 26:3). God's already given you everything you need for this moment in time.

Rest securely today in the personal, powerful, and ever-present hope found in the person of Jesus Christ.

Heavenly Father, thank You for the eternal hope I have through Jesus Christ. Help me to live for that day with great expectation both for my good and for Your glory. In Jesus' name, amen.

WEEK 43—MONDAY
Refrigerator Friends

Now we exhort you, brethren, warn those who are unruly, comfort the fainthearted, uphold the weak, be patient with all. See that no one renders evil for evil to anyone, but always pursue what is good both for yourselves and for all. Rejoice always, pray without ceasing, in everything give thanks; for this is the will of God in Christ Jesus for you.

1 THESSALONIANS 5:14–18

Our enemy is an isolator. This has been his plan from the beginning. In isolation we are easy targets of the enemy and can more easily fall back into old flesh patterns. Our reading today reminds us as believers that we are connected to each other. Being involved in a healthy body of believers is not just a good idea—it is a necessity for spiritual survival.

Being involved in a body means we are responsible for each other. Paul's use of "brethren" was not merely church jargon but a deep understanding of our connectedness in Christ. Every believer needs what I call "refrigerator friends" in his or her life. A refrigerator friend is one who comes into our house and grabs a bite to eat or something to drink without even asking. Having friends like this allows us to speak into their lives when we see them drifting from Christ or when they are discouraged. These friends also need to feel the freedom to speak into our lives as well.

I provide correction and encouragement to my children without hesitation because they are my responsibility. In much the same way, Paul encouraged us to take responsibility for the brothers and sisters in Christ whom God has placed in our lives. When we do this, we cultivate a healthy body of believers.

Father, help me to cultivate some refrigerator friends in my life so we can provide care and correction for each other. Amen.

BRADY COOPER, NEW VISION BAPTIST CHURCH, MURFREESBORO, TN

Week 43—Tuesday
Fan the Flame

Do not quench the Spirit. Do not despise prophecies. Test all things; hold fast what is good. Abstain from every form of evil.

1 THESSALONIANS 5:19–22

There are few things in life I enjoy more than a good fire. I have a fireplace in my den, a fireplace in my bedroom, a fire pit on my porch, and a digital fire playing on my computer screen. The crackle of the fire, the smell of the wood, and the warmth are amazing. Great fires take attention, but they are so worth it.

When I am at home sitting by the fireplace in the evening, anybody who does anything to quench my fire is public enemy number one. Per our reading today, we know the Holy Spirit can be quenched. It's like putting out a fire. In our personal walk with the Lord, let's be reminded that our actions and attitudes can quench the Spirit's fire. As we walk in obedience to the Lord today, we should fan the flame of the Spirit. We do this by being wise in our actions, studying the Scriptures, cultivating a relationship with Jesus, and avoiding all forms of evil.

Father, today I am aware that through my faith in Christ Your Holy Spirit dwells inside me. Today, Holy Spirit, I want to live more aware of Your presence within me, and I want to fan the flame of Your power in my life for Your glory and my good. Amen.

WEEK 43—WEDNESDAY
Make Yourself at Home

Now may the God of peace Himself sanctify you completely; and may your whole spirit, soul, and body be preserved blameless at the coming of our Lord Jesus Christ. He who calls you is faithful, who also will do it.

1 THESSALONIANS 5:23–24

Having grown up in the South, I have heard these four words uttered every time I've entered someone's house: "Make yourself at home." Some folks, I am sure, really mean that but for many it's just a figure of speech. In our reading today Paul referred to God as "the God of peace." This peace comes from the Holy Spirit's making Himself at home in our lives.

Can we stop for a moment and take inventory? Are there rooms in our hearts where the Holy Spirit may not be at home? We often compartmentalize our lives: our spiritual lives, social lives, professional lives. We have all been in someone's home and not felt at home. When this happens we are not ourselves at all. Thus we must welcome the Holy Spirit into every room in our hearts.

Paul continued by saying God wants to sanctify us completely—not merely one compartment of our lives. As we open our hearts to Him, confess the sin that has resided there, and give Him access to every room the result will be peace, which is a by-product of God's presence.

Do you desire more peace? Surrender every area of your life to the sanctifying work of the Holy Spirit!

....

Father, will You reveal, through the power of your Holy Spirit, a room in my life where You are not at home? Will You grant me the grace to surrender that room to You completely? In Jesus' name, amen.

WEEK 43—THURSDAY
Ball Security

I urge you in the sight of God who gives life to all things, and before Christ Jesus who witnessed the good confession before Pontius Pilate, that you keep this commandment without spot, blameless until our Lord Jesus Christ's appearing, which He will manifest in His own time, He who is the blessed and only Potentate, the King of kings and Lord of lords.

1 TIMOTHY 6:13–15

As a kid I moved from basketball season to baseball season to football season. The sports changed but one thing stayed the same: ball security. My baseball coaches encouraged me to use two hands when catching the ball, my basketball coach taught how to protect the ball when dribbling, and on it went. In like manner, Paul coached young Timothy when he told him: "Keep this commandment." Timothy had been called to preach the gospel and care for the church. Paul didn't want Timothy to fumble his calling but rather to value and protect it.

We all have been called into ministry if we claim the name of Jesus as Savior. Just as the athlete has to value the ball in competition, so we must value our role in ministry. Nothing in our lives is more important than following God's will for our lives.

While God calls all of us into ministry, we all have different gifts to use. This allows us to play different positions on the team. Part of valuing our callings is discovering, developing, and deploying our gifts in ministry. Ball security is the difference between winning and losing on the athletic field, and often the way we value our spiritual gifts determines success or failure in our work for the Lord.

Father, help me to value my calling as never before. Amen.

WEEK 43—FRIDAY
Pick the Right Fight

I have fought the good fight, I have finished the race, I have kept the faith. Finally, there is laid up for me the crown of righteousness, which the Lord, the righteous Judge, will give to me on that Day, and not to me only but also to all who have loved His appearing.

2 TIMOTHY 4:7–8

In life are many fights or causes to which we can commit ourselves. For some, politics is the fight of their lives. For others, building their careers is the fight of their lives. I am not saying anything is wrong with these fights, but they are not what Paul referred to when he talked about the "good fight."

The key to a good life is in picking the right fight. The good fight for Paul was giving his life to making disciples. He spent his time in evangelistic efforts in church planting and encouraging struggling believers with his writing. He fought the good fight of the gospel.

Fighting connotes training and then stepping into the ring. Paul spent his life working diligently and running the Christian marathon every day. It is a daily struggle that is not easy. Paul wrote that if we fight the good fight, we also will enjoy the rewards the Father has for us one day. Paul knew he had fought well. Can we say the same?

. . . .

Father, strengthen me to fight the good fight. Encourage me to be willing to step into whatever disciple-making ring You have for me. Amen.

BRADY COOPER, NEW VISION BAPTIST CHURCH, MURFREESBORO, TN

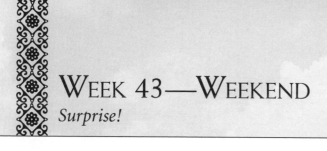

WEEK 43—WEEKEND
Surprise!

But when the kindness and the love of God our Savior toward man appeared, not by works of righteousness which we have done, but according to His mercy He saved us, through the washing of regeneration and renewing of the Holy Spirit, whom He poured out on us abundantly through Jesus Christ our Savior.

TITUS 3:4–6

Many of us love surprises because they mean people were thinking of us and were willing to go out of their way for us. We probably all have stories where we opened a door expecting one thing only to hear our closest friends and family members yell, "Surprise!"

Surprises shatter our expectations. And nothing in all of life has surprised me and continues to surprise me as much as the gospel.

> *That the Creator of the universe knows me . . . Surprise!*
> *That God loves someone like me . . . Surprise!*
> *That I can't get to God on my own effort . . . Surprise!*
> *That I deserved judgment but He offered me grace . . . Surprise!*
> *That He gave me the Holy Spirit for my growth . . . Surprise!*
> *That He pours out His grace on my life . . . Surprise!*

As we think about the surprises of the gospel, let's get our hearts ready to worship an amazing God this weekend!

Father, thank You for surprising me with Your grace! Help me never to take Your grace for granted. Amen.

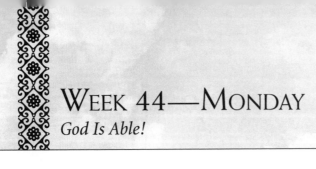

Week 44—Monday
God Is Able!

Beware, brethren, lest there be in any of you an evil heart of unbelief in departing from the living God; but exhort one another daily, while it is called "Today," lest any of you be hardened through the deceitfulness of sin. For we have become partakers of Christ if we hold the beginning of our confidence steadfast to the end.

HEBREWS 3:12–14

The heart of every problem is a problem of the heart. The context of this passage is unbelief. God had performed great and powerful miracles for Israel when He set His people free from Egypt. But when the opportunity came for the same people to enter the promised land, they hardened their hearts and would not trust God to deliver this new land to them. Even though God had revealed His faithfulness over and over again, the people remained faithless.

Anytime someone loses perspective on who God is and what He can do, the result will always be a hardened heart. Frustration, anger, disappointment, and fear are usually connected to a wrong perspective. That is why the Bible challenges us to encourage one another to trust God firmly.

Remember today the same God who brought fire from heaven, who calmed the storms, who healed the sick and lame is still available to you. Your situation may seem impossible, overwhelming, or even worse, but God is attentive, available, and able!

....

Father, help me today to see with the eyes of faith. Enable me to see from Your perspective what I cannot see from mine. I trust You to lead and provide in all areas of my life. Amen.

CHRIS DIXON, LIBERTY BAPTIST CHURCH, DUBLIN, GA

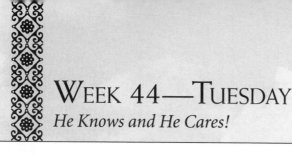

Week 44—Tuesday
He Knows and He Cares!

Seeing then that we have a great High Priest who has passed through the heavens, Jesus the Son of God, let us hold fast our confession. For we do not have a High Priest who cannot sympathize with our weaknesses, but was in all points tempted as we are, yet without sin. Let us therefore come boldly to the throne of grace, that we may obtain mercy and find grace to help in time of need.

Hebrews 4:14–16

Have you ever felt like giving up? Sometimes life can become so challenging and difficult we feel as if nothing is ever going to change or get better. That is how many of the Christ followers felt when they first received the letter of Hebrews. With this knowledge in mind, let's reread the three verses from today's text.

Because of who Jesus is (God), because of what He experienced in this life (our experiences), and because He is attentive to our lives, we can trust that He will help us in our times of need. The theme this week is simple: God is attentive, God is available, and God is able. And this theme fits in perfectly with the text from Hebrews.

Don't focus on your problem, your position, your timing, or your pain. Remind yourself over and over again today of the truth God reveals throughout the Scriptures. God is attentive, God is able, and God is available! If this is your focus, you will find mercy and grace to help you in your time of need.

Take time today to cast your cares on the Lord. Tell Him your hurts, concerns, and needs. Then acknowledge your faith that He is attentive, available, and able.

....

Dear Father, thank You for caring for me. I cast all my cares on You. Amen.

WEEK 44—WEDNESDAY
His Promise

Thus God, determining to show more abundantly to the heirs of promise the immutability of His counsel, confirmed it by an oath, that by two immutable things, in which it is impossible for God to lie, we might have strong consolation, who have fled for refuge to lay hold of the hope set before us.

HEBREWS 6:17–18

I n verse 18 the writer spoke of how we have a "strong consolation." The word *consolation* speaks of exhortation and encouragement. When one thinks of the word *strong,* he or she might think of something that is powerful and mighty, such as an army. The writer in today's text told Christians they have a mighty source of encouragement. This source of encouragement acts like an army or fortress against discouragements in life.

How can you stay encouraged during the discouraging times of life?

There is one fact you can be absolutely certain about: God will never lie. He cannot lie! In verse Hebrews 6:13, the writer used Abraham as an example of this truth. Just as God gave Abraham a promise and delivered on it, God has also given you certain promises and you can trust He will deliver. He wants you to experience the reality of His faithfulness.

Do not overlook this thought. God may not deliver what you need today, tomorrow, next week, or this year, but if He promised it, He will deliver eventually!

Take time today to thank God for His faithfulness and to acknowledge your full confidence that you can trust Him.

Dear Lord, I am so grateful for the truth that You can never tell a lie. I know I can trust You with everything. Amen.

CHRIS DIXON, LIBERTY BAPTIST CHURCH, DUBLIN, GA

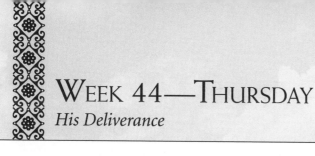

Week 44—Thursday
His Deliverance

Thus God, determining to show more abundantly to the heirs of promise the immutability of His counsel, confirmed it by an oath, that by two immutable things, in which it is impossible for God to lie, we might have strong consolation, who have fled for refuge to lay hold of the hope set before us. This hope we have as an anchor of the soul, both sure and steadfast, and which enters the Presence behind the veil.

HEBREWS 6:17–19

The book of Hebrews was written to Christians who were facing very difficult times. They were under persecution and probably discouraged, so the author wanted to give them words of encouragement. Today's passage offers great hope to all those who are struggling through a storms in their lives.

It would take a book to reveal all the truth in these verses, but I will simply share this: the wind may blow and the rain may fall, but we will reach heaven's harbor safely. The seas may be rough and dangerous, but Jesus, our Forerunner, has already gone ashore, dropped His anchor, and is bringing us home. He will keep every promise He has ever made.

It is impossible for Him to lie, so we know He will keep His promises. He is our Refuge, and He is watching over us until we get home. Better days are ahead for the children of God, and the writer of Hebrews assured that we will arrive home safely. These glorious truths light our way home! They are the believer's strong consolation. Praise the Lord!

. . . .

Father, thank You for the promises in Your Word that give me encouragement for today and hope for tomorrow. Amen.

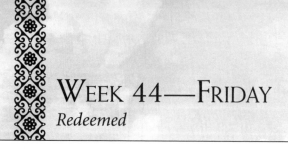

Week 44—Friday
Redeemed

But Christ came as High Priest of the good things to come, with the greater and more perfect tabernacle not made with hands, that is, not of this creation. Not with the blood of goats and calves, but with His own blood He entered the Most Holy Place once for all, having obtained eternal redemption.

Hebrews 9:11–12

Redeemed! *Redeem*: the word means to free from captivity by payment of ransom, to release from blame or debt. That is what Jesus Christ did for you! He freed you from the penalty of your sin! The life, death, and resurrection of Jesus Christ freed you from your sin debt.

Do not miss the power of these verses. A place of worship, an act of service or sacrifice cannot redeem—only Jesus can redeem! It does not matter where you have been or what you have done. He made the payment for your debt with His sacrifice.

In the words of the classic hymn: "Jesus paid it all, all to Him I owe, / Sin had left a crimson stain. He washed it white as snow." These words speak of the great blessings Christians receive when they ask Jesus to forgive them of their sins.

Do not live in doubt; do not live in discouragement; do not live in defeat. Because of Jesus you have been set free from your sins!

Take time today to thank God for all He has done for you. Do not allow the distractions of pain and problems to keep you from praising God for His sacrifice and forgiveness.

....

Dear heavenly Father, thank You so much for redeeming my soul from hell by forgiving me of my sins. Amen.

CHRIS DIXON, LIBERTY BAPTIST CHURCH, DUBLIN, GA

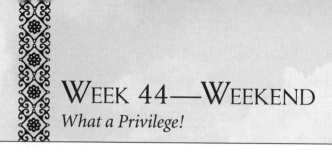

Week 44—Weekend
What a Privilege!

Therefore, brethren, having boldness to enter the Holiest by the blood of Jesus, by a new and living way which He consecrated for us, through the veil, that is, His flesh, and having a High Priest over the house of God, let us draw near with a true heart in full assurance of faith, having our hearts sprinkled from an evil conscience and our bodies washed with pure water.

Hebrews 10:19–22

In the Old Testament, the Israelites followed a system of religion that kept them out of the direct presence of God. So when the Jewish believers read for the first time that because of the death of Jesus on the cross they could come into the presence of God, a powerful truth confronted them that we often take for granted today.

Jesus' sacrifice for us on the cross was an open invitation from God Himself: "Let us draw near."

We often have a hard time believing that God—the Creator of the entire universe—is interested in the daily concerns and decisions of our lives. And we don't realize how much prayer matters to God and how He wants to work through prayer. If we find prayer is a duty or ritual we don't enjoy, it means we don't have the right perspective on how God works through prayer.

When I bring my life to God, God begins to work in all aspects of my life. He goes to work with this outlook: *I am going to take this situation or problem and I am going to answer in such a way that everyone involved will see I did this! And through this I will show the world what kind of Father and Friend I am.*

When I communicate with God, He communicates through me!

....

Dear heavenly Father, help me not to take prayer for granted. Amen.

WEEK 45—MONDAY
Exhorting Faith

Let us hold fast the confession of our hope without wavering, for He who promised is faithful. And let us consider one another in order to stir up love and good works, not forsaking the assembling of ourselves together, as is the manner of some, but exhorting one another, and so much the more as you see the Day approaching.

HEBREWS 10:23–25

I am so thankful for the faithfulness of God to save me from my sin. I am so thankful for the faithfulness of God to send me the Holy Spirit. I am so thankful for the faithfulness of God to seal me for all eternity. I am so thankful for the faithfulness of God!

Although we have received the incredible mission of directing people toward a relationship with Jesus, we were never given this mission with a dependency on our faithfulness. You and I can't be faithful to God on our own. Yet God is faithful, and because God is faithful, we can be faithful to Him. He does for us what we cannot do for ourselves.

As we hold fast the confession of our hope, we are also encouraged by God's provision of faithfulness through the church. The Christian life is a "one another" life. The Holy Spirit connects us as the body of Christ, and we are to enjoy the faithfulness of God together. When we prioritize one another, it stirs us up in love, it inspires us to do good works, and we receive encouragement to remain faithful until the coming of Jesus.

....

Lord Jesus, thank You for this reminder of Your faithfulness. I commit to holding fast together with Your church as we all anticipate Your return. Amen.

DR. ROB WILTON, VINTAGE CHURCH, NEW ORLEANS, LA

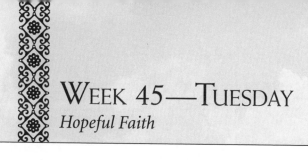

WEEK 45—TUESDAY
Hopeful Faith

Now faith is the substance of things hoped for, the evidence of things not seen. For by it the elders obtained a good testimony. By faith we understand that the worlds were framed by the word of God, so that the things which are seen were not made of things which are visible.

HEBREWS 11:1–3

Even the most cautious of us displays moments of faith throughout life. As we get in our cars for work, we have faith that our wheels won't fall off. We drop off our kids at school and have faith in their safety. We make decisions each week at our jobs that are calculated risks in hope of success. We eventually go to bed at night and have faith the roof won't collapse.

So much of life is unseen, yet we make daily decisions to trust the unseen. I still don't understand fully how airplanes work, yet I spend a lot of my life flying. The level of our faith will always depend on the reliability of the objects of our faith. I trust flying because most airplanes fly successfully.

Followers of Jesus should have stronger faith than others because God will never fail. Faith is being sure of something, and God declared in His Word that He will be victorious forever. Our hope is not in anything or anyone from the world; our hope is in the One who created this world. Our trust is not in chariots and horses; it is in the name of the Lord. Our faith is not in the wind and the waves; it is in the One who controls the wind and the waves.

. . . .

Lord Jesus, give me faith to trust You through all the unseen moments of life. May my faith in You move mountains for Your glory. Amen.

WEEK 45—WEDNESDAY
Pleasing Faith

By faith Enoch was taken away so that he did not see death, "and was not found, because God had taken him"; for before he was taken he had this testimony, that he pleased God. But without faith it is impossible to please Him, for he who comes to God must believe that He is, and that He is a rewarder of those who diligently seek Him.

HEBREWS 11:5–6

What an amazing testimony: Enoch pleased God! Because of his great faith in God, he didn't experience death on this earth. Instead, God took him away.

Pleasing God should be the ultimate aim of our lives. The heroes of the Old Testament didn't please God because of their work for Him—they pleased God by placing their faith in Him as they worked for Him. Placing faith in God involves a pursuit of God and His glory first and foremost.

As one who is extremely driven to accomplish great things for God, I am saddened by the number of times I've forgotten about God. The Great Commission is not just about the work we do for Jesus; rather, it is the enjoyment of God that we experience as we work for Him. As we serve God, we should seek to develop a closer relationship with Him. This will be very pleasing in His sight, and this will also motivate us to work even harder for Him.

....

Lord Jesus, forgive me for being so busy for You that I forget about You. Give me a pleasing faith that delights You as I serve You and this world. Amen.

DR. ROB WILTON, VINTAGE CHURCH, NEW ORLEANS, LA

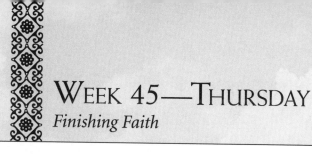

WEEK 45—THURSDAY
Finishing Faith

Therefore we also, since we are surrounded by so great a cloud of witnesses, let us lay aside every weight, and the sin which so easily ensnares us, and let us run with endurance the race that is set before us, looking unto Jesus, the author and finisher of our faith, who for the joy that was set before Him endured the cross, despising the shame, and has sat down at the right hand of the throne of God.

HEBREWS 12:1–2

Every follower of Jesus has a specific calling for his or her life. In today's verses the author compared this calling to a race.

As with any race, there are important things to remember if we hope to finish well. In order to run this race skillfully, we need the Word of Jesus to reveal where we should go. Jesus gives us directions throughout the Bible. We also need the strength of Jesus to sustain us to the end. Jesus does for us what we cannot do for ourselves.

Because this race of faith has been victoriously run by a great cloud of witnesses of the past, we can have the confidence to finish this race as well. The heroes of the faith mentioned in Hebrews 11 serve as great examples for us to follow. Because of the gospel of Jesus, we are set free from a life of sin and are made alive as we look to Jesus, the Author and Finisher of our faith. Jesus pioneered and perfected the path of faith for us, so we must never take our eyes off Him.

....

Lord Jesus, as I look to You I am thankful for my salvation in You that equips me with the power to finish the race that is set before me. Amen.

WEEK 45—FRIDAY
Guaranteed Faith

Therefore, since we are receiving a kingdom which cannot be shaken, let us have grace, by which we may serve God acceptably with reverence and godly fear. For our God is a consuming fire.

HEBREWS 12:28–29

Jesus came to give us the guarantee of a kingdom that will last forever, which refers to eternity in heaven. We can have everything this world has to offer, but nothing in our lives or in this world will satisfy the way Jesus will. Jesus promised entry into this kingdom with the following guarantees and expectations:

Our lives are not our own.

This world is not our home.

We gain entrance into this kingdom when we deny ourselves, take up our crosses, and follow Jesus. To deny ourselves is to surrender completely to Jesus. To take up our crosses means we sacrifice all for Him. To follow Him speaks to a complete submission to His plans. Jesus gave us His all and He expects our all.

We also find entrance into this kingdom when we lay up treasures in heaven. As followers of Jesus our citizenship is in heaven. Nothing will ever separate us from this promise. Jesus saved us in order that we might serve Him faithfully on this earth with the provision of eternity with Him.

Lord Jesus, thank You for Your provision of a kingdom that will never be shaken. I commit to obeying Your expectations as I trust the guarantee of Your kingdom. Amen.

DR. ROB WILTON, VINTAGE CHURCH, NEW ORLEANS, LA

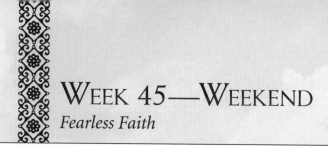

Week 45—Weekend
Fearless Faith

Let your conduct be without covetousness; be content with such things as you have. For He Himself has said, "I will never leave you nor forsake you." So we may boldly say:
"The Lord is my helper; I will not fear. What can man do to me?"

HEBREWS 13:5–6

W e will never find true peace in the absence of problems; rather, we will find true peace in the presence of Jesus. That ultimate peace is found through the gospel.

The Lord promises He will never leave us or forsake us. Because of this declaration, we are free from the cravings of this world, we are free from fear, and we are free from covetousness. In other words, this peace brings contentment, consistency, and courage through His presence in our lives.

We find contentment when we rest securely in His presence. I've been blessed to be around people who endured struggles in this world yet still had peace. This is a testimony to a peace that passes all understanding.

We find consistent peace in Christ. So many people, seasons, and experiences in this world change and are inconsistent. But the consistency of the Lord remains forever.

We find courage when we boldly declare and trust the Lord is our Helper. Jesus is completely victorious over sin and death and nothing is too great for Him to overcome.

....

Lord Jesus, thank You for bringing contentment, consistency, and courage to my life. I will not fear! In Jesus' name, amen.

WEEK 46—MONDAY
Because He Lives

Therefore by Him let us continually offer the sacrifice of praise to God, that is, the fruit of our lips, giving thanks to His name. But do not forget to do good and to share, for with such sacrifices God is well pleased.

HEBREWS 13:15–16

"The root determines the fruit." Much truth is in that statement, from both agricultural and spiritual standpoints. I once planted some tomato plants in my yard using the Japanese Tomato Ring method; it was incredibly successful. The plants grew more than six feet tall, and I could not give the tomatoes away as fast as the four plants produced. The most interesting thing about this method is I did not water the plants themselves. I planted them in a circle, and the fertilizer and water went in a ring in the center of the plants. The roots of the plants would seek the nutrients and grow toward the center. I watered the roots only, not the leaves or stalks. As a result, the branches produced beautiful, delicious fruit because I provided proper nourishment to the roots.

Much like the roots of the tomatoes I planted, your heart is the root of your speech. Feed and water your heart today with the truth of who Jesus is and what He did for you on the cross. At this very moment, consider how great and powerful He is, then allow that realization to produce the fruit of praise from your lips. Tell God how great and awesome He is. Do something special for someone else today, then take the opportunity to share the love of Christ with him or her.

....

Father, You are worthy of my praise and so much more. I pray that every word formed by my mouth this day will be pleasing to You. Help me to glorify You by serving someone else today. Amen.

TIM SIZEMORE, LIGHTHOUSE BAPTIST CHURCH, MACON, GA

WEEK 46—TUESDAY
Heavenly Hope

Now may the God of peace who brought up our Lord Jesus from the dead, that great Shepherd of the sheep, through the blood of the everlasting covenant, make you complete in every good work to do His will, working in you what is well pleasing in His sight, through Jesus Christ, to whom be glory forever and ever. Amen.

HEBREWS 13:20–21

Have you ever felt you were a lost cause? Have you ever felt as though you could never measure up to what Christ has called you to be? I have felt that way many times, and the truth is we are correct. We can never reach the perfection of Jesus on our own. The truth of this passage, however, gives us tremendous hope. The author of Hebrews told us that if God has enough power to raise Jesus from the dead, then certainly He can handle humanity's problem with sin.

When I look back, I am amazed at the work Christ has done in my life. I also realize Christ is not shepherding me so I can gather accolades. God is perfecting me so that I can be more effective for Him. He gives me talents to serve Him with—not so I can fulfill my own desires.

Everything we do should be for the glory of God. He gives us breath so we can praise Him—not so we can be glorified.

....

God, thank You for Your work in my life. Give me focus today to use all You have provided me with to advance Your kingdom. Amen.

WEEK 46—WEDNESDAY
The Joy of Trials

My brethren, count it all joy when you fall into various trials, knowing that the testing of your faith produces patience. But let patience have its perfect work, that you may be perfect and complete, lacking nothing. If any of you lacks wisdom, let him ask of God, who gives to all liberally and without reproach, and it will be given to him.

JAMES 1:2–5

When I was a child, my family had a small vacation place on Jackson Lake in Jackson, Georgia. Across the street from our single-wide trailer was a place called Kersey's. It had a small store, pinball games, and a restaurant. Mrs. Kersey made the best hamburgers ever. She would let me sit up on a wooden stool beside her as she cooked on the flat griddle. I knew as soon as we completed the two-hour trek from our home in Phenix City, Alabama, to the lake, I would get the best cheeseburger known to man and a cold Yoo-hoo. I always hated the drive, but I rarely complained because I knew what the outcome would be.

It is tough to consider hard times as joyful. I do not enjoy the journey to patience, but the taste of it, in the end, is incredible. Trials are our mode of transportation to patience and completeness in Christ. Ask God today for the wisdom to embrace the journey to patience, and He will not only give it to you but will give it liberally. The more patient you become, the more peace will fill your life.

....

Lord, I sometimes wish I could take a nap on the journey and wake up patient. Help me count the trials as joy, realizing they bring me closer to You. Fill me, Lord, with Your wisdom! In Jesus' name, amen.

TIM SIZEMORE, LIGHTHOUSE BAPTIST CHURCH, MACON, GA

WEEK 46—THURSDAY
It's All Good . . . When It's from Him

Do not be deceived, my beloved brethren. Every good gift and every perfect gift is from above, and comes down from the Father of lights, with whom there is no variation or shadow of turning. Of His own will He brought us forth by the word of truth, that we might be a kind of firstfruits of His creatures.

JAMES 1:16–18

Some people might accuse me of having a touch of OCD at times. I like for all of my pants to hang together in the closet. All of the jeans are with the jeans and the slacks hang with the slacks. Dress shirts should be together, and they should all face the same direction. I get a little perturbed when I go to get the creamer for my coffee and it is not where it is supposed to be. Sometimes I think my family moves things around just to drive me crazy. I find comfort in consistency.

Nothing is more consistent than God! James assures us in this passage that there is no "variation" in God's blessings to His children. Whatever He gives us will be good and perfect for us. Do not be deceived by Satan that anything is good apart from the Lord. Or that God will give you something that will injure you. Whatever God gives you today will be good; you can bank on that. Trust Him today.

....

Father God, thank You for the gifts You give me. Thank You for being consistent always. Help me to be that way as well. Amen.

Week 46—Friday
Cooler Heads Prevail

So then, my beloved brethren, let every man be swift to hear, slow to speak, slow to wrath; for the wrath of man does not produce the righteousness of God.

JAMES 1:19–20

My dad says it is better to keep your mouth shut and let people think you are stupid than to open it and remove all doubt. I hate nothing more than when I make a quick and wrong assessment of a situation before I get all of the information—and then proceed to make an utter fool of myself through anger. It is the worst feeling in the world.

This past Wednesday we learned that trials bring forth patience, which makes us more like Christ. Yesterday we saw God is consistent in giving us only what is good for us. Today James says since all of that is true, maybe we should hold our tongues when we are tempted to blow steam. Since God is consistent in giving only what is good to His children, it stands to reason that Romans 8:28 is true and all things will work together for our good.

No one has ever grown closer to God by having a quick temper. Think about the godliest person you know. Would you characterize him or her as a hothead? Every time you lose your temper and speak too quickly, you lose credibility and the opportunity to influence those around you for Christ. God gave you two ears and one tongue for a reason.

Father God, help me to listen to You more and not become angry. Amen.

TIM SIZEMORE, LIGHTHOUSE BAPTIST CHURCH, MACON, GA

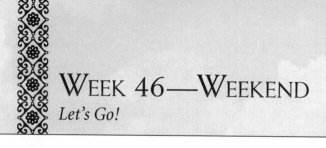

WEEK 46—WEEKEND
Let's Go!

But be doers of the word, and not hearers only, deceiving yourselves. For if anyone is a hearer of the word and not a doer, he is like a man observing his natural face in a mirror. . . . But he who looks into the perfect law of liberty and continues in it, and is not a forgetful hearer but a doer of the work, this one will be blessed in what he does.

JAMES 1:22–23, 25

Early in my adult life, I was a deputy sheriff and SWAT team member. SWAT stands for Special Weapons and Tactics. Some of those special tactics involved using pressure points to control individuals as well as various hand-to-hand combat maneuvers. We began learning these moves by listening to the instructor give directions on how to use them properly and the science behind why they work. We would often watch video demonstrations, and sometimes the instructors would even model the moves on each other. All of that was cool to see and usually drew cheers and chants from those watching. But it never failed to silence the room when the instructor said, "Okay, who wants to go first?" Reading about SWAT team maneuvers and watching others perform them is one thing, but sooner or later I had to put to practice what I had learned in order to be effective.

I cannot encourage Bible study enough. We must put what we read into practice in order to make the Bible real in our lives. If we are only hearers of the Word and not doers of the Word, our Christian walks are ineffective. We must do what the Bible teaches if we want to please God.

Scan over this week's study to refresh, and then put what you learned into practice. Who wants to go first?

....

God, help me today to practice what I preach. Amen.

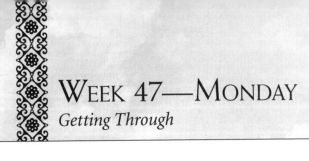

WEEK 47—MONDAY
Getting Through

Therefore submit to God. Resist the devil and he will flee from you. Draw near to God and He will draw near to you. Cleanse your hands, you sinners; and purify your hearts, you double-minded. Lament and mourn and weep! Let your laughter be turned to mourning and your joy to gloom. Humble yourselves in the sight of the Lord, and He will lift you up.

JAMES 4:7–10

Many of us struggle with developing a closer relationship with God. We have difficulty praying and connecting with God. We wonder if God hears us. Are we even getting through?

We must pray! A prayer-less Christian is a powerless Christian.

James told us how we can get through to God and see supernatural activity take place when we pray. Submitting to God, resisting the devil, and being humble are all the key factors. To submit means to fall in under rank or to know our place. When we submit to God, the devil flees.

We must be careful to have a spirit of humility. God hates pride and self-sufficiency. When we are dependent on God and not ourselves, God moves on our behalf.

James encouraged us to draw near to God and He in turn will draw close to us. What a promise! Don't we long for a deeper relationship with Jesus? It starts with submitting to Him.

....

Lord Jesus, help me to have the right attitude when I come into Your presence. I desire intimacy, and I long to see Your power demonstrated in my life. Amen.

DR. STEVE FLOCKHART, NEW SEASON CHURCH, HIRAM, GA

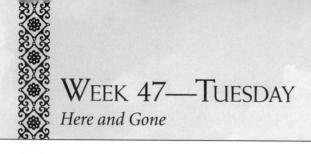

WEEK 47—TUESDAY
Here and Gone

Come now, you who say, "Today or tomorrow we will go to such and such a city, spend a year there, buy and sell, and make a profit"; whereas you do not know what will happen tomorrow. For what is your life? It is even a vapor that appears for a little time and then vanishes away. Instead you ought to say, "If the Lord wills, we shall live and do this or that."

JAMES 4:13–15

At some point in our lives, we all have asked, "Where did the time go?" For example, I look at my grown children in amazement. They were just crawling around in diapers a while ago. Now my children are adults, married, and have children of their own. It seems like only yesterday. . . .

I hear many people make remarks about time flying by. Life is short. James said life is a vapor, a mist. It is here, and then it is gone. None of us is promised tomorrow. Life is uncertain—it is short and gone before we know it.

This reality struck me a couple of years ago. I was listening to people sing "Happy Birthday," and it hit me: *I'm fifty years old.* The fact that life is brief here on earth and I have very little time to make a difference arrested my attention. I must impact today because I may not have tomorrow.

I'm sure you want your life to count and you want to make a difference. So stop with the petty things that frustrate you. Love unconditionally, forgive graciously, and be thankful for all God has done. Make a difference while you can!

....

Father, thank You for this amazing gift called life. Help me live it to the fullest, bringing glory to You in all that I do, and making a difference for You! In Jesus' name, amen.

WEEK 47—WEDNESDAY
Does Your Faith Hold Up to the Test?

The genuineness of your faith, being much more precious than gold that perishes, though it is tested by fire, may be found to praise, honor, and glory at the revelation of Jesus Christ, whom having not seen you love. Though now you do not see Him, yet believing, you rejoice with joy inexpressible and full of glory, receiving the end of your faith—the salvation of your souls.

1 PETER 1:7–9

In today's text Peter told us we will all face trials. All of us will experience pain and hurt. Disappointment, distress, and discontentment will be a part of our lives.

Peter gave us a picture of a prospector bringing in gold to be tested. This process reveals whether it is real gold. Peter then challenged us with a question: Even in the midst of unbearable circumstances, will our faith hold up to the test? Real faith triumphs when tested! Trusting Him builds our faith.

Do we have fair-weather faith? When things get rough, do we thrown in the towel or reach for our Bible? Do we fall away or do we fall on our knees?

Peter used gold in his analogy because it is one of the most valuable and precious of all metals. Just as fire separates gold from the dross, God uses life's trials to purify us. God does not send trials to harm us or to hurt us, but rather to grow us and make us more like Jesus. When those trials come, run to Jesus. Cry out to Him. Trust Him!

....

Father, please help me see Your divine purpose and to rejoice even in the midst of trials. Amen.

DR. STEVE FLOCKHART, NEW SEASON CHURCH, HIRAM, GA

WEEK 47—THURSDAY
True Identity

But you are a chosen generation, a royal priesthood, a holy nation, His own special people, that you may proclaim the praises of Him who called you out of darkness into His marvelous light; who once were not a people but are now the people of God, who had not obtained mercy but now have obtained mercy.

1 PETER 2:9–10

One of the greatest challenges in our lives is to understand, believe, and live out our true identities as believers. People often define themselves by what they do for a living. Many find their identities in having lots of possessions or certain statuses. But knowing who we are as Christians and living that out is critical to our Christian walks.

Peter told us who we are: we are chosen by God. We are unique. God has a special purpose for each of us.

Peter said we are a royal priesthood. Exodus 19:6 says, "You shall be to Me a kingdom of priests." Thus as believers we have a honorable position with certain privileges.

We are a holy nation—holy, different, and set apart. A people for God's own possession. God has called us and equipped us for a reason. He took us out of darkness and out of the sinful state we once lived in. We were spiritually blind, and Jesus called us into the light. Because of what He did and who we are now, we belong to God. We once were lost and undone in our sin, but we have been redeemed. We have new identities in Christ!

....

Lord Jesus, it is so easy to lose my identity and focus instead on people, personal status, or the accumulation of stuff to define my identity. May I look to You to determine who I am. In Jesus' name, amen.

WEEK 47—FRIDAY
How to Be a Member of God's Family

Finally, all of you be of one mind, having compassion for one another; love as brothers, be tenderhearted, be courteous; not returning evil for evil or reviling for reviling, but on the contrary blessing, knowing that you were called to this, that you may inherit a blessing.

1 PETER 3:8—9

In this text, Peter told us how to treat one another in the family of God. We need to have the same mind. We are to live in harmony with one another. Unity never means uniformity; it means cooperating in the midst of diversity. Peter told us to have compassion for each other. We need to sympathize with the pain of others. Peter told us to love each other like family because we are part of a family. We are to display humility and kindness, looking and acting like Jesus.

Then he told us to forgive others, to release the hurt we have experienced. We all struggle with the proper reaction when we or someone we love has been mistreated, but Peter made it clear we must learn to forgive.

Peter told us not to return evil with evil or insult with insult. We can choose to live on a different level and take the high road. We cannot live with bitterness in our hearts toward other people. Can you think of someone or some situation where you need to make things right? Perhaps you need to make a phone call, write a letter, or go see someone face-to-face. Do it today. You will be blessed!

....

Father, it is so hard to forgive sometimes. Help me show forgiveness to my brothers and sisters in Christ. I want to be a loving member of Your family. In Jesus' name, amen.

DR. STEVE FLOCKHART, NEW SEASON CHURCH, HIRAM, GA

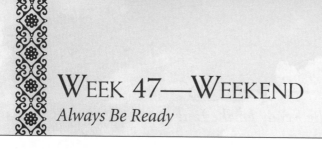

WEEK 47—WEEKEND
Always Be Ready

But sanctify the Lord God in your hearts, and always be ready to give a defense to everyone who asks you a reason for the hope that is in you, with meekness and fear; having a good conscience, that when they defame you as evildoers, those who revile your good conduct in Christ may be ashamed. For it is better, if it is the will of God, to suffer for doing good than for doing evil.

1 PETER 3:15–17

Many of us can quote the exact stats of our favorite sports team. We might know all the facts, the numbers, the players, and the wins and losses. But when it comes to the Bible, many Christians border on being illiterate. Yet Peter told us to be ready to give a defense. We must be ready to share what we believe and why we believe it. We need to be able to provide a reason for our faith in Jesus.

In order to obey the instructions from Peter, we must study diligently so we can state intelligently what we believe. Instead of being intimidated, we must know what we believe and communicate it clearly.

In the world today, we must be educated and confident in defending our faith. The purpose of this is not to win an argument but to win souls! We must also heed Peter's warning about being humble in our defense of the gospel. We don't want to come across as arrogant or condescending. Neither will help in defending our faith. The goal should be that our defenses of the gospel are both strong and humble at the same time.

....

Jesus, please give me a godly, humble spirit to represent You and to speak the truth in love. Amen.

WEEK 48—MONDAY
Three Ways to Be Ready for the End

But the end of all things is at hand; therefore be serious and watchful in your prayers. And above all things have fervent love for one another, for "love will cover a multitude of sins." Be hospitable to one another without grumbling. As each one has received a gift, minister it to one another, as good stewards of the manifold grace of God.

1 PETER 4:7–10

In the maze of modern Christian beliefs, mania swirls concerning end-time events. The Bible doesn't speak on this topic for the sake of spiritual entertainment, but for spiritual edification. The reality concerning Christ's return should serve as a catalyst for kingdom building. Consider these responses we should have to truths about the end times:

Get serious about prayer. Most believers are familiar with Bible instructions concerning prayer (1 Thessalonians 5:17), but many fail to maintain a steady discipline. Prayer is a value many honor in theory but don't practice often. If we are going to spend eternity with God, shouldn't we talk to Him regularly now?

Love like Jesus. Love is the hallmark of the Christian faith (Matthew 22:37–40). Tragically, many believers operate according to the world's standards of relationships. In light of Christ's imminent return, we should be conscious of how we treat others (Matthew 25:31–46).

Use the gifts God has given you. At salvation, each believer receives the Holy Spirit. With the Holy Spirit, believers also inherit spiritual gifts (Romans 12:6–8). When Christ returns to earth, He desires to find His people using His gifts for His glory and for the good of others (Matthew 25:14–30).

....

Father, please return to earth soon, and help me to be prepared in the meantime. In Jesus' name, amen.

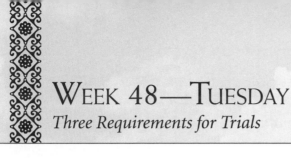

WEEK 48—TUESDAY
Three Requirements for Trials

Beloved, do not think it strange concerning the fiery trial which is to try you, as though some strange thing happened to you; but rejoice to the extent that you partake of Christ's sufferings, that when His glory is revealed, you may also be glad with exceeding joy. If you are reproached for the name of Christ, blessed are you, for the Spirit of glory and of God rests upon you. On their part He is blasphemed, but on your part He is glorified.

1 PETER 4:12–14

I once heard a preacher remark that every believer is either in a trial, coming out of a trial, or going into a trial. It's a fact of life—we will face suffering. Since this is true, believers must be equipped appropriately. Consider these three requirements for trials:

First, don't be surprised. As a new Christian, I naively assumed I would no longer experience hardship. How little did I know! Being a believer actually ensures more difficulties. Not only do Christians have the consequences of the fall to deal with, they also face reproach from unbelievers (Matthew 5:11).

Second, choose to be joyful. Rejoicing is required to face trials well (James 1:2). This may seem counterintuitive, but the Scriptures teach such joy gives us strength (Nehemiah 8:10). When you quit praising God in the storm, you are likely to quit persevering in the storm.

Third, remember Jesus. You are not alone in your suffering. You have a Savior who experienced all the horrors and hurt of human life. His Spirit now lives within you, and He can help you stay strong during the storms (Hebrews 4:15–16).

....

Father, when I face trials, help me to lean on You and to learn from You. Amen.

WEEK 48—WEDNESDAY
Three Marks of Humility

Likewise you younger people, submit yourselves to your elders. Yes, all of you be submissive to one another, and be clothed with humility, for "God resists the proud, but gives grace to the humble." Therefore humble yourselves under the mighty hand of God, that He may exalt you in due time, casting all your care upon Him, for He cares for you.

1 PETER 5:5–7

Humility is a difficult yet necessary virtue to obtain. Humility is difficult because it requires the death of self-love. It is necessary because no one can relate to God without it. Only those who empty themselves of all pride and pretense can experience and enjoy the exalted Lord.

Humble people show respect for others. Jesus taught we should love others as we love ourselves, and we should treat them as we desire to be treated (Matthew 7:12; 22:39). Such kind regard is evidence of humility. Those who detach themselves from inordinate self-love place priority on others (Philippians 2:4). The prideful don't.

When we make little of ourselves in humility, we experience much of God. This is a universal axiom that cannot be compromised. The eternally infinite God loves to bless those who are lowly and contrite (Isaiah 66:1–2). He resists puffed-up people and draws near to humble people.

Finally the humble trust in God. An abiding confidence in Christ characterizes the contrite. Prideful people manipulate and strive to secure the life they desire. Humble people don't have to because they trust in the Lord's sovereign leadership (Proverbs 3:5–6).

....

Father, teach me to be humble so I might experience Your presence and provision. Amen.

WEEK 48—THURSDAY
Three Pieces of Advice for Spiritual Warfare

Be sober, be vigilant; because your adversary the devil walks about like a roaring lion, seeking whom he may devour. Resist him, steadfast in the faith, knowing that the same sufferings are experienced by your brotherhood in the world. But may the God of all grace, who called us to His eternal glory by Christ Jesus, after you have suffered a while, perfect, establish, strengthen, and settle you.

1 PETER 5:8–10

The topic of spiritual warfare intrigues many. Speculation and sensationalism abound as people obsess over the subject. Fortunately, God's Word provides some solid truths for your soul.

Spiritual warfare is real. With startling imagery, Peter depicted the devil as a hungry, maniacal animal in pursuit of prey. Don't be deceived: Satan is real. Though many scoff at the idea, a spiritual enemy truly desires to distract you from God's plan for your life (2 Corinthians 4:4).

Faith is the key to victory in spiritual warfare. A steady reliance upon Christ is the means of overcoming the enemy (Galatians 2:20). Never forget— you haven't been called to figure out all the theological concepts related to demons and the devil. You've simply been called to a faith relationship with your heavenly Father.

Christ can help you overcome. If you keep your eyes on Jesus, you will experience victory over the temptations the adversary throws your way. The Lord will build you up and make you strong. Like a finely tuned athlete who is able to compete at a high level, you will be equipped for spiritual endurance (2 Corinthians 9:8).

....

Father, thank You for strengthening me for spiritual battle. Amen.

Week 48—Friday
Three Keys to Abundant Christian Living

Grace and peace be multiplied to you in the knowledge of God and of Jesus our Lord, as His divine power has given to us all things that pertain to life and godliness, through the knowledge of Him who called us by glory and virtue, by which have been given to us exceedingly great and precious promises, that through these you may be partakers of the divine nature, having escaped the corruption that is in the world through lust.

2 PETER 1:2–4

An abundant life is available to all who know Jesus (John 10:10). Sadly, many Christians never realize this. They exist as mere shadows of what God intended, maintaining lives similar to those of unbelievers. How can we experience abundant life?

Stay focused on Jesus' peace. Peter referenced a peace that comes from the knowledge of God. Jesus also promised to give us tranquility of the soul, but we have to focus on Him in order to experience it. Christ's confidence won't calm our hearts if we don't maintain a steady faith.

Stay focused on Jesus' power. Jesus' final promise to His disciples was a promise of power (Acts 1:8). Through the Holy Spirit, we have strength to face all types of circumstances (Philippians 4:10–13). Abundant life can't be quenched because of Jesus' presence within us.

Stay focused on Jesus' promises. The Bible is replete with assurances concerning God's blessings, and all of them have or will come true (2 Corinthians 1:20)! We simply have to appropriate them. If we want to experience an abundant life in Jesus, we must rely on the promises of Jesus!

Father, thank You for the abundant life You offer. Help me to experience it fully. Amen.

WEEK 48—WEEKEND
Three Ingredients for Spiritual Growth

But also for this very reason, giving all diligence, add to your faith virtue, to virtue knowledge, to knowledge self-control, to self-control perseverance, to perseverance godliness, to godliness brotherly kindness, and to brotherly kindness love. For if these things are yours and abound, you will be neither barren nor unfruitful in the knowledge of our Lord Jesus Christ.

2 PETER 1:5–8

God calls for Christians to grow spiritually. Such development, however, can seem elusive from time to time. Some complicate the matter, while others settle for mediocrity. What's required for the growth God desires? Let's consider three essential ingredients:

Peter's challenge began with the phrase "for this very reason." The words point back to his description of salvation in 2 Peter 1:3–4. Blossoming believers have minds that are mindful of the gospel. The good news compels them to new levels of devotion. Thus one ingredient is a gospel awareness.

A second ingredient is intentional effort. Salvation is a result of grace (Ephesians 2:8). But if properly understood and appreciated, grace will motivate believers to work toward spiritual growth. Believers will exhibit diligence and put forth an intentional effort in growing spiritually (Titus 2:12).

A third ingredient is a transformed life. Peter listed numerous virtues that result from a grace-motivated pursuit of growth. His list wasn't meant to be all-inclusive. It simply identified some of the virtues that appear in the lives of those who are committed to spiritual transformation. If we grow spiritually, our lives will show it (see John 15:5).

....

Father, thank You for the relationship I have with You. Amen.

Week 49—Monday
The Confidence of Heaven

Therefore, brethren, be even more diligent to make your call and election sure, for if you do these things you will never stumble; for so an entrance will be supplied to you abundantly into the everlasting kingdom of our Lord and Savior Jesus Christ.

2 Peter 1:10–11

How confident are you of your salvation? I knew a guy who kept saying, "I hope I can get into heaven by the skin of my teeth." (The irony of it all is the guy who made the statement had false teeth.) That is not way people who are confident of their salvation talk. People who have assurance of their salvation want more than anything to be obedient and growing in their faith.

Confident Christians understand when they "add to [their] faith virtue, to virtue knowledge, to knowledge self-control, to self-control perseverance, to perseverance godliness, to godliness brotherly kindness, and to brotherly kindness love" (2 Peter 1:5–7), the results are Christians who have assurance in their faith.

You see, secure Christians are not content just to do the minimum to get into heaven; they have a deep desire to be all God wants them to be. God doesn't want people to be saved just by the skin of their teeth. He wants to supply confidence for those entering His everlasting kingdom, and He wants to do it for every one of His children.

....

Father, thank You that I can have assurance of my salvation. Today I commit myself to being all You want me to be. Help me to walk in confidence as I serve You. Amen.

DR. LEE SHEPPARD, MABEL WHITE BAPTIST CHURCH, MACON, GA

Week 49—Tuesday
Use Your Time Wisely

But, beloved, do not forget this one thing, that with the Lord one day is as a thousand years, and a thousand years as one day. The Lord is not slack concerning His promise, as some count slackness, but is longsuffering toward us, not willing that any should perish but that all should come to repentance.

2 Peter 3:8–9

When our twins were very young, we took a family vacation to the Smoky Mountains. It was about a seven-hour drive, and we hadn't been on the road very long when the question came, "Daddy, are we at the mountains yet?"

I said, "Not yet. It's going to be this afternoon when we get there." But of course they asked the same question repeatedly before we finally arrived.

As humans we are slaves to time. Time is everything to us. To us a day is a day, an hour is an hour, a month is a month, and a year is a year. God, however, dwells in eternity. To Him a day is as a thousand years, and a thousand years is as a day.

Using God's formula of computing time, Christ has not been gone very long. Using God's time schedule, Jesus was here just the day before yesterday.

While many may grow weary with the passing of time since Jesus first promised to return, in God's eyes it hasn't been that long. Further, He affords us the opportunity to spread the good news and see many come to repentance. God's desire is that no one should perish but for all to come Christ in repentance.

Father, thank You for the time You have given me to share Jesus with others. Amen.

WEEK 49—WEDNESDAY
Make the Most of Every Day

Therefore, beloved, looking forward to these things, be diligent to be found by Him in peace, without spot and blameless; and consider that the longsuffering of our Lord is salvation—as also our beloved brother Paul, according to the wisdom given to him, has written to you.

2 PETER 3:14–15

The ancient Mayans were fascinated with time. They marked their days with three distinct calendars. The Tzolkin calendar lasted 260 days and marked their religious ceremonies. The Haab lasted 365 days, much the same as ours—minus that pesky February 29. But the calendar that had the world in an uproar was their Long Count calendar, which expired on December 21, 2012. Many believed this meant the world would end on that date.

Many others today have theories about when the world will end. Some believe the world will self-destruct. Others who hold to doomsday prophecies expect Planet X, an undiscovered planet in our solar system, to slam into the earth. Some predict we will have some sort of self-induced catastrophe that will incinerate the planet.

The truth is no one knows when the world will end. But Peter stated we have clear instructions. We are to live every day for the Lord and live holy lives that please Him. As we do this, we know that every day we have is an exercise of God's patience and an opportunity to live out our faith to bring glory to our heavenly Father.

Father, You know when the world will end, and You have a perfect plan. I pray that as I live for You and walk in peace that I will be reminded of Your grace and love. Amen.

DR. LEE SHEPPARD, MABEL WHITE BAPTIST CHURCH, MACON, GA

WEEK 49—THURSDAY
This Little Light of Mine

This is the message which we have heard from Him and declare to you, that God is light and in Him is no darkness at all. If we say that we have fellowship with Him, and walk in darkness, we lie and do not practice the truth. But if we walk in the light as He is in the light, we have fellowship with one another, and the blood of Jesus Christ His Son cleanses us from all sin.

1 JOHN 1:5–7

As a boy I remember singing the song "This Little Light of Mine." I would go through the motions as if I were holding a candle to illuminate the darkness. I sang that I wouldn't hide it under a bushel or let Satan blow it out. Then I would sing that I was going to let it shine until Jesus comes—let it shine, let it shine, let it shine.

Our lives should be like candles in the darkness of this sin-sick world. As we walk in the light, we have fellowship with the Father and one another, we can see the traps and snares of the enemy, and we keep from stumbling in our faith. The source of our light is Jesus. He keeps us on the narrow path that leads to righteousness until He calls us home.

The fuel for our lives is found in Psalm 119:105: "Your word is a lamp to my feet and a light to my path." As we focus on God's Word and walk in obedience, we will mature in our faith journeys and reflect Christ to others.

Father, as I intentionally walk in obedience to Your Word, help me to reflect You to others and grow in my faith. Amen.

WEEK 49—FRIDAY
How Callous Is Your Heart?

If we say that we have no sin, we deceive ourselves, and the truth is not in us. If we confess our sins, He is faithful and just to forgive us our sins and to cleanse us from all unrighteousness. If we say that we have not sinned, we make Him a liar, and His word is not in us.

1 JOHN 1:8–10

When I was young, one of the best things about summer was taking our shoes off and going barefoot. At first it was a little rough because our feet were tender and hadn't become calloused. But in a short time they became toughened and we could walk or run without feeling discomfort.

Our hearts are a lot like our feet. The longer we continue living a lie and deceiving other people, the more calloused our hearts become. One lie leads to another. One wrong action leads to others. All the while our hearts become more hardened until we aren't able to hear God anymore. This is why it is essential that we keep our hearts free from sin. We don't want to impede our relationship to God because of unconfessed sins.

Believe it or not, confession is a good thing. When we sin we feel guilty, dirty, and unclean. But true confession brings forgiveness and removal of guilt. So when we sin and come under conviction, it is important to confess it! The more we confess, the closer we walk with God. But to say we have not sinned when God says we have sinned is to call God a liar.

....

Father, thank You that as I confess my sins, Jesus forgives and cleanses me. Amen.

DR. LEE SHEPPARD, MABEL WHITE BAPTIST CHURCH, MACON, GA

WEEK 49—WEEKEND
Knowing God

Now by this we know that we know Him, if we keep His commandments. He who says, "I know Him," and does not keep His commandments, is a liar, and the truth is not in him. But whoever keeps His word, truly the love of God is perfected in him. By this we know that we are in Him.

1 JOHN 2:3–5

Are you a dyslexic Christian? A dyslexic Christian reads these verses and says, "I want to know God, so I must keep His commandments." But in reality these verses say just the opposite. Keeping God's commandments becomes possible through knowing God. It is possible to live a law-abiding life without knowing God; the Pharisees proved that. But you can't know God without living a holy life as a result. When God's love is perfected in you, the result will be your keeping God's Word.

Any attempt to reverse this order is getting the cart before the horse. It won't work, yet this is what so many try to do. They seek to know the Lord better by living holier lives. But just the opposite is true. If they experience God's love, then they will produce holy lives.

This dyslexic condition causes many to tie God's love for them to their performance. When they do well, they feel as though God's favor shines upon them. When they do poorly, they condemn themselves. They think God condemns them, but He doesn't. God loves Christians unconditionally.

We all need a greater revelation of God's unconditional love for us. He loves us!

Father, thank You for Your unconditional love. Today I want to walk closer and know You more. Amen.

LIVING IN THE LIGHT

WEEK 50—MONDAY
The Darkness That Blinds

He who says he is in the light, and hates his brother, is in darkness until now. He who loves his brother abides in the light, and there is no cause for stumbling in him. But he who hates his brother is in darkness and walks in darkness, and does not know where he is going, because the darkness has blinded his eyes.

1 JOHN 2:9–11

Hatred, or ill will harbored within, has detrimental effects. If left unchecked, hatred can spiritually blind us, ultimately proving one has not truly come to know Christ as Lord and Savior.

Sometimes we are tempted to hate our brothers or sisters because of the transgressions committed against us. It is a fact: Christians can hurt Christians. Other times we are tempted to hate people because of their advancements or accomplishments. While someone's transgression against us may have caused great pain, and while jealousy is a real emotion that every believer must face and fight, no scriptural justification exists for harboring those feelings. We must be mindful of Christ's perfect example (Ephesians 4:32), offer forgiveness, find reconciliation, and move on from hatred.

We must remember that hatred toward another will soon boil over and surface, hurting those around us, if it is not confessed and addressed before God. If we desire to walk in the light as Christ is in the light, we must allow the light of His presence to drive out the blinding darkness of sin and hatred.

....

Father, I ask You to forgive me for times I have harbored hatred toward my brother or sister in Christ. Help me to love others as You have loved me in Christ Jesus. In Jesus' name I pray, amen.

STEVEN BLANTON, EBENEZER BAPTIST CHURCH, HENDERSONVILLE, NC

WEEK 50—TUESDAY
The Way of the World

Do not love the world or the things in the world. If anyone loves the world, the love of the Father is not in him. For all that is in the world—the lust of the flesh, the lust of the eyes, and the pride of life—is not of the Father but is of the world. And the world is passing away, and the lust of it; but he who does the will of God abides forever.

1 JOHN 2:15–17

The use of "world" in verse 15 refers to the things of the world that are opposed to Christ and His kingdom. John reminded us: "If anyone loves the world, the love of the Father is not in Him." Does this mean that if one has a love for the things of the world, God no longer loves him? Or when one falls into sin, God stops loving her? Of course not! God is love and He loves His children forever and always.

The meaning of verse 15 is this: if one loves the world and the things in the world, that person has no love for the Father. As believers, we must remember that like a scene in a play, this present world is passing away, "but he who does the will of God abides forever." As obedient followers of King Jesus, we have been called to forsake "the lust of the flesh, the lust of the eyes, and the pride of life" so we might set our hearts on things above, which is where Christ resides (Colossians 3:1–4)!

....

Father, I ask You to help me forsake the passing lusts of this present world so I might fulfill Your plans for my life. In Jesus' name I pray, amen.

WEEK 50—WEDNESDAY
The Hope of God's Love

Beloved, now we are children of God; and it has not yet been revealed what we shall be, but we know that when He is revealed, we shall be like Him, for we shall see Him as He is. And everyone who has this hope in Him purifies himself, just as He is pure.

1 JOHN 3:2–3

As God's children, we hope in the promised return of Christ and the transformation that accompanies it. Just as Jesus resurrected in glory after His death on the cross, in like manner every believer who has repented of his or her sins and confessed Jesus Christ as Lord and Savior has been promised resurrection in Him.

We know not in full all that awaits believers at the return of Christ. But until that day, we know this: Jesus will come back in glory, and when He does, believers will receive glorified bodies. Jesus will return in authority, and when He does, believers will reign with Him in eternity. Jesus will return in perfect righteousness, and when He does, believers will live in perfect righteousness with Him forever in heaven. We shall be like Him!

While waiting for Christ's return, we have been called to purify (consecrate) our hearts in this hope. Knowing that Christ could return any minute should cause faithful believers always to be ready for the "blessed hope and glorious appearing of our great God and Savior Jesus Christ" (Titus 2:13).

....

Father, knowing that the return of Your Son, Jesus, grows nearer by the day, help me always to be ready for that day as a faithful and devoted follower of Christ. In Jesus' name I pray, amen.

STEVEN BLANTON, EBENEZER BAPTIST CHURCH, HENDERSONVILLE, NC

Week 50—Thursday
Love in Deed

My little children, let us not love in word or in tongue, but in deed and in truth. And by this we know that we are of the truth, and shall assure our hearts before Him. For if our heart condemns us, God is greater than our heart, and knows all things.

1 John 3:18–20

Genuine love for others must be demonstrated rather than just discussed. The instruction from verse 18 calls us to put our words into action and to demonstrate our love for others to the glory of the Lord.

Consider our perfect example, Jesus Christ. The Scriptures say in Romans 5:8, "God demonstrates His own love toward us, in that while we were still sinners, Christ died for us." In the greatest act of love ever displayed, God sent His Son to the cross to lay down His life willingly for sinners. Thus Jesus demonstrated His perfect love for sinners in action.

In verse 19 John provided a precious promise for us when we express God's love to others in word and deed. Actively loving others builds our confidence that we have truly come to know Jesus Christ as Lord and Savior.

With heightened sensitivity, we must pray, watch, and be ready for opportunities to represent Him. Love in action builds our faith and helps reassure us that no matter our past, we can have forgiveness and be used by God to demonstrate tangible acts of love toward others because of what He has done for us.

Father, I ask You to open my eyes and stir my heart for opportunities to demonstrate Your love to others. In Jesus' name I pray, amen.

Week 50—Friday
Loving One Another

Beloved, let us love one another, for love is of God; and everyone who loves is born of God and knows God. He who does not love does not know God, for God is love. In this the love of God was manifested toward us, that God has sent His only begotten Son into the world, that we might live through Him. In this is love, not that we loved God, but that He loved us and sent His Son to be the propitiation for our sins.

1 John 4:7–10

An authentic love for God and His people is proof of a genuine born-again believer. One may claim to have faith in Christ, but if his or her life doesn't bear the spiritual fruit of love, this person is only posing as one who has experienced the saving love of God.

God manifested His love for humankind when He sent His Son, Jesus, to earth. On the cross Jesus paid the ransom when He gave His life for sinners. When considering Jesus as the propitiation for our sins, we must understand how His perfect, sinless life and death satisfied the wrath of God toward sinners (2 Corinthians 5:21). Because of His death on the cross, sinners can be saved and know the love of God by grace through faith in Christ Jesus.

When one truly comes to know Christ as his or her Savior, the power of the Holy Spirit compels and enables that believer to love others to the glory of God.

....

Father, as I seek to display the love of Christ toward others, help me to do so in such a way that the power of Your Son may be revealed through me for Your glory. In Jesus' name I pray, amen.

STEVEN BLANTON, EBENEZER BAPTIST CHURCH, HENDERSONVILLE, NC

WEEK 50—WEEKEND
Fearless Love

Love has been perfected among us in this: that we may have boldness in the day of judgment; because as He is, so are we in this world. There is no fear in love; but perfect love casts out fear, because fear involves torment. But he who fears has not been made perfect in love. We love Him because He first loved us.

1 JOHN 4:17–19

Second Corinthians 5:10 reminds Christians of the judgment seat of Christ that awaits every believer when his or her work on earth is complete. Certainly we will all answer for what we've done, or failed to do, in this life. Following this, we will receive our eternal reward in heaven because we trusted Christ's work to save us by His blood.

It is a fact: either upon His return or as a result of our individual deaths, we all will stand before the judgment seat of Christ. But if we devote our lives to abiding in the love of Christ, we will have no reason to dread Judgment Day.

The love of Christ in a believer's heart makes one bold in his or her faith and fearless throughout life and death. Because God has first loved us, we are empowered to share His love without fear. In the courageous love of Christ, believers find strength to love others when the cost is steep, the sacrifice great, and the risk high. The perfect love of Christ casts out any anxiety of loving God and others deeply and sacrificially. The fearless Christian simply lives to hear the Savior say, "Well done, good and faithful servant" (Matthew 25:21).

....

Father, I ask that Your perfect love would cast out every fear I may have of sacrificially serving You. In Jesus' name I pray, amen.

WEEK 51—MONDAY
Loving and Overcoming

For this is the love of God, that we keep His commandments. And His commandments are not burdensome. For whatever is born of God overcomes the world. And this is the victory that has overcome the world—our faith. Who is he who overcomes the world, but he who believes that Jesus is the Son of God?

1 JOHN 5:3–5

John continued to drive home a major point over and over again so his readers wouldn't miss what he was saying. His point? Those who love God will also love other people. As a matter of fact, John had already made the statement that we will know we have passed from death to life because we love our brothers and sisters (1 John 3:14). John's point couldn't be clearer—if we love God, we will love people. John learned this teaching from Jesus when He had taught that the two greatest commandments were to love God and love people (Matthew 22:36–40).

But here in this passage, John also reminded us loving God isn't only about loving people. It is also about obeying God. Again, Jesus taught this when He said, "If you love Me, keep My commandments" (John 14:15). Our obedience to God demonstrates our love for God, which might appear to be difficult because God's commandments are hard to keep. But John said His commandments are not burdensome. They may seem demanding, but they are not oppressive and crushing. God's commands are not to be seen as rules keeping us from something but as guidelines given to us from the heart of our heavenly Father.

....

Father, thank You for Your commandments. They lead me to a better way of life. Help me to obey You today! In Jesus' name, amen.

TREVOR BARTON, THE CREEK CHURCH, LONDON, KY

WEEK 51—TUESDAY
The God-Man

This is He who came by water and blood—Jesus Christ; not only by water, but by water and blood. And it is the Spirit who bears witness, because the Spirit is truth. For there are three that bear witness in heaven: the Father, the Word, and the Holy Spirit; and these three are one. And there are three that bear witness on earth: the Spirit, the water, and the blood; and these three agree as one.

1 JOHN 5:6–8

John declared for all who read these words that Jesus wasn't simply a man: He was also divine. He was fully human and fully divine at the same time. Jesus had to be both God and man in order to accomplish the work of redemption He came to perform.

What is interesting is that throughout Jesus' ministry we see expressions of both of these natures: As a man, He slept in the bow of the boat, but as God He commanded the winds and waves to obey. As a man, He experienced hunger, but as God He took a lad's lunch and fed thousands of people. As a man, He was tempted in all points even as we are, but as God He was without sin. As a man, He wept, but as God He will one day wipe all tears from our eyes. As a man, He died, but as God, He defeated sin and death and arose to die no more. As a man, He was a like a Lamb led to the slaughter, one who opened not His mouth, but as God He is the victorious Lion of the tribe of Judah.

Jesus our Savior was both God and man. He was the God-Man. This is one of the essential tenets of Christianity.

....

Father, thank You for sending Jesus, the perfect Savior, who knows what it is like to be me, but as God He redeems me and rescues me from being me. In Jesus' name, amen.

Week 51—Wednesday
Only in Jesus

If we receive the witness of men, the witness of God is greater; for this is the witness of God which He has testified of His Son. He who believes in the Son of God has the witness in himself; he who does not believe God has made Him a liar, because he has not believed the testimony that God has given of His Son. And this is the testimony: that God has given us eternal life, and this life is in His Son.

1 John 5:9–11

As Christians, we love to read the accounts of Jesus' first followers. We love the Gospels and what they tell concerning Jesus Christ. They record for us the stories He told and the sermons He preached. They preserve for us the accounts of His many miracles. They paint for us the vivid details surrounding Jesus' last days before He was crucified. They account for us the death of Jesus and His resurrection. They give insight into those days that led up to Jesus' ascension back to heaven. Their witness of Jesus is powerful, dramatic, and credible. Yet as much as we love their writings, John reminded us that God's witness is greater!

At Jesus' baptism, God testified concerning His Son, saying, "This is my beloved Son, in whom I am well pleased" (Matthew 3:17). God repeated this assertion at the transfiguration of Christ (Matthew 17:5). John said that to reject this testimony is to call God a liar. Likewise the apostle Paul told us when the Spirit of God raised Jesus from the dead, it was actually a declaration that Jesus was the Son of God (Romans 1:4). God consistently testified throughout the New Testament that Jesus is His Son. To believe God's witness concerning His Son is to receive eternal life. This eternal life is found only in God's Son, Jesus Christ.

Father, I receive Your testimony concerning Your Son. I believe that He is Your Son and eternal life can be found only in Him. Amen.

TREVOR BARTON, THE CREEK CHURCH, LONDON, KY

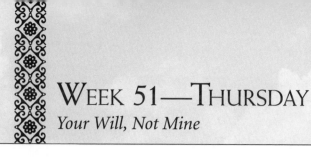

Week 51—Thursday
Your Will, Not Mine

Now this is the confidence that we have in Him, that if we ask anything according to His will, He hears us. And if we know that He hears us, whatever we ask, we know that we have the petitions that we have asked of Him.

1 John 5:14–15

So much of John's theme throughout his letter has been about our love for God and how our love for God results both in a love for people and obedience to God. As we grow in our love for God, we don't just love Him for who He is or what He has done; we also grow in love for what He desires. In other words, the more we love God, the more we find ourselves loving what He loves and wanting what He wants. It becomes more about Him and less about us.

Loving what God loves affects our prayers. John said we will pray with confidence because we seek things in alignment with God's will. As our hearts position themselves toward God, our prayers become less about insisting our will be done but more about His will being done. Our prayers will have an added comfort as we rest in the providence of our heavenly Father who knows all things, controls all things, and works all things out for our good according to His own will and purpose.

John reminded us that aligning our wills with God's will brings our prayers into focus and targets them toward what we know about God's heart and desires. We pray such things as "Your will be done on earth as it is in heaven," and doing so isn't merely lip service. Rather, the desires of our hearts flow from our love for the Father.

....

Heavenly Father, I want to love the things You love and desire the things You desire. Amen.

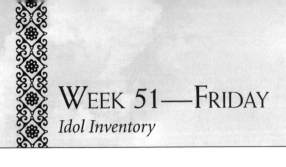

WEEK 51—FRIDAY
Idol Inventory

We know that we are of God, and the whole world lies under the sway of the wicked one. And we know that the Son of God has come and has given us an understanding, that we may know Him who is true; and we are in Him who is true, in His Son Jesus Christ. This is the true God and eternal life. Little children, keep yourselves from idols. Amen.

1 JOHN 5:19–21

John, speaking to followers of Jesus, reminded all of us to keep from idols. This isn't always easy to do, and we know this if we are honest with ourselves. Idols in our culture are a bit more sophisticated and seemingly respectable than in ancient times. We don't have statues or monuments that serve as our idols. Rather, we have idols that are often discussed as virtuous things, such as family or careers.

If we are serious about wanting to make an idol inventory of our lives, some easy, practical steps will help us know if we have turned from Jesus. First, our calendars help us discover if idols have crept in. How much time does God get in our lives? Do we find ourselves too busy to get involved in church? If so, maybe we should do as Jesus taught and do something drastic about our calendars. Second, our financial statements tell us if idols have slipped in. Are we able to give to God's kingdom? Are we able to be generous to others? We may discover that our treasures have led our hearts toward idols. Third, our passions will tell us much about our hearts and if they have begun to drift. What do we get most excited about? We must not let our passion for God abate.

Let's all take a long look so we can keep ourselves from idols.

....

Father, help me turn to You and away from idols in my life. Amen.

TREVOR BARTON, THE CREEK CHURCH, LONDON, KY

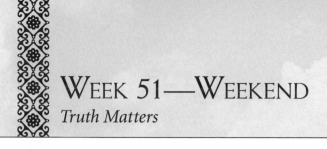

WEEK 51—WEEKEND
Truth Matters

Whoever transgresses and does not abide in the doctrine of Christ does not have God. He who abides in the doctrine of Christ has both the Father and the Son. If anyone comes to you and does not bring this doctrine, do not receive him into your house nor greet him; for he who greets him shares in his evil deeds.

2 JOHN VV. 9–11

John taught us that what we believe matters. It matters much! Fidelity to God, in this case, is also fidelity to truth. To love God is to love truth, even when the truth isn't to our liking or comfort. Many of us are prone to drift toward beliefs that excuse our behavior. There is a part of us that wants to do whatever we want. But this isn't an option for those who know God and love Him. And even though truth isn't always convenient or what we want to hear, we embrace it because we love the One from whom truth comes. We trust the heart of our Father to know best. We trust that truth, though it may feel at moments confining and restrictive, is ultimately the path to freedom and better lives.

The encouragement is for all of us to seek truth. We know that Jesus was the very embodiment of truth. We know that the Scriptures are truth. So as we follow Jesus, hear His words, and study the Scriptures, we come face-to-face with truth and a choice to receive or reject the truth. To reject truth is to reject the Author of truth. Thus we must make sure the closest influences in our lives are also those who know and love the truth.

Father, show me Your truth. Help me to open my heart and mind to Your truth. My heart's desire is to obey Your truth and to enjoy the freedom only it can bring. Amen.

Week 52—Monday
Faultless Before Him

Now to Him who is able to keep you from stumbling, and to present you faultless before the presence of His glory with exceeding joy, to God our Savior, who alone is wise, be glory and majesty, dominion and power, both now and forever. Amen.

Jude vv. 24–25

I love the way this passage begins by giving credit where credit is due: "Now to Him." It is God alone who saves the sinner, sanctifies the sinner, and ultimately one day will present the sinner as "faultless."

When the Bible speaks of God's ability, it simply refers to Him "who is able." God is all-powerful and He displays His omnipotence in the way He cares for His own.

In this text Jude magnified the God of salvation in all He does. We cannot save ourselves or keep ourselves safe, but He can and He does. He guards what belongs to Him.

It seems on a daily basis I struggle with some burdensome weight or some ensnaring sin. But how encouraging and glorious to know He will present me "faultless before the presence of His glory with exceeding joy." This is a very reassuring promise!

Jude closed his book in verse 25 with this significant reminder: God alone is wise. He is the one who knows what is best for all of His children, and all power, glory, and dominion belong to Him forever.

....

Lord, I am grateful I can rest in the knowledge of who You are. You are worthy of all majesty and glory. Amen.

WEEK 52—TUESDAY
He Is Coming Soon

Behold, He is coming with clouds, and every eye will see Him, even they who pierced Him. And all the tribes of the earth will mourn because of Him. Even so. Amen.

"I am the Alpha and the Omega, the Beginning and the End," says the Lord, "who is and who was and who is to come, the Almighty."

REVELATION 1:7–8

The book of Revelation is a book about Jesus: His person, His provision, and His purpose. John wrote the book circa AD 95, while Rome was under the wicked rule of Domitian. This book unveils who Jesus is and what's in store for the world.

I love the fact that Revelation reveals our Savior and King is coming back again. This book is full of hope all based on His promise. A day is coming when His return will be visible: "Every eye will see Him, even they who pierced Him." All will see the triumphant Savior. To some people His return will be glorious. To others His return will be gloomy: "All the tribes of the earth will mourn." This speaks of the unrepentant unbelievers. But those who love Him now will love His appearing.

As we read and reflect on Revelation 1:8, we quickly realize there has never been a time that He has not been: "who is and who was and who is to come, the Almighty." What a joy to serve an almighty God who knows our pasts, is with us in the present, and already inhabits our futures.

....

Lord, You are glorious. Amen.

WEEK 52—WEDNESDAY
Jesus Is Knocking

As many as I love, I rebuke and chasten. Therefore be zealous and repent. Behold, I stand at the door and knock. If anyone hears My voice and opens the door, I will come in to him and dine with him, and he with Me. To him who overcomes I will grant to sit with Me on My throne, as I also overcame and sat down with My Father on His throne.

REVELATION 3:19–21

One way we can know for sure that we belong to Jesus is His discipline in our lives when we are disobedient. Those whom He loves, He chastens (Hebrews 12:6). When the Lord rebukes, He exposes, convicts, or punishes. He chastens us to train, discipline, or educate us. This shall lead us to desire earnestly His best for our lives. When we repent, which is a change of mind that leads in a change of direction, we restore our relationship with God.

The church in Revelation 3:14–22 was a church that had become lukewarm in its faith. Revelation 3:20 explains how Jesus wants lukewarm Christians to return to Him. Those who used to be on fire for Him sometimes lose their fervor and drift away from Him. But Jesus wants these people to return to Him, and He knocks on the doors of their hearts so they can be reconciled to their Savior.

In this text Christ is seen outside the church, seen as the waiting Guest, seeking and knocking. If we will listen, we can hear Him knock at the door of our hearts. If we will open our hearts to Him, He will open heaven to us. God doesn't want lukewarm Christians; He wants Christians who are on fire for Him and working hard to build His kingdom. We must let Him in!

....

Lord, You are welcome to come in and take over. Amen.

DR. JOHNNY HUNT, FIRST BAPTIST CHURCH WOODSTOCK, WOODSTOCK, GA

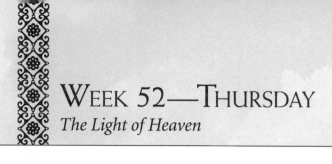

WEEK 52—THURSDAY
The Light of Heaven

The city had no need of the sun or of the moon to shine in it, for the glory of God illuminated it. The Lamb is its light. And the nations of those who are saved shall walk in its light, and the kings of the earth bring their glory and honor into it. Its gates shall not be shut at all by day (there shall be no night there).

REVELATION 21:23–25

John told us that the overwhelming glory of God will literally be the light of heaven, which is none other than Jesus Christ. There will be no need for the sun or moon in heaven because He will light up its skies. Jesus has served as the Light of my life for the last forty-four years, and when this life is over, He will continue to be my Light in heaven.

Revelation 21:22–27 presents Jesus as the Lamb. All throughout eternity, we will be reminded as to why we are in heaven and how we got there: the Lamb! It was His sinless life, His vicarious (substitutionary) death, and His victorious resurrection that purchased our place and sealed our standing with the dear Lamb of God.

Not only will I be there, I will be joined with people from every tribe, tongue, and nation on the globe. One day we all will walk in the light of His radiant presence in heaven.

His presence shall not only be radiant but eternal. There will be no night in heaven. We talk about waking up to a new day—what a day that will be!

....

Lord, being grateful is not enough to describe how thankful I am for Your salvation. Thank You! Amen.

Week 52—Friday
Heavenly Rewards

"And behold, I am coming quickly, and My reward is with Me, to give to every one according to his work. I am the Alpha and the Omega, the Beginning and the End, the First and the Last."

Revelation 22:12–13

John taught that Christians will receive rewards for their kingdom work they accomplished while on earth. Jesus taught us we cannot give a drink of cold water in His name that He will not reward (Matthew 10:42). I am convinced that every deed and every dollar we give precede us to heaven.

We will be in heaven in the first place because of the debt His death paid. As the hymn says, "Jesus paid it all, / All to Him I owe, / Sin had left a crimson stain, / He washed it white as snow."

When we get to heaven, He will reward us for all we did that passed the examination of 1 Corinthians 3:10–15. Martin Luther challenged us with this truth: "I have held many things in my hands, I have lost them all; but whatever I have placed in God's hands, that I still possess." Nothing we give away in the name of Jesus is ever lost in light of eternity.

When we see Him for who He is, then and only then will we receive the rewards of heaven and spend eternity in Jesus' presence. We will be able to do this because He is God and has all power and glory. What a great day this will be!

....

Lord, I praise You for who You are! Amen.

WEEK 52—WEEKEND
Come!

"I, Jesus, have sent My angel to testify to you these things in the churches. I am the Root and the Offspring of David, the Bright and Morning Star." And the Spirit and the bride say, "Come!" And let him who hears say, "Come!" And let him who thirsts come. Whoever desires, let him take the water of life freely.

REVELATION 22:16–17

The book of Revelation paints a beautiful picture of the deity of Christ. He is indeed Lord of all. His deity is gloriously made known to all who believe. He is the Son of Man and the Son of God. He has all authority and power, and He is worthy of all praise.

As the apostle John wrote in today's text, Jesus is the "Bright and Morning Star." He lights the world with His arrival, and He lights our lives when we by faith invite Him into our darkened lives.

I cannot read Revelation 22:17 without thinking about God's invitations. In Genesis 7 we see God's first recorded invitation in the Bible, when He invited Noah and his family to enter the ark. Now here in the last book of the Bible we find His final invitation to humankind. Many times throughout Scripture, God invites people to come to Him and find salvation. According to John in Revelation, both the Holy Spirit and the church invite lost souls to be saved. Thus God's invitation to salvation extends through the whole Bible.

What a joy to preach a gospel that invites the thirsty to the water of life. Jesus graciously offers eternal life to all who will heed His words and come to Him.

Lord, how can I ever thank You enough? Amen.

CONTRIBUTORS

Scripture Index